# THE MIRACLE OF ISTANBUL

## LIVERPOOL FC FROM PAISLEY TO BENÍTEZ

JOHN WILLIAMS AND STEPHEN HOPKINS

MAINSTREAM
PUBLISHING

EDINBURGH AND LONDON

First published in Great Britain in 2005 by
MAINSTREAM PUBLISHING COMPANY
(EDINBURGH) LTD
7 Albany Street
Edinburgh EH1 3UG

ISBN 1 84596 083 1

A catalogue record for this book is available
from the British Library

Typeset in Stone Informal and Stone Sans

Printed in Great Britain by
Clays Ltd, St Ives

# THE MIRACLE OF ISTANBUL

# CONTENTS

# Chapter One

# SIX MINUTES

Football is football: one small thing can change everything.

Rafa Benítez

## ATATÜRK OLYMPIC STADIUM, NEAR ISTANBUL, 25 MAY 2005, 8.15 P.M.

We had noticed this fella right away when we first got into the ground, into the new white-elephant Atatürk Stadium: this rather fraying old Liverpool guy sitting right behind us, amidst all the seething madness. He seemed to be on his own, the very eye of a red storm. He also had the look of a supporter who had seen some games, a man who had done the European rounds with Liverpool. So he would have been to many grounds like this one before. And this was one of those truly horrible, functional, multipurpose new arenas: a sunken stadium with a vast running track enveloping the field, uncovered seating at the goal ends and a pitch at a disconcerting, off-centre angle to the distant main stands. From the outside, at night, it looked a little like a great illuminated concrete oyster, laid open in the middle of some abandoned muddied field in Turkey: somewhere near, we were told, the very point where Europe meets Asia. How symbolic. Though, to be truthful, we were much more concerned tonight about marking the spot where Liverpool Football Club, back in the European Cup final for the first time in 20 years, were meeting the mighty Italians from AC Milan.

You will already have noticed that no one of our generation – in fact, no serious Liverpool fan at all, in our view – calls this affair the 'Champions League' final. For us this is, and will always be, the European Cup. So this was not the first time for Liverpool on this stage. Sky Sports and all the rest of the UEFA Champions League public relations crew might want to tell you differently, but there was no end of sporting history for us when satellite TV and its sponsors arrived to offer wall-to-wall European football coverage for a new mini-League format. TV cash was secured as long as, of course, the 'big' clubs were protected from early elimination. Business is business. You can argue all you like about the relative merits of the old European Cup knockout format – a one-chance stop, for league champions only – compared to the gruelling league and knockout combination of today, which also includes the also-rans of the top European leagues. The truth of the matter is that the luck of the draw meant that, occasionally, Liverpool had their easier European Cup runs in the 1970s and 1980s, but they also had no protection from fierce rivals: Clough's English champions Nottingham Forest in the very first round in 1978, and the brilliant Georgians Dinamo Tbilisi at the same stage the following year. Both ties were lost.

But whichever way you fall on this one, it made no difference to us. However you measure it, this was actually Liverpool's *sixth* European Cup final. Count them: '77, '78, '81, '84, '85, and then 2005. No other British club has played more than two. So far we had won four of them – Paisley three, Fagan one – and disgraced ourselves in another, the last one, at the piss-poor Heysel Stadium in 1985. Judging by the ludicrous arrangements and the near-Biblical setting for this final match in 2005, UEFA had not learned very much in the past 20 years that might have made a difference. Big Joe Fagan cried and retired right after that awful Brussels night 20 years ago, suddenly a broken man. It was also the crushing, violent end of a great Anfield football era. We were here tonight, perhaps as many as 40,000 Red souls, to rehabilitate ourselves as fans – and to start another.

In the two decades since the Heysel catastrophe, a period in which Liverpool had, allegedly, fallen pitiably behind the top English clubs, only once had an English club even reached this final again – Manchester United in 1999. And Bayern Munich fans, to this day, still bleat on about how this outplayed, outclassed United side *stole* the European Cup in injury-time on that fetid Barcelona night – rather like the way Michael Owen blissfully snaffled the FA Cup from Arsenal in Houllier's Treble year in 2001, or Arsenal themselves did from United in Cardiff, just a few days before this one. What this record in Europe means for United is, for all their 'richest club' millions and their 'global fan base' and 'merchandise opportunities', their multiple Premiership titles and even their knighted, gnarled old manager – a man squarely in the honourable tradition of Shankly, Busby and Paisley, by the way – Manchester United have chalked up just *one* European Cup win in the past 30 years of trying – hardly a European footballing odyssey.

And what about Wenger's Arsenal: a club steeped in tradition and so dynamic and yet so cerebral when casually trashing the opposition at home? These thoroughbreds must surely have laid Europe to waste at least once? Not a hope. Not even a European Cup semi-final to discuss; not one in the entire history of this champion club, with its great Marble Halls, its own Underground station and its aristocratic airs – a club never once, mind, relegated from the top English flight. But Arsenal is an institution that unfailingly fails in Europe: it crumbles when it all comes on too heavy. By the same token, our ambitious neighbours Everton, and even the lordly Chelsea with their new Russian fortunes, can still only dream of European Cup glory. So, yes, you could say it was special to be here again tonight. Not unusual – but very special.

So, back to this old Liverpool fan behind us. He was wearing a dirty, once-white baseball cap, which he might have needed for the hot sun that we'd seen a little of in Istanbul earlier on. But he was probably wearing his little hat now to try to keep warm as the night wind threatened to whip across this strange, oddly soulless open bowl. (We would kick off here at 9.45 p.m., and only return to dreamy Istanbul by 3.30 a.m. the next morning. But that was all still ahead.) He also wore one of those zipped-up little jackets, this guy; it was rather crumpled looking now, a bit stained from the day's excesses. And I think he might have had a stick. He might well have been approaching that terrible time when he would have to stay at home with all the other TV suckers, the people who would curse themselves later for not being here tonight – but he wasn't there yet. Not by a long chalk. No, he was happy enough, this old Liverpool fella, twinkling quietly away in the wild wastes of Turkey, taking it all in. He was alone among his closest friends. He *loved* all this.

And you have to think what a great night it was, especially for guys like this one: for a man who had probably seen some of the great Liverpool European Cup matches in the 1960s at Anfield: such as the first time Liverpool wore their famous all-red strip, against Anderlecht in 1964; or the tightest of early battles against 1 FC Cologne, a tie finally bizarrely settled on the toss of a red-and-white token in Holland, well before anyone had even thought of the penalties option; the bittersweet semi-final home victory against Inter Milan in 1965, just three days after Liverpool had won the FA Cup for the first time (some people who were there still say that this 3–1 win is Liverpool's greatest ever European Cup performance); and even the 2–2 draw against Cruyff's Ajax, when Bill Shankly almost convinced the Kop that Liverpool could still retrieve a 1–5 foggy first-leg rout. We would have to call on the ghost of Shankly later tonight.

Our good man in Turkey, he had probably seen all of the 1970s Liverpool European treats too: an early Anfield football lesson learned from Red Star Belgrade; Davy Fairclough's dousing of the St Etienne fire in '77; the routine crushings of Benfica, Bilbao and all the rest. He would also recall all the winning Liverpool European Cup finals; he was the type. He'd remember, for sure, Alan Kennedy's unlikely goals, Smithy's Rome header, Kenny's Wembley chip, and Brucie's wobbly legs in '84. He probably still had nightmares about the dreadful misery of Heysel. Had he – had we – ever truly believed that, after the awful carnage of that night, when many of us thought, 'Is it really worth it any more, any of it?', this sweet European Cup moment might come around again for Liverpool. And before he was just too old to care.

Since 1985 he had, no doubt, despaired many times about Liverpool in Europe – like most of us had. After all, we were banned under Kenny in the 1980s, disunited under Souness in the early 1990s, and just too brittle under the great servant Roy Evans in the years that followed. We ended up frustrated under Gérard Houllier into the new century, though we had a wonderful UEFA Cup party in Dortmund in 2001 as an hors d'oeuvre for tonight. And none of us thought that the Liverpool FC, once built around tanner-ball Scots and the determined Irish – but with an English core – would one day be a truly *international* football club. Did this old man ever imagine, for a second, that it would take Spaniards and Czechs and a Croatian and a Pole, a Finn and a German and Frenchmen, as well as Scousers, to get us here again? Did any of us? So this was *his* great night, his gently smiling, battered old football face saying just about enough. It was every ageing Liverpool fan's last dream, to be here among the red flags and the banners and the great Liverpool songs that wrapped around this stadium tonight. That is, at least, how this crazy night in Istanbul had begun.

Of course, we could have – perhaps we should have – seen coming some of what was about to happen. After all, when Rafa Benítez, Xabi Alonso and Sami Hyypiä had arrived for the UEFA pre-match press conference the day before at the Atatürk, they were turned away because they had incorrect accreditation. They were made to wait outside in the pouring rain while officials searched out someone – anyone – who recognised them. 'They tried to chase us away,' joked Sami, grimly, 'but we are here now. Nobody has been able to keep us away. They tried on the gate, but we got in.' Liverpool were clearly unconsidered – probably unwelcome – gatecrashers in Turkey. The fear was that they would ruin UEFA's shopfront TV spectacle by actually shutting up the shop – or else by embarrassing themselves with their ineptitude, with their utter mediocrity. *The Times* described the pre-match image now seeping out from the Milan camp before the final like this: 'The widespread view of Liverpool was as a remorselessly dull side with the attacking instincts of a neutered tabby cat.' Thanks for that, Milan – do you mean you didn't rate us?

One British commentator described this final as likely to be 'a night to test the power of innocence'. Some test. Who had the answers? Ancelotti, the Milan coach, saw it differently: as a contest between a team 'dedicated to attacking play' (Milan) and one 'committed to defence' (Liverpool). 'But strong defence is not a defect,' he had argued, charitably, 'this is a quality.' But you did have to know *how* to defend. His captain, the ageless Maldini, incredibly four times already a European Cup winner, was much more derisory. He told the press that his children, not fear of Liverpool, were the only things that kept him awake at night: 'We play the game properly and we attack,' he said (this seemed a novel Italian trait). 'Liverpool do not play forward at all. Caution is at the heart of their game. They are very much defensive in their tactics. Once they have the advantage, it is very difficult because they have eight or nine players in defence. It is very hard to find space against them.' So Milan – like everyone else – expected a grinding, tight contest, probably with few goals, and with Liverpool as spoilers – a boring European Cup final (and let's face it, most of them are). As we know now, they were *almost* right.

## TOUCHING THE VOID: 10.35 P.M.

More than two hours had now passed since we'd first entered the Atatürk Stadium. The climate had perceptibly altered. It was chilly now, more of a typical British football night. And looking at our Reds history fan again, other things had clearly changed too. The guy had sunk visibly deeper, much deeper, into his seat (there was barely any crowd noise now, no players on the field, except, that is, for one tall Liverpool man, Hamann, who was being sternly warmed up alone in front of us by a barking Spanish coach). The old man's shoulders had slumped, noticeably so, and his eyes were now hooded. He looked much older than before, suddenly worn out, and was absent-mindedly stroking the back of the seat next to him, gazing into a void. There may even have been a single tear gently threading its way down the route of the smile marks he was showing us much earlier. And he was not alone here, because around him pretty much all the Liverpool faces now looked the same. They all had the same numbed stony stare, the same glassy-eyed despair and rueful head shaking. They were all in shock, because something quite terrible had just happened here, out in the wilds of the Europe–Asia border, something we had feared but not planned for, something we had earlier pushed to the very recesses of our minds because the possibility of it happening was just too painful even to contemplate. But we still knew it *could* happen.

Our fella – Liverpool's senior 'Everyfan' – was actually gazing now to his right, over the heads of the thousands of Liverpool fans who were collapsed, like him, over their seats or with heads collectively bowed on the North Tribune. Above them a giant red electronic scoreboard beamed out the message of our stay so far, which was, in fact, the story of the blues. It carried the badges of the two competing clubs but it said this, if you can bear to take it in: *Half-time – AC Milan 3 Liverpool 0.*

Our captain and leader, Steven Gerrard, had walked to the touch-line towards his coach at half-time, slumped, with palms open, as if to say, 'What can we do now? This is all fucking wrong.' Which meant that 20 long years after we'd last reached this European pinnacle, after we'd last played in the final with the real football elite, we were no longer dreaming of winning the European Cup for a British-record fifth time. UEFA had even said that we could keep the trophy if we defeated Milan. *Defeat* Milan? What, tonight? Cancel that Brasso order, and also that night of dancing and singing we had lined up for ourselves along the Bosporus. Get us the earlier flight home after all. For the next 45 minutes, instead of preparing to party, we would simply be waiting for the final whistle, fighting for our self-respect – and to avoid global sporting humiliation.

The Anglican bishop of Liverpool, James Jones, recently described the people of Liverpool as 'a strange mixture of pessimism and optimism. Go into a meeting announcing great news and they will gloomily retort that it will never happen. Go in announcing terrible news and they'll say, "Don't worry, it will work out brilliant."' To be sure, the man is not very far from the truth: we can be a contrary bunch, wary of promises, too many of them unfulfilled, but absurdly defiant in the face of adversity. But not on this night, not in chilly Istanbul. Not even when the sardonic 'We're gonna win 4–3' chants began to surface all around us and a brave and tearful 'You'll Never Walk Alone' was sung so loudly that it was even heard way down in the Liverpool changing-room. I can tell you that no one in red, not our old fella behind us, nor any of the people who were gloomily surrounding us now with their questions and fears, was thinking that this carnage would turn out 'brilliant'.

Already three goals down and light years from being even competitive, we talked coldly, instead, at half-time in this surreally awful venue even by UEFA's standards, about what we could possibly hope for in part two of this unfolding nightmare. *Hope* for? We just wanted this to end right now, maybe get back to the warm, spaced-out Pete Wylie concert we had been listening to outside in the hours before kick-off, or even get back onto those rickety single-decker buses that had got us here and that we knew would take hours to get us back to the friendly bars of downtown Istanbul. Some Liverpool fans had already left, had commandeered taxis or started yomping, distractedly, into the Turkish country darkness and back towards town, hoping that by putting distance between themselves and the site of this catastrophe it would, somehow, erase its very existence. We too wanted to be somewhere else. But we had to stay: a supporter's duty (we had nowhere to go). We came up, instead, with a mental shortlist, a despairing set of targets we could now hope to achieve in this harsh new world of impending – no, certain – defeat:

- Avoid a European Cup-final record loss. Benfica had scored five goals in the 1962 final – after falling two goals behind – and Di Stefano's Real had scored seven in 1960 at Hampden. Seven! But even these sorts of scores were realistically looming for us now, and on both occasions in that earlier football era of great attack and little defence, their opponents had at least managed to score three goals of their own. On a few more occasions since, the European Cup winners had scored four times in the final, Milan twice among them. Liverpool might just avoid conceding seven goals tonight, but none of us were actually counting on it. The Ukrainian Shevchenko, the €70 million man, looked frightening, full of movement and goals – and he was still to score. But, you see, modern elite football players these days tend to wind down anyway when the real damage is done: they try to conserve, and to save their fellow professionals on the other side from complete humiliation. A one-sided hammering is also plain bad for the TV viewing figures. Surely Milan just didn't *need* to score any more goals tonight; they had already wiped Liverpool out. But could we possibly score even *one* goal against Jaap Stam, Nesta and Maldini and all their rock-solid, film-star-looks mates?

- No, come on; show some ambition. We really did *need* a goal here – a consolation at least, something to cheer. For Christ's sake, what about Liverpool's millions around the globe watching this live, in sunshine and snow, in darkness (real darkness) and in light? What about these tens of thousands of fantastic Liverpool fans who were here? Look at their devastation. They had taken a trip all the way to the Asian border from Bootle and Huyton, Kirkby and Speke, for 90 minutes of head-in-hands torture. They *deserved* something.

- Get a solid shape to the team. At least, Rafa, get Didi Hamann onto the field now, for Christ's sake; shore things up a little and make that Brazilian schemer Kaka realise he's not in one of those Rio beach 90-minute training workouts. Dig in for 20 minutes, at least. Show us some decent organisation and some heart.

Apart from for ourselves, we felt sorry mostly now for Hamann, a player who seemed to be strangely distrusted by his club managers even though his resolve and the quality of his play produced few complaints from us. His game always soared with the importance of the occasion. Few Liverpool fans doubted him, so how absurd it was to start without him tonight, without one of our few experienced warriors. Benítez might have opted for Kewell, of course, for the width and pace he threatened to offer against ageing Milan full-backs. But maybe all those early Milan press conferences and mind games had got to the Liverpool manager.

Maybe he was actually really irked by all that stuff about 'boring' Liverpool and the supposed defensive mindset of his team. He was a great coach. Maybe vanity had made him really want to show something else tonight: perhaps even that he could outsmart Ancelotti and all those know-all English football journalists who had expected to see only dull Liverpool solidity and caution against Milan's invention. He, Benítez, would prove them all wrong.

OK, Hamann had already played in a World Cup final for Germany, so why should we have cared so deeply for him right now? Well, because of his team ethic, his hard-yards reliability for Liverpool and for his sheer guts. But here he was, already in his 30s and now a non-starter in the biggest club game in any player's life. He was usually our defensive midfield fulcrum, the obvious choice, the man who should have been first on the team-sheet after Gerrard. But, because of the manager's perverse logic, Didi had been forced to sit out – just like the rest of us – in a first half in which Milan players had been running free, causing merry havoc in just the spaces he usually patrolled brilliantly for us.

And now the manager – a 'tactical genius', we were told by better judges, but a man in danger of ruining our lives tonight – had basically said to him, to his German shield, 'You need to take care of Kaka.' Hamann admitted later that he had had no thoughts at all of actually turning this game around. What Benítez had, effectively, said to the midfielder was, 'OK, this game is over now. But it's the European Cup final. Go and have a run-out and save us from a complete thrashing.' So we were watching Hamann going through his solitary routines on the pitch. He looked resigned, but just seeing him out there produced both anger and hope among the Liverpool fans. A few may even have been daring to think that the impossible was still possible.

At half-time in the clotted VIP areas in the Atatürk, UEFA's Michel Platini – remember him from 1985? – was putting his hand gently on the shoulder of the Liverpool chairman David Moores. The Scouser's hangdog expression was even more pronounced than usual. 'It looks like a damage-limitation exercise,' offered the Frenchman. It was the best he could do. Liverpool's odds had already drifted to 350–1 with some bookmakers. After the match one of the British journalists present asked the Liverpool chief executive, Rick Parry, what he was thinking at half-time: what was racing through *his* mind as he strolled among the UEFA caviar nibbles and cava – and the Liverpool sobs. 'Basil,' said Rick. What, thought the press, as in *Fawlty Towers* and the clueless waiter Manuel, a dead ringer tonight for our hapless Spanish manager? No, not at all, he smiled. That was not what he'd been thinking at all.

He'd actually meant *Basle*. In 2002, and in the midst of an appalling run under Gérard Houllier, Liverpool had actually once before recovered from a 0–3 deficit in a European Cup tie, against the Swiss side. Here, thought Parry, was something perhaps to hold on to, a straw to clutch (though the fragile Vladimir Smicer had scored one of the Liverpool goals in Basle, so don't hold your breath). But Basle were true European Cup greenhorns: they had begun to shudder long before Danny Murphy scored the first goal for Liverpool, around the hour mark that night, and they collapsed soon after. Even at 3–3 in a terrible tie Liverpool were still eliminated. And, let's face it, the occasion in hand was quite a different matter. This was AC Milan, Europe's finest, in the European Cup final. Traditionally these guys would rather kill their own mothers than concede goals, even in consolation. Did you not see some of their players actually *laughing* going down the tunnel at half-time beneath us? (Traoré would say later that Liverpool players could hear the half-time celebrations in the Milan dressing-room).

There *was* something else, though – just a glimmer. Last season this same Milan side arrived in La Coruña in the European Cup quarter-finals with a thumping 4–1 first-leg lead – and lost. By half-time in Spain a rampant Deportivo were already leading 3–0: Fran's late goal, Deportivo's fourth, simply sealed the tie. Milan were quite wretched that night, gutless. And just a few weeks ago hadn't we watched on TV as Milan had taken a lucky 2–0 advantage to Eindhoven in the semi-final? We were hoping PSV could turn the tables to meet us here, but by the point extra-time was looming, we were beginning to wonder. The Dutch side had easily clawed back those two goals, and Milan looked slow and old, worn out, while PSV were dangerously quick, hungry. Milan eventually toughed it out and sneaked a late goal which made Cocu's third PSV goal meaningless. But PSV's *was* a third goal against this vaunted Italian defence. Milan had looked desperately tired in Holland and they had played more Italian league matches since then. Although they looked beyond challenge here, maybe they were just a tiny bit vulnerable.

Was Benítez going through *any* of this now, down in the Liverpool dressing-room bunker, where a head-in-hands Steven Gerrard later recalled hearing precisely *nothing* of what the manager had said about reshaping the team for the second half? Benítez was too humble later to talk about all of what he'd said. Or maybe he was even a little ashamed. No player spoke in the Liverpool dressing-room at half-time. This was a losers' space, a sporting morgue. No one said later, either, that they really believed that Liverpool could still win from here, not even the usually unquenchable Carragher. The manager was calm, undemonstrative even. There was no point in bawling people out from where Liverpool were now: the whole Benítez project might even have collapsed if he'd gone down this route. He had planned to replace the struggling Traoré with Hamann, but Finnan was injured, a thigh problem, so that would now have to be the exchange. Liverpool would move to three at the back, with Gerrard pushed on, Hamann dealing with Kaka and general rubbish-clearing, Carragher would press up on the right when he could as Smicer moved inside, and Riise would have to do a double shift on Liverpool's left-hand side.

## BENÍTEZ'S LIVERPOOL HALF-TIME CHANGES

But there was no great coaching masterplan available to turn this game around. You don't retrieve three goals in situations like this with mere tactical readjustment. It was all far too late for that.

Instead, you must ask for your real men to stand up and be counted. And you hope for luck. Benítez did point out that Milan would definitely tire if Liverpool could just get back in the match with a goal. Psychologically the Milanese were weak, he argued: remember their collapse in Eindhoven; remember their slump in their final weeks of the Serie A campaign? Liverpool needed to sow these seeds of doubt now: make Milan fear the shaming possibility of their own capitulation from a position of apparently

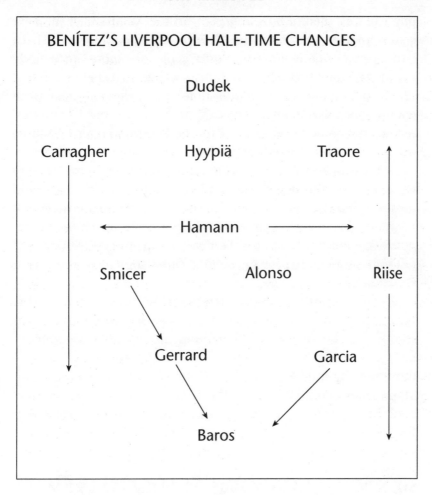

BENÍTEZ'S LIVERPOOL HALF-TIME CHANGES

Dudek

Carragher          Hyypiä          Traore

←——— Hamann ———→

Smicer          Alonso          Riise

Gerrard          Garcia

Baros

insurmountable strength – bully them. But, mainly, Benítez merely pleaded now for some self-respect; he appealed to the Liverpool players' pride: 'We are Liverpool FC,' he said. 'We have so many fans we are not going to be slaughtered. If we can score a goal quickly, we can push on from there.' The Spanish technocrat was back to tribal basics – do it for your mates and for the crowd. Cut all the coaching mumbo-jumbo: football, in the end, as it was for Paisley and the rest, is about selecting the right players and getting them to play with real heart.

If there was one at all, *this* was Liverpool's plan to escape the despair that now engulfed the dressing-room, the TV millions, the Liverpool VIP areas and the great unwashed who were close to physical and mental breaking point in the Atatürk. Get the next goal – and see what happens. Now the Liverpool players at least had a target again, an achievable goal once more. Their body language had lifted, slightly, from the beaten rabble who had sloped off, individually, at half-time. They were together once again, which was Benítez's major contribution in the 15 minutes' repair time he had had at his disposal. Returning after half-time, the Milan players looked relaxed – a little cocky even: completely sure of themselves, certainly. In Italy, any side in this position, any team that was 0–3 down and had been outplayed like this, would lie down and take defeat, honourably. Their 'reward' for accepting the inevitable in such a professional and uncontested manner was not to be utterly humiliated. Perhaps the men of AC Milan were not entirely prepared for an English club's spirited response to a situation of such utter hopelessness.

Steven Gerrard's black-dog depression had also lifted a little. When the second-half kick-off was set, he looked around at his winning opponents, at his teammates and at this extraordinary Liverpool crowd that had decamped to Turkey in their tens of thousands by land, sea and air. Perhaps his manager was right about what might still be possible if Liverpool could get an early goal. In any case he might never play in another European Cup final and he had nothing to lose right now. He was going to give the next 20 minutes some stick, shit or bust.

## SIX MINUTES: 25 MAY 2005, 10.59 P.M.–11.05 P.M.

Six minutes. Think about it for a moment. What, exactly, can you do in six short minutes? Run a bath, perhaps; take your time on that welcome half-time toilet break; or, if you're watching on TV at home, make a nice cuppa, change a plug, or else you could cruise eBay for that oh-so-difficult-to-find special gift? It will probably take about six minutes for you to read four or five pages of this book. Six short minutes. They can easily disappear, drift away unspent, even while you think. Or else, while you dream.

Alternatively, you might just try turning the summit of European club football on its head in these 360 seconds. This might involve, for example, confounding your own downtrodden travel-weary supporters and every single global football pundit in the process. As a precursor to this you might try, as our man Benítez had done, selecting for your raw, inexperienced team in their biggest ever club match abroad against dangerous, hardened European opponents, a fragile and distrusted forward, Kewell, over one of your few match-proven and experienced battlers, Hamann. Or try giving a brutal AC Milan team – representing a club six times European Cup winners themselves – a three-goal half-time start in a European Cup final. And this was an even *better* Milan side, remember, than the Ruud Gullit and Marco Van Basten version that the current Milan manager, Ancelotti, had also played for in the early 1990s. It was also better, it had been claimed, than the one that had gone on, in 1994, to humiliate Barcelona 4–0 in a showpiece final. Hadn't the Italian manager foolishly told us as much just before the 2005 final?

The Italian press later described Liverpool's second-half revival in Istanbul as '*Sei minuti di follia*' – 'Six minutes of madness'. But no single period of play can be extracted from the context of the match in which it is embedded, not even a segment as mind-boggling or as apparently distinctive as this one. This little sub-plot was still part of the wider narrative of this, thus far, lop-sided football match. At the start of the second half Liverpool were at least visibly competing again, suggesting that their spirit was still strong, that they were not yet broken. Gerrard was playing just behind Baros – where Kaka had been causing havoc against Liverpool. The Liverpool crowd had also found its voice again. But Dudek was soon clumsily kneeing away a bouncing Cafu cross and his muddling mate, Traoré, was soon at it again, too, losing a simple pass from Sami on halfway, who then had to bring down Kaka. Sami (somehow) convinced the referee this was no booking. Pirlo and Seedorf set up Shevchenko's free-kick, which seemed to go through the onrushing Baros and a Banshee-like Carragher, forcing the Polish keeper to save low at his left-hand post. Frankly Milan still looked dangerous in any forward movement, but Liverpool's own mini-resurgence meant that there were no definitive signs yet about at which end another goal might arrive. But then, after nine minutes of the second half – Milan probably only had to survive the same again to be absolutely certain of victory – the real possibilities for this night began to be unveiled for the first time.

The real story of this match begins with Liverpool's Norwegian, sometimes red-headed, left-sided midfielder John Arne Riise. After making a strong early impression at Anfield from August 2001 with his enthusiasm, pace and his shooting, Riise, a £4-million buy from Monaco, had lost his way a little in the latter period of Gérard Houllier's time in charge at Liverpool. With Harry Kewell's arrival at Anfield in the summer of 2003, Riise was forced to switch between left-back and midfield and, as a result, he seemed to have lost some confidence and, under instructions about his defensive responsibilities, some of his zest for attacking. He had also occasionally lost his place in the squad. But under Benítez, and with Djimi Traoré now in defence, Riise had since rediscovered some of his most consistent Liverpool form once again in midfield, though he frequently struggled to complete a full 90 minutes' work. Benítez was fond of calling him off after 70 minutes, seemingly almost irrespective of the state of the match or the quality of Riise's contribution to it. In the new Liverpool second-half formation in Istanbul Riise now had to try to offer support for the unstable Traoré wide on the left at the back for Liverpool, as Djimi tucked in to a three, as well as getting forward whenever he could to support the Liverpool attacking options out wide. His was now a crucial dual role – and he would have to compete for rather more than 70 minutes. But here we are concerned only with six.

It was the Brazilian Cafu who directly faced Riise for Milan, a quality, but ageing, wing-back, a man who could be vulnerable on both sides to determined attackers with power and real pace. Liverpool had successfully 'got at' Cafu in a UEFA Cup tie in Rome in 2001, so they knew that he was potentially dangerous, but also vulnerable. Riise fancied him. The Norwegian's usual job for Liverpool from wide positions was not necessarily to whip in quick crosses from deep areas – after all, Liverpool had no great forward headers of the ball, certainly not without the cup-tied Spaniard Morientes in their ranks. Instead, he aimed to get round the back of opposing defences or else play himself into areas inside in order to draw fouls, or into decent shooting positions. Riise had a real hammer of a left foot, which, on good days, he could deploy with real accuracy and control. However, with Steven Gerrard now free to sneak forward and between Milan's centre-backs in attack, the early-lofted cross from the left was back in play as a Liverpool option. In these critical circumstances it was, at least, worth trying. Three hundred and sixty seconds start here.

Liverpool's six-minute revival in the 2005 European Cup final that begins nine minutes into the second half starts not with a red shirt but with a white one, and the great Paolo Maldini, high up on Liverpool's right-hand side. Here, Maldini robs Xabi Alonso but then unaccountably slices his cross-field pass horribly, and it is picked up by Riise, who exchanges passes with Steven Gerrard near Liverpool's penalty area and then tries to outrun Gattuso on Milan's right. But there is no losing this determined little midfielder yet, so Riise doubles back and finds Gerrard again. Stevie G. is right in front of us now, across the running track, near the halfway line. Why isn't he more forward? The ball now goes across the field in Milan's half: Gerrard – Alonso – Hamann – back to Alonso. Three goals down: do we have time for this? Riise has now drifted wider again and Xabi finds him with a low, curling pass. The referee, Mejuto González, lifts his right leg with a flourish to allow the ball through to Riise, a cute little footnote in an astonishing tale of European Cup history that is about to unfold in front of our disbelieving eyes. Gerrard has continued his movement forward towards the Milan box – no one has yet picked him up.

Riise is closed down immediately by Cafu and his first attempt at a left-footed cross is telegraphed and easily blocked by the defender. But the ball falls comfortably again to the Norwegian's left side and this time the cross is arrowed in – not with any real pace, but aimed directly at the space in the 18-yard box between Stam and Nesta. As often happens in a sport that has football's fluidity and pace, the initial blocked cross and the momentary resetting of the Liverpool attack has actually briefly unsettled the Italian defence and has also allowed Steven Gerrard the vital extra time he needs to get in position to attack the flight of the ball. It now dips towards him. His powerful, twisting header redirects the looping delivery high into the left-hand side of Dida's goal: Gerrard has watched it every yard into the Milan net. Dida has too: he ends up chasing the header across his goal before he careers, stumbling, beyond the far post. It was a perfectly placed cross by Riise and a precise header by the Liverpool captain, with the Brazilian keeper and the entire Milan defence helpless to intervene. From the moment Maldini sliced his kick 70 yards away, it has taken *29 seconds* for Liverpool to score.

There is a view in football punditry – you even hear top coaches saying this sort of stupid stuff – that, somehow, being, say, 0–2 down in a football match is not necessarily a bad thing. The coaching 'logic' here goes that if you get just one goal back early enough, you can irreparably undermine the resolve of your opponents and use their negative energy to push past them and onwards to victory. So why not do that from 2–0 *up*?

But what does a goal back from *0–3* down mean? How do you read it? Context, baby; context is everything. What it means tonight, with over half an hour still remaining in a concrete container outside Istanbul, where the life has been sucked out of you by Milan, where no one has been able to buy food or drink now for hours, and where every Liverpool fan is looking for a sign, any sign, that this huge airlift has not been in vain: what it means is hope.

And as we cautiously hug each other and ourselves on the East Tribune – these are not yet full-blown celebrations, of course, merely a statement of intent – everybody looks now for a sign from the Liverpool players and especially from the scorer, from the Scouse engine, Gerrard, the man who has toyed with our loyalties and his own emotions all season long. How should *we* respond now? What can we do? A few Liverpool players are offering only the most perfunctory of high fives to their captain as he returns to halfway. But what we get back from the pitch at this moment are waves of huge energy and belief: and just a little frustration and anger. The captain is frantically waving at us along the touch-line, his flailing arms screaming at us – at Benítez's famous 'twelfth man', the Liverpool crowd – to pump up the volume, to get involved again: 'C'mon, you Scouse fuckers,' he's saying. 'We can still win this, but we need you. So get off your arses, open your lungs, and do your job.' And you know something? We, the ordinary foot-soldiers, we the messed-around, hungry infantrymen of European excursions from Moscow to Marseille, we the great unfed who have been hanging our flags all over Istanbul for three days, we are collectively *thrilled* by this wild and affectionate abuse from our leader. And the *noise* around us is deafening.

Liverpool press forward strongly now, as Milan can establish no control of the ball high up the field: Hamann is already dominating Kaka. We, the Liverpool crowd, Stevie Gerrard's humble servants, are just babbling anything, making some sound, anything, as if it is the decibel count alone that is driving Liverpool on. Even now, if Milan can hold on for the next ten minutes, or even five, this putative Liverpool 'revival' might easily fizzle out, especially as tiredness begins to set in. This means we must score the second goal soon – and when it comes it involves a couple of huge breaks for Liverpool. The first happens immediately after the kick-off. Traoré constructively and accurately plays the ball forward to García, who then flicks it on first time to Baros. The Czech is offside. The Spanish linesman waves frantically – we can see him even from where we are on the other side of the stadium. But the Milan defence collects the ball and the referee either doesn't see the offside or plays the advantage – of which there is precisely and brilliantly none. In fact it is the opposite, because the ball breaks left to Riise, who has another cross blocked and then directs the resultant throw-in to Alonso, who passes inside to Hamann in a central position about 25 yards out from the Milan goal.

The second lucky break for Liverpool happens as this attack is building. The midfield man Pirlo – or is it Kaka? It's no. 21 or 22 – mysteriously stops playing and is kneeling down to fix his pads or his socks, as if he is hacking around in a Sunday League fixture. Has he lost his mind? Shevchenko has seen this but is back too late and Milan are now one man down in midfield. The white-booted Vladimir Smicer points at a spot in front of himself and Hamann delivers the five-yard pass – his speciality. Smicer takes one touch to steady himself. *Two minutes and 25 seconds have passed since Maldini sliced his cross outside the Liverpool penalty area.*

Born in Decin in 1973, Vladimir Smicer signed as a 14 year old with Slavia Prague before moving to Lens after Euro '96, from where he was signed for Liverpool by Gérard Houllier in 1999. He came with the reputation of being a goal-scoring, technically adept and clever, international-quality wide midfielder. But he had struggled to win over sections of the Liverpool crowd right from the start. Vlad had two main problems in the eyes of his many L4 (Anfield) critics: first, he didn't over-relish the physical side of the English game, too often ducking out of the sort of wild tackles we expect all English players to fly into. If Vlad sometimes looked for ways out of the sort of front-on conflict that was still integral to the Premiership, if not abroad, then there were plenty of young English players – such as Liverpool's rising Stephen Warnock, for example – who were perfectly happy to oblige: to the crowd's satisfaction but sometimes also to their own cost.

Second, even with his various avoidance strategies in play, Vlad's body was simply not built for the attrition levels involved in football in England. He had barely gone a season at Anfield without missing rows of matches through injury and he had made his first League appearance in the 2004–05 campaign only as a sub at Charlton Athletic on 1 February 2005. He had made but a couple of League starts by the season's end – more injuries. When he finally returned to the Liverpool squad this season – a swansong – Vlad's hair was shoulder length and his boots a provocative white: these are not easy traits to love by a crowd that wants its well-paid foreign stars to show themselves willing to spill blood.

To be fair, on his day Vlad did have real star quality, and he had scored important goals for Liverpool – in the League Cup semi-final in 2001 against Crystal Palace, and a famous last-minute League winner against Chelsea at Anfield among them. Smicer had also shown his mettle in Europe: he had scored in Basle to almost rescue Liverpool in the European Cup in November 2002 and had been absolutely outstanding against Roma in the European Cup earlier that year on the famous Anfield night that Gérard Houllier returned from illness. But with just 180-odd games – including plenty as sub – in 6 seasons and with a goal only every 10 games, this was not what we thought we were paying £4 million for when Gérard Houllier took over the club and brought in the man from the Czech Republic.

Rafa Benítez felt the same way about Vladdy. He had already told the Czech that his Liverpool contract would not be renewed in the summer of 2005. We all knew that this was his last match for the club and that he would probably now go back to France, where he would have more room and more time to play, and fewer psychopaths blocking his way. Vlad had even asked the manager if he was needed, or could he have these last few weeks of his contract off on holiday! And yet here he was, already off the Liverpool bench for Harry Kewell as early as the 23rd minute, playing in the biggest club match in a footballer's life and for a regime that had already discarded him. Not that his emergence off the bench actually thrilled many of us here in Istanbul: we simply presumed that Kewell's withdrawal would allow the manager to rectify his original mistake and bring on Didi Hamann. Instead, to groans all around us, we saw Vlad's unconvincing shape step up with Benítez on pitch side as the dejected Kewell trooped away to boos (did the crowd think Harry was faking injury?). But what we were about to see now from old 'Vlad the Impaler' would at least wipe out all of his earlier perceived misdemeanours. It was free drinks in the Flat Iron pub in Anfield from now on: all previous Czech offences were about to be, very favourably, taken into consideration.

As far as we know on all past evidence at Liverpool – although philosophers will tell you that seeing the sun rise on one day does not absolutely prove it will also happen on the next – Vladimir Smicer has no serious shot on him. He is a scuffer: he can get into decent shooting positions but can seldom finish. Here, picking up a short ball from Hamann, he is at the very limits of his range – beyond it, actually – but he is going to try a shot nevertheless. We expect to see it screw harmlessly wide to his left, maybe bounce off a white Milan body for a corner, if we are lucky. Hell, why not, we are now in charge here, pressing on desperately for another goal. Instead, Vlad catches this shot cleanly, and not only does it avoid the Milanese defence, but it also whips past another Milan (Baros) who, milliseconds earlier, has been calling for a pass from his Czech mate, but who is now curving his body forward and around the silver UEFA ball in order to avoid being struck by Smicer's swerving shot. Maybe goalkeeper Dida is unsighted or thinks Baros is going to divert this attempt, because the Brazilian seems to get down too late to the shot and, with two hands, tries to push it away from goal. Instead he can only divert it, on the dipping half-volley, into the side of the Milan net.

'GOALLLLLARRRRRGH!'

This is us, right here, right now: the crazy people. This is us, now, in the quite ridiculous and suddenly rather marvellous Atatürk Stadium miles outside of Istanbul: the people who, not three minutes before, would probably have traded anything for a trip home for a quiet pint and a place in an empty bar, or in any darkened room in Walton or Old Swan. Now we look around us and, where once we saw only doomed expressions, we see hundreds of expectant Liverpool faces filled with hope. And, honestly, who would you rather be now? The silky-smooth team, the European aristocrats that were once 3–0 up and strolling? Or the side that was being humiliated and has now scored twice in just over two minutes out of nothing, and who are now being urged to score again by 40,000 complete lunatics? We know who we would rather be – the team that is still behind: the team that if the game ended right now would lose. It's mad, isn't it? And simply wonderful; it's just great being 2–3 down in the 2005 European Cup final. Vladdy has now done his bout of public badge-kissing: how could we have misjudged him so cruelly? Red flares are being lit on the North Tribune, dramatically illuminating the faces of all those crazies who clamour round. To our left, in contrast, the Milan fans on the South Tribune, rowed in neat little red, white and black plastic tunics and only minutes ago themselves rocking with joy and certainty about what was happening here, are now stilled and utterly silent. They know – as we know – that this is not finished after all.

Liverpool pour forward now, almost like a fighter does when he knows that he is completely on top of an opponent, ignoring the blows of his rival, swept onwards by adrenalin and a complete lack of fear. Since Shevchenko's free-kick Milan have barely had possession and have threatened nothing in Liverpool's half. Their play is suddenly aimless, full of doubt, and Kaka and Pirlo, so dominant in the first half, now seem overrun. With the veterans Maldini and Cafu at full-back, Milan also lack width and pace on the flanks, so their play is cramped into the middle of the field, which is suddenly populated by confident and energetic Liverpool midfielders – and soon by Bootle's Jamie Carragher. Because, as Smicer drifts inside, Benítez has told Carragher to offer support on the right, and this happens now as a ballooned Sami Hyypiä clearance ends up with Smicer in the middle of the Liverpool half of the pitch and he releases Carragher. The Liverpool man – a true Anfield hero this season amidst all the talk about so-called star names leaving the club – goes galloping forward unmarked, initially on Liverpool's right flank but then driving inside, the guttural sound of thousands of Liverpool voices urging him on.

Steven Gerrard now makes his own early start forward in the middle of the field. Ahead, Luis García makes an expectant run to the right flank, the obvious pass, but Carra ignores him and, instead, feeds a low ball inside to Milan Baros on the edge of the Milan penalty box. Baros has run hard and long already tonight, but his decision-making has been poor: a perennial problem. But, for once, he senses the run of Gerrard behind, who has motored through and beyond a startled Gattuso, and the Czech now flicks a delicate little pass into Steven's path inside the Milan box. Even from our foreshortened vantage point we can see that our man is running at pace and is flexed to shoot from close quarters. Given what has happened in the last few minutes, we now fully expect to see Dida's net bulge with Liverpool's equality. Except that Gerrard collapses, *Platoon* style, a man comprehensively corpsed from behind. A hidden sniper, perhaps? In fact, Gattuso has snagged at him, pulled the Huyton boy marginally off-balance – and in today's football world you really have to fall for this sort of thing, a professional's duty. PENALTY – for Liverpool! *It is now exactly 5 minutes 59 seconds since Paolo Maldini lost the ball, unknowingly, to start this Liverpool comeback.*

How do you respond to the award of a penalty kick in football – a cheque awarded but not yet cashed? I'll tell you how: you celebrate as if it were a goal – and then you catch yourself, reel yourself back in, and you become introspective and fearful. Self-doubt soon invades your head; you have to fight it off or it will kill your soul. It's starting here. First, why is Carra so upset with the referee? Has the ref, who pointed directly to the spot, now changed his mind and given something else? Oh shit! This once happened for us at Anfield in 2001, in the UEFA Cup with Roma, when another Spanish official, a Señor García-Aranda, pointed to the spot for Roma – and then offered them a corner instead. The

Italians weren't happy. If this guy changes his mind here, he soon might find 20,000 people in red trying out this protective Turkish running track. No, hold on, it is a pen; thank Christ for that. But Carra is still going wild, demanding that Gattuso is sent off: last man, goal-scoring opportunity, and all that. Benítez has actually told Carra to go and badger the ref on this one, to push him around – but Gattuso stays on, with a yellow. Panic over. But another one soon takes its place.

Who will take this kick? Under Houllier, Liverpool got into real problems for a while on this score. When Gary McAllister was in the side, a penalty kick meant that you could safely line up again for a restart kick-off. He never missed. But, later, Houllier decided that a reluctant Michael Owen should take the kicks and it all came off the rails. Michael, a consummate striker, of course, was less convincing with a stationary ball and with no defenders snapping at his heels. Fortunately Houllier eventually got the message and Danny Murphy then took over where Gary Mac had left off. Spud loved taking kicks for Liverpool, was ice cool, scored them all. But since Murphy got sent off, by Benítez, to the arid lands of south-east London, Steven Gerrard has recently been stepping up for Liverpool – and has been missing. He won't be risked here. So who? Baros can't be trusted. García would fancy it, but is he secure? Riise would get our vote, but he never comes forward. What about Carragher? He scored at Cardiff in 2001, even though he said he was shitting himself. But it is none of these. Instead, in his first major final, it is a man who has never won a winner's medal of any kind in football. It will be our Spanish coach's football 'son' who steps up. God help him.

Xabi Alonso, 23 years old, central midfielder, was Benítez's £10 million gift to Liverpool. His father, Periko, a tough midfielder himself, won two Spanish league titles with Real Sociedad and Alonso followed in his father's footsteps in San Sebastian until Benítez brought him to Anfield from under the noses of Real Madrid. Initially the passing midfield leader feared coming to England because of its reputation for the long-ball game and a lack of sophistication, but he soon knew he had come to the right club: 'Liverpool have always been a bit more Continental,' he said. 'You can see and hear the reaction in the stadium when you make three consecutive good passes. Anfield supporters have been taught good football.'

Liverpool pass-master Jan Molby watched Alonso play in Euro 2004 for Spain. He liked what he saw: 'Every pass he made, I was saying, "That's the right one; that's the right one." I knew this kid was special.' Jan knew his stuff all right – and Xabi even got used to missing the fresh-fish meals he so loved back home on the northern Spanish coast.

Mourinho's Chelsea had figured large in Xabi's first season in England, because Alonso had broken an ankle in a League match against the Londoners at Anfield in January, so missing much of the League season. Liverpool slumped. He also missed out on the second leg of the European Cup semi-final against Chelsea because of a harsh first-leg yellow card. But here he now stands, with Liverpool FC's future almost literally at his feet: a silver ball on a creamy white spot, and nine metres away from a man who is desperate to frustrate Red dreams. It looks pretty easy – easy, that is, if you can still swallow and move your legs at all. Because in this kind of situation, an emotional switchback ride of a night, a penalty miss now by Liverpool virtually settles the match again for Milan. This is how we see it. This comeback has been so extraordinary, but also so physically draining, that the psychological effect of missing a chance like this to get level again would be completely disastrous. It would absolutely deflate the Liverpool players, make them feel their legs, and infect even the fans who have dragged themselves up into believing again. It would also lift the Milan players: the gods have not deserted us after all.

So this is the match, right here. We can't say at this moment whether a levelling Liverpool goal will mean a win for our heroes – getting level often acts as a weird psychological barrier to going on positively to win the game. But we can say that a penalty miss will mean certain defeat. It's that simple. And it is also why, when we look around us in the Liverpool crowd now, people have got hands clasped around their faces and there is fear in the eyes of those half-watching through their fingers; some people are not even looking at all. Twenty years in the waiting, thousands of pounds spent and hundreds of miles travelled to a field of light in the middle of nowhere. And now this torture: who could blame them?

Alonso now steps forward. Mercifully, there is no fancy stuff here: no 'broken' run-up, no waiting for the keeper to move, no wild slash at the ball. He places the kick low down to Dida's right side. But the Brazilian goalkeeper has correctly read Alonso's intentions and he has stretched a long, right arm along the ground to block the ball's path. The action of this intervention actually rolls up his goalkeeper's green jersey on that arm, so that he looks strangely lop-sided when he stands up again. A gasp begins to escape around us as the ball now returns to Alonso's feet. It's a save! But the Spaniard has not stopped his forward movement and he is calm enough, even with Nesta hacking at him from behind and the crowd going wild, to meet the ball on the rebound, but this time with his left foot and, crucially, to loft it high into the net over the rising Dida.

Benítez said later that it was a 'terrible feeling' missing a penalty kick in such a situation: 'If Xabi had not shot in the rebound, I feared the sky would have fallen on him.'

But our sky is all red. It takes us barely a microsecond to make sense of all of this – the shot, the save, the rebound, the Nesta hack, the goal, the net. Exactly 6 minutes 47 seconds ago AC Milan were cantering through the 2005 European Cup final, leading 3–0 and threatening more. Now it is 3–3! And the Liverpool celebrations are, at last, unconditional, unrestrained, chaotic. On the pitch, Baros is threatening to strangle Alonso in near-sexual ecstasy. He should try it with us. Everywhere we look there are people wrestling each other, falling over exhausted, delirious bodies. We look wild-eyed, tugging at each other, as if to ask: are we *really* here? We must be because when we look later in the shower or in our beds at the bruises and grazes on our legs, it is back here that we picked each other up. But who feels any pain now?

The old fella behind us, our Liverpool 'History Man', he is just sitting on his seat, head bowed, as the world goes quite mental around him. He might be crying again, but this time it is a very different set of tears. We check our watches: is it injury-time yet? In fact there are still 30 minutes left of what some insane folk might call 'normal' time in the European Cup final that knowledgeable people will describe later as possibly the greatest of all time. How will we make it back home from here – or even through the next half-hour? And what might Liverpool's great European guru Bob Paisley be thinking now about all of this, as he looks down upon us from these pitch-black Turkish skies?

## Chapter Two

# FROM BOOT ROOM TO BIG SCIENCE: PAISLEY, EVANS, HOULLIER

### UNCLE BOB

If any individual can be said to have embodied and encapsulated the 'Liverpool Way' over the course of the decades from the 1960s through to the 1990s – especially, perhaps, for major matches in Europe – then Bob Paisley is that man. Working at Liverpool FC, in one capacity or another, throughout the post-war era until the early 1990s, Bob Paisley was regarded, uniformly by the coaching staff and the players, as a deep thinker about the game, an excellent (and at times uncanny) judge of a player's physical condition, but generally a poor communicator. But was Paisley's image carefully honed, perhaps to lull opponents into a false sense of security? Stories abound of his uncomplicated tastes, whether in clothes, food or football. His captain Graeme Souness recalls Paisley's flat cap and carpet slippers, the latter worn whenever possible because of an injured ankle. In Paris, after the European Cup final victory against Real Madrid, Paisley looked incongruous in the palatial splendour of the team's hotel, and Souness recalls him 'sitting back with a cigar, a glass of whisky and wearing those old-fashioned slippers . . . Completely relaxed and apparently not at all excited.'

Before training every morning, Paisley would stop in at a local garage for a cup of tea, while he picked out his horses from the paper, and Souness used to meet him there for a chat. The journalist and writer Stan Hey argued, however, that 'it would do Paisley a disservice to try to define him as the last true football man, with its connotations of centre-partings, boot-room camaraderie and home-spun values, because, although he embraced all of these, he was also one of the great thinkers and modernisers of the English game'.

Souness agreed that Bob was, in fact, a 'football "intellectual". Had he been more articulate, he would have been hailed as one of the greatest thinkers and managers of the game.'

Stan Liversedge, Liverpool's programme editor for many seasons and ghost-writer of successive manager's notes, wrote that, 'anyone who took Bob Paisley for a fool would have spent his money badly . . . He was a canny fellow, all right – and don't let that woolly-cardigan image fool you.'

It didn't fool Liverpool fans – not for a moment.

Paisley's image as a 'kindly . . . favourite uncle type' should not, therefore, distract us from his ambitions for Liverpool, and his willingness to gently, but firmly, remind commentators of his prowess. When Liverpool won the European Cup in 1977 and became the first British side to retain it the following year, Paisley acknowledged that Bill Shankly 'had to take a lot of the credit for what happened . . . But on the other score, there is a bit of credit due to me and the staff [including Joe Fagan, Ronnie Moran and Roy Evans], because we changed the whole team over.' In 1978, before the defence of the European Cup, Paisley pointed out, and not immodestly, that 'in their history, Liverpool have now won or been runners-up in the League, FA Cup and European Cups 36 times. And I've been involved on 26 of those occasions, as player, assistant manager, or manager.' It is not hard to see how this record inspired the players, and despite his apparent uncertainty with the media, he commanded real respect among them. Souness argued that although 'he may have been regarded as a fatherly figure by the supporters . . . let me tell you, he ruled at Anfield with a rod of iron . . . He was a commanding man and there were few who dared mess around with him. If we looked as though we were becoming a little complacent . . . Bob would say, "If you have all had enough of winning, come and see me and I will sell the lot of you and buy 11 new players."' He meant it.

A crucial aspect of Paisley's approach was the search for players who could display flexibility out on the pitch, who were intelligent enough to make decisions and communicate with each other during the maelstrom of fiercely competitive matches and the chess-like European games, and who did not 'hide', but actively sought out responsibility. As Tom Saunders, long-serving youth development coach, observed, 'I can't recall a time here where players have been looking towards the bench for advice for what should happen next . . . It's a decision-making game, and you want men who can assume responsibility and make decisions on the pitch while the game's going on.' The Liverpool Way emphasised the hard work involved in winning, and then repeatedly winning over and over, season after season. As soon as the Championship or a cup was safely tucked away, the celebrations barely over, Bob or Joe Fagan would be moving on, the slate wiped clean, reminding the players that it would be more difficult next year. Ronnie Moran's deliberately low-key reaction to a hard-won victory was, 'I've got a job for another week.'

## *ALLEZ LES ROUGES!* LEARNING FROM EUROPE

This philosophy of the game was exported to good effect to the European arena, with a UEFA Cup success in 1976, followed by back-to-back European Cups in Rome and London, and a final swansong for Paisley in Paris in 1981. Liverpool's emphasis upon passing the ball, maintaining options for the player in possession through unceasing movement of (and off) the ball, and defending collectively when the ball was lost, was not necessarily European in its inspiration. However, Liverpool's style did develop through the assimilation of new ideas and tactical ploys, as they qualified annually for European competition from 1964 until 1985, when, after Heysel, the club was banned from Europe until 1991.

Liverpool took several significant lessons from early controversial European experiences (dubious refereeing at Inter Milan in 1965, for example). From then on, when playing abroad, there was a strong sense of suspicion regarding the conditions, both on and off the pitch, which awaited the visitors. Undoubtedly, travel and facilities in the 1960s and '70s were not comparable with the standards enjoyed by the teams of subsequent years. Paisley and his staff tried to come up with ways to combat these, perhaps exaggerated, concerns and fears, including taking their own food and bottled water, arriving at their destination only the afternoon before the match and trying to isolate the team from any problems that might arise. These precautions maybe served a dual purpose, in building team spirit in perceived conditions of adversity and concentrating the players' minds. Eventually, on the pitch, Liverpool were capable of absorbing any intimidation, settling themselves and imposing their own game. Off the pitch these European trips were not occasions for the players and staff to broaden their cultural horizons, and foreign climes were always treated as potentially hostile. But, Paisley reassured, 'We don't go around with our eyes shut.' If there were footballing lessons to be learned on these trips abroad, Bob and the staff were only too willing to gather information.

## THE REDS IN TURKEY (PART ONE)

Before the 2005 European Cup extravaganza in Istanbul Liverpool had played twice before in Turkey, both times in the European Cup: once against Galatasaray in the Champions League in 2002, and once in a second-round tie in the autumn of 1976, en route to the glory that was Rome later that season. That first trip represents a good illustration of some of the themes mentioned above. The Reds were drawn with Trabzonspor, an unknown quantity from the Black Sea port of Trabzon, 500 miles east of Istanbul. Paisley talked about 'getting the atlas out' and flying into 'the unknown' for this fixture. When Liverpool arrived, he was less than impressed. Bob, a football man of his time, was bordering on the xenophobic in his distinctly unflattering description of Trabzon, 'with its Eastern atmosphere, yashmaks and wailing Muslims and no Turkish delight'. On arrival at the hotel Bob's mood darkened further: 'I told everyone to stay on the bus while I went to make an inspection, and I was horrified by what I saw. It was a doss-house, and if you said it had a star rating it was only because you could see them through the holes in the roof . . . It was a squalid place, with food to match . . . The players existed just on chocolate they had brought from England . . . It was a thoroughly nasty experience.'

Paisley went on to argue that enduring these conditions 'made us all the more determined to beat the Turks where it mattered – out on the pitch'. Unfortunately, this determination came to naught, and the Reds were beaten 1–0. On a pitch that was 'as rough as everything else . . . uneven, with dangerous potholes in it', with 'an old bladder of a ball', the Reds could not muster a shot. The Trabzonspor goal was a 'dubious' penalty (you guessed it!), but Bob said, 'We weren't too concerned, however, because the Turks hadn't shown anything to be alarmed about, and we were confident we could turn the tables in the return leg at Anfield. We were just glad to take off from Trabzon and head for home.'

A 3–0 blast in the first 20 minutes at Anfield confirmed Paisley's view, but he still managed one last dig: 'the only disappointment was the attitude of the Turks in defeat. When they realised they were on their way out of the competition, they kicked up rough.' The lesson Paisley drew from the 'worst conditions I have ever come across' was that 'it's when you face that kind of thing that you look for the character and spirit in the side. Without it your chances are next to zero.'

Liverpool also learned the virtues of patience and possession. Arguably, it was through the experience of playing over two legs in European competition that Liverpool refined their playing style, adopting elements of the Continental game that were complementary to the acknowledged strengths of the English game. This produced what has been described as a 'measured aggression': one that emphasised control of the tempo of the match, self-discipline and a ruthless streak. Away from home Liverpool teams attempted to maintain possession in a systematic fashion, often moving the ball around the back four (and including the goalkeeper, as was possible before the change to the back-pass law), frustrating the opposition and quietening the crowd. Attempting to 'draw the opposition onto them', Liverpool hoped to exploit counter-attacking opportunities as they arose, but they wouldn't be unduly concerned if the match was played at a slow tempo. If, by chance, they fell behind, Liverpool learned through bitter experience that they risked more misery by 'chasing the game', throwing caution and discipline to the wind. A 1–0 defeat was not disastrous, and could often be repaid with interest at Anfield. Drawing lessons from a 1973 defeat by Red Star Belgrade, Paisley pointed out, 'Our approach was a bit frantic. We treated every match like a war. The strength of British football lay in our challenge for the ball, but the Continentals took that away from us by learning how to intercept. We discovered it was no use winning the ball if you finished up on your backside.'

Liverpool learned from these experiences. 'The top Europeans showed us how to break out of defence effectively. The pace of their movement was dictated by the first pass. We had to learn how to be patient like that, and think about the next two or three moves ahead when we had the ball.'

Even when playing English opposition in Europe – as they would, of course, in 2005 – Liverpool still needed to adopt a 'European' mentality. According to Paisley, the Reds still managed to commit a costly error against Nottingham Forest in the away leg of the first round in 1978–79. 'When we were a goal down, we were looking for an equaliser instead of accepting that as a reasonable result in the first leg of a European Cup tie . . .' said Paisley.

However, the value of an away goal was also quickly learned. One of Liverpool's best-ever results in Europe, in the European Cup semi-final in 1981, proved the point. A 0–0 home draw with Bayern Munich was followed by a thrilling 1–1 result away, with Ray Kennedy scoring with fewer than ten minutes left. Sammy Lee had famously man-marked Bayern's most dangerous creative force, Paul Breitner, out of the game, illustrating that Liverpool were now also prepared to adjust their tactics to take account of opposition strengths. These lessons from playing in Europe had to be re-learned, sometimes painfully, for a new era and by new players, when Liverpool were re-admitted to European competition in 1991. For instance, defeat by the single goal at Anfield, in the second leg of a second-round UEFA Cup tie, against the moderate Danish side Brondby in 1995–96, had followed what many considered a 'tie-winning' scoreless draw in Copenhagen.

On Liverpool's return to European competition after the 1985–91 ban – manager Kenny Dalglish had no opportunities to lead the club in Europe – Graeme Souness inherited the task of making

Liverpool competitive here once more, but the record was not particularly impressive, at least initially. Liverpool lost 1–4 on aggregate to the moderate Italian side Genoa. The world of Continental football had moved on in the meantime, perhaps particularly in Italy, where the great AC Milan side of Arrigo Sacchi was sweeping all before it. A young Rafael Benítez looked on admiringly from Spain, as Milan, inspired by the Dutch triumvirate of Van Basten, Gullit and Rijkaard, played a new, high-tempo 'pressing' game, very different from Liverpool's European style, at least away from home. In the late 1990s the insular, suspicious, but nevertheless highly successful traditional Liverpool Way in Europe, exemplified in the boot-room culture, would meet the technocratic and scientific approach of a new breed of Continental coach. With Roy Evans as manager, joined in 1998 by Gérard Houllier, this clash of footballing cultures was made flesh; it proved hard to reconcile these philosophies, at least in the short-term.

## GOOD EVANS

Arguably, the real roots of Liverpool's recent European renaissance are located in the mid-1990s, when the club briefly rediscovered the sort of style and rhythm that was quite in tune, once more, with the Liverpool Way. This was very much a case of a progressive and sympathetic move by the Liverpool board 'back to the future', to a servant from the famous Melwood boot room of Bob Paisley: but it also produced some of the best football and nurtured some of the best young talent seen at Anfield in a generation.

The loyal Bootle boy Roy Evans, a self-effacing ex-player, club coach, reserve-team manager and assistant manager at Liverpool, had never wanted, or expected, the manager's job at Anfield. He was in very good company, of course: Bob Paisley, Joe Fagan, Ronnie Moran and even Kenny Dalglish had all felt the same way when the management call at L4 came down from above. But after the collapse of Graeme Souness's Liverpool project in 1994, Evans was finally pitched by his friend and club chairman David Moores into the Big Office, into the managerial role at troubled Liverpool. His first match was on 5 February 1994, an entertaining but typically frustrating 2–2 draw at Carrow Road with Norwich City.

In the East Anglian winter sunshine that day – on yet another new Anfield dawn? – Liverpool's always trembling back line creaked in the face of a young Chris Sutton's endless boring and fouling.

After the convulsions under the impatient moderniser, Souness, the Liverpool board had returned, once again, to the comfort of the past to try to revive the club's ailing fortunes. After all, Liverpool's last League title was still warm, won only a paltry three years ago, though memories were more strained to recall the club's last great European triumph, now almost a decade distant. Evans quickly got rid of some of the unstable forces Souness had championed – Dicks, Hutchinson and Stewart were soon despatched – and he remodelled his new Liverpool around the talents of a fading, but still influential, John Barnes, revitalised after the departure of Souness, and three emerging young Liverpool talents: the film-star-looks midfielder Jamie Redknapp, the loping cross-country runner Steve McManaman, and an icy teenage striker, the left-footed Toxteth genius Robbie Fowler.

Now if you like your football cerebral and smooth, a calm masterclass in passing and patience, these were halcyon days indeed in L4. With Evans and Barnes in charge, and McManaman directing attacks, Liverpool kept the ball with ease and even controlled matches: a feature that had been increasingly lacking under Souness. Between 26 November 1994 and 11 March 1995, Liverpool lost just one match in twenty-four – though too many matches were drawn, provoking accusations that Evans's team was pretty to watch, sure, but lacked real focus and devil. A McManaman-inspired League Cup triumph against Bolton Wanderers in 1995 seemed like it might be the springboard to greater things, and the recruitment of the mercurial Stan Collymore from Nottingham Forest in the summer of 1995 for a British-record transfer fee of £8.5 million looked like an emphatic statement of intent. In 1995–96 on the field Collymore and Fowler wrecked opposing defences but off it, like a computer virus, Stanley was also a threat to Liverpool's team spirit and harmony, as well as the still fragile credibility and authority of Roy Evans. Worse was to come: a white-Armani-suited surrender to Manchester United in an execrable Wembley FA Cup final.

In the 1996–97 season, with player power an emerging new

feature of the game, salaries rocketing and celebrity culture infesting football dressing-rooms everywhere, but especially, the press argued, at Anfield – Roy Evans seemed increasingly like a man from a very different, more decent era. He began to lose his way. Out went John Barnes and the 3–5–2 formation after an especially cowardly Liverpool defeat in France to Paris St Germain in the European Cup-Winners' Cup semi-final and, for 1997–98, in came 4–4–2, marshalled by the more destructive Paul Ince and a new, potent challenger to the still adolescent Robbie Fowler, the irrepressible England schoolboy star Michael Owen. Despite Owen's immediate impact it was third place again for Liverpool, but this time they were a distant 13 points behind Double-winning Arsenal. Arsenal's Championship success also carried with it a new warning for local boot-room boy Evans: Arsène Wenger, a full-blooded European technocrat, a new footballing *professeur,* was now established at the Highbury helm, having imported foreign talent and completed an impressive stable-cleaning job inside the old Marble Halls. With Champions League cash now flowing into north London and Old Trafford, Anfield, by comparison, suddenly looked outdated and disorderly – and in danger of being cut adrift by the new European football elite.

## *ENTENTE CORDIALE* – OR *GLACIALE* ?

Roy Evans may well have looked ahead to the 1998–99 league season believing he was unlikely to start it as manager of Liverpool Football Club. But the Liverpool board is loyal – some might argue to the point of uncertainty – and lacking some of the necessary ruthlessness that was increasingly identified as being absent in their chosen manager. Evans knew he was unlikely to be sacked – it would be like discarding a favoured son – and he was also loath to resign because of his deep sense of duty to the club. Instead Liverpool needed a third way, a new departure.

The wily old club secretary Peter Robinson found it. Robinson thought Liverpool needed their own Wenger, but without the pain of discarding Evans. Both he and chief-executive-in-waiting Rick Parry knew and admired Gérard Houllier, one of the respected architects of the French youth system that had fashioned the 1998 World Cup-winning French team. Houllier, a schoolmasterly and civilised disciplinarian, but with no playing career to shout about, certainly looked like another Wenger in the making. Houllier had taught in the city and was a long-standing admirer of Liverpool FC.

When the smoke eventually cleared, Roy Evans was as willing and amenable as ever: *share* the manager's job? Why not? If it will help the Liverpool club, sure. Was this naivety, or simply decency? Probably both. Peter Robinson had attracted Houllier back to Liverpool with the promise that he would, initially at least, share manager's duties with Evans – but if it didn't work out, the Frenchman would have his opportunity alone. Evans was led to believe that Houllier was being recruited for his European knowledge and expertise to replace the retiring Ronnie Moran as club coach. It was only when the two men actually met and sat down with the board and job titles were discussed that someone suggested 'joint manager' would probably best reflect the new working arrangement. This was, at best, disingenuous, back-door diplomacy. The experienced Gérard Houllier was, justifiably perhaps, unwilling to be subordinate to Roy, and Roy, being Roy, as the board knew he would, had reservations about the new deal but swallowed them for the sake of unity of purpose. Tellingly, Houllier was also allowed by Liverpool to bring with him his own coach, Frenchman Patrice Berguès. Although Evans little knew it, the battle lines were already being drawn up inside the club.

Working together as joint managers in a context as hierarchical and potentially full of conflict as an elite football club is difficult enough, but trying to combine differing managerial *styles* is simply a step too far. This became clear soon enough. For all his soft words and his cerebral approach, Gérard Houllier was also a tough and deceptively powerful presence, a man who could be autocratic and high-handed. In his eyes, the power of the football manager was absolute. Houllier immediately sacked a man recruited by Evans, the Liverpool fitness coach Andy Clarke, because Clarke was allegedly 'too close' to the players. Houllier also disliked dealing with players directly himself when they were angry or upset about being dropped or disciplined because he thought that this was demeaning to management – it showed a lack of authority and respect. Evans was more democratic and more up-front than the Frenchman, occasionally damagingly so: he wanted to be *liked* by his players as well as respected, and he found it difficult to give up the collective camaraderie and banter of the dressing-room, which were among the things he most enjoyed about being involved in the game.

The two men – different personalities, different philosophies of management – soon began to irritate each other. Houllier, keen to make an impact, tinkered with players' diets, and he seemed to interfere with their preparations almost for the sake of taking a hand. More damagingly, Houllier also seemed to Evans and to the players to be obsessed by the new coaching bible on player rotation. Sports science had told the Frenchman that elite professional players needed regular resting in order to perform at optimum mental and physical levels. Years of successful work under Shankly and Bob Paisley had, by contrast, taught Roy Evans that changing a winning team was the resort of losers. This was a major early point of disagreement, especially when Liverpool began changing a winning team – and losing. Houllier's more 'open' Continental coaching consciousness also seemed to conflict with the battle-hardened, self-sufficient British approach of Paisley's era. Already it seemed that this unstable marriage simply couldn't last.

Matters came to a head in European competition, in a typically fraught UEFA Cup second-leg tie at Valencia in November 1998. Liverpool had failed to score at home in a cagey 0–0 stalemate with the Spaniards and were favourites for elimination, especially when Valencia went ahead in the tie before half-time at the Mestalla. But an unexpectedly gutsy show by the visitors produced late goals from McManaman and Patrik Berger and an unlikely and seemingly secure Liverpool lead: this tie was now over. Until, that is, the usually placid Macca and the abrasive Paul Ince managed to get themselves sent off by the French referee in a 'handbags' skirmish with Valencia's Carboni. This debacle left enough time for David James to concede a crazy late own goal for 2–2. Chaotic, nine-man Liverpool then hung on, inelegantly, for the finish.

Roy Evans – Paisley's footballing son, of course – now wanted to leave Spain and the UEFA-appointed officials as soon as possible. Gérard Houllier was much less agitated: he was humming to himself and calmly collecting Liverpool team shirts from the dressing-room floor that he had already promised to give to the French referee and his assistants as souvenirs. Evans exploded. This piece of apparently minor symbolic betrayal was just too much for a man who had been in the football trenches abroad many times before. The Bootle man was hardly celebrating Liverpool's survival in Europe. Instead, he deliberated hard about his future on the flight home from Spain. How could he work with a man who seemed so flagrantly disloyal to the visceral club cause: someone who could be so coldly professional and detached? Roy Evans decided that he was on his way out of Anfield for the last time.

## DANGER: FRENCHMAN AT WORK

Roy Evans's departure was an awkward, but clearly not an unexpected, turn of events. Gérard Houllier immediately accepted Roy's decision go and Evans's departure merited an editorial in *The Guardian*, no less, about how it signalled the passing of the decent, but limited, British manager and his replacement by the more technical and educated Continental equivalent. It was rather more than Evans eventually got from the Liverpool board. Initially he was offered a job upstairs, but said he had no desire to hang around Anfield like a 'ghost on the wall', perhaps as Bill Shankly had threatened to do in the early 1970s. But there was no presentation or other acknowledgement of loyal service for Evans, as there had been for other club boot-room men like Paisley, Fagan and Moran. Maybe Houllier and the board now simply wanted a clean break with the past, in order to get the club moving fast in a new direction, unencumbered by its recent history. In any event it left a bitter taste for Evans, one he admitted he had problems overcoming in the unemployment years that followed.

Houllier was also very cute, as Evans later commented, because the Frenchman was soon talking loudly about how it would be at least a four- or five-year job to 'turn Liverpool around'. What – when the club had actually finished in the top four in each of Evans's four seasons in charge and was third in the table when Houllier took over? This patient had major problems all right, but it seemed to have a stubborn virus rather than some potentially terminal illness, as the Frenchman was now implying. Liverpool eventually finished an unacceptable seventh in the league in this disrupted season, with 14 games lost. A highly publicised 'romp' at the club's Christmas party, starring an unsuitably roused Jamie Carragher, provided further proof – if it were needed – that indiscipline was rife within the L4 organisation. Houllier probably smiled faintly at the stupidity and backwardness of it all – and set to work.

He first needed a devoted 'hit man': Tom Saunders suggested Phil Thompson should be recalled for duty. The Kirkby man jumped at the chance to reconnect with Anfield after his massive earlier falling out with the then manager Graeme Souness. So far, so good. Houllier also wanted what he regarded as the disruptive Liverpool dressing-room influences out of the club: the British barrack-room lawyers (Ince); the erratic (James); the occasionally indisciplined (McAteer, David Thompson); and the seemingly uncommitted (McManaman). McManaman's departure on a 'Bosman' – the first in the English game – was an expensive early lesson about the peculiar economics of 'new' football. Houllier took careful note: within a year he had signed experienced German international Markus Babbel by the same method.

With a strong local core already in hand – Carragher, Owen, Fowler, the ex-Crewe man Danny Murphy and the impressive, emerging Huyton boy Steven Gerrard – Houllier's early recruits for season 1999–2000 also signalled an entirely new direction for Liverpool, a confident step into the new globalised football age. One of the early arrivals, the leggy French youngster Djimi Traoré, made it all the way to Istanbul. He was followed to Anfield by the much more reliable Finn Sami Hyypiä, arguably Houllier's best Liverpool signing, and his defensive partner, the dogged Swiss international Stéphane Henchoz. For just over £6 million the Frenchman had now recruited the linchpins of his early successful Liverpool defence – good business by any measure. The aloof Sander Westerveld, from Vitesse Arnhem, was bought for £4 million to replace David James in goal, while the German international Dietmar Hamann cost £8 million from closer to home Newcastle United. Hamann was also a crucial Houllier signing, a lasting Anglophile success in what was to become an increasingly important central-defensive midfield position in the modern game. Hamann would also play a crucial role in the 2005 final.

Houllier's multiple defensive signings signalled his likely approach to the game: conservative and cautious. But for the Liverpool attack he also brought in for £4 million Vladimir Smicer, a talented but fragile Czech. Houllier's signings made up £27 million worth of new blood and, early in 2000, he laid out another £11 million, this time on Leicester City's coltish Emile Heskey for the seasonal run-in. A muscular and uncomplicated young forward, Heskey was bought to complement the defter striking skills of Michael Owen and Robbie Fowler.

The key to all these signings for Houllier – with the exception perhaps of Hamann and, to an extent, Smicer – was that they all still had their reputations to make in the game. The Frenchman preferred to recruit youthful and relatively undiscovered talent, players he could mould and shape to his Liverpool project, rather than deal with well-known established players who might have more 'completed' personalities and thus offer challenges to his authority via strong ideas about playing styles and tactics.

This policy was partially financially driven, of course: both Houllier and Rick Parry now stressed that Liverpool could no longer match the outlays of the European football giants. But Houllier also enjoyed the prospect of developing young players and improving their game. He believed, quite unselfconsciously, in the value of top coaches and had sufficient ego to be willing to talk publicly about the ways in which he could help improve the match performances even of top Liverpool international players. Few other top managers in the English game spoke openly in this way about themselves, preferring the on-field credit to be taken by players, while also fielding criticism for them when it came. Later it seemed to some that Houllier actually preferred to do the reverse: grab praise when it was being offered but avoid responsibility when things went awry.

## TREBLE CHANCE

With Liverpool's new global recruitment policies and the new manager's more 'scientific' methods – players' diets and behaviour were now closely monitored, alcohol was banned for players at Anfield and Houllier pored over statistical analyses of their performances late into the night – the team's approach under

Houllier had little of the free-flowing qualities often seen under the unfortunate Roy Evans. Back to a rigid and more solid 4–4–2, Houllier – like the early Bob Paisley – championed a tough defensive core at the heart of his team, but unlike Bob he also had problems converting defensive solidity into truly penetrative and sophisticated counter-attack. Fans of other clubs even teased Liverpool supporters with hurtful jibes about their club 'hoofing' the ball under the Frenchman's direction. While Liverpool was winning football matches, this was just about bearable, but with Champions League qualification in sight in April 2000 Liverpool's challenge inexplicably collapsed in the last five league fixtures, with no goals scored and no wins. It was a huge disappointment – but at least this failure also offered Houllier one more year's welcome preparation before facing the major challenge of top European competition.

With Markus Babbel already added to the Liverpool squad, Houllier spent big again in 2000: Diomède, Barmby and Christian Ziege all arrived at Anfield. By November they had been joined by the unheralded Igor Biscan, a much sought after and puzzlingly languid 22-year-old Croatian international, for £5.5 million, and also a skilful 18-year-old French left-back, Gregory Vignal. These were signature Houllier signings of the time: young, relative unknowns designed to be honed to carry his new Liverpool into the new century. By 2005 the once-derided Igor Biscan had partially revived his fading Liverpool career under Rafa Benítez and had made the 2005 European Cup final squad.

Later in the 2000–01 season the experienced and talented Finnish Liverpool fan Jari Litmanen was added to the forwards but, alas, this was probably a couple of years too late for him to make any real impact in the fast-paced and physical British game. Houllier certainly showed little trust in his new acquisition. But one signing stood out amongst all of these, a man who cost nothing in transfer fees and who was recruited essentially to improve the overall professionalism in the young squad. At 35 years of age, midfielder Gary McAllister, apparently drifting into full-time football management at Coventry City, set off in a new direction: he was actually about to have the season of his football-playing life at Liverpool.

Much – too much – has already been written about Liverpool's amazing 2000–01 cup and league campaign under Gérard Houllier. In the 2001 Worthington Cup Liverpool rode their luck in the draw and in the final to eventually overcome plucky First Division Birmingham City, if only on penalties. Michael Owen sat out his first major final on the bench, while his rival Robbie Fowler captained and scored – just a little early lesson for Michael about the benefits of patience and a manager's absolute authority. In the FA Cup Liverpool also had good fortune with the draw before positively stealing the final from Arsenal in Cardiff. This time Michael Owen was brilliantly inspired at the last. In Europe, in the 2001 UEFA Cup, Liverpool astonished with a victory in Rome against AS Roma; appalled the European elite with a 0–0 semi-final bore draw in Barcelona, remaining rooted in their own penalty area in the Camp Nou; and then wore down little Alaves from Spain 5–4 in an emotional and dramatic final in Dortmund. By any measure this was an incredible return to grace after the fallow Liverpool years of the 1990s – and it was one led from the front by the studious, meticulous Houllier. The Red half of Merseyside rejoiced – and looked forward to the league title residing once more at Anfield, surely, in 2002. But, as it always does, fate was to intervene, damaging both the triumphant Gérard Houllier and the ambitions of his football club.

## HEART OF DARKNESS

In the summer of 2001 John Arne Riise arrived from Monaco for £4 million. It was money very well spent – Riise was a key Liverpool player in the successful 2005 European Cup campaign, though by now in a left midfield role. Houllier also signed the precocious 18-year-old Czech Milan Baros from Banik Ostrava in August 2001. Baros was just the sort of raw talent Houllier enjoyed honing: a forward with real pace but little team sense or native football intelligence. Even in 2005 he remained a paradox: an important but largely frustrating presence in the Liverpool European Cup-winning team. Houllier – and later Rafa Benítez – seemed to make relatively little coaching progress here. However, poor goalkeeping by Sander Westerveld in an early-season Liverpool league defeat at Bolton Wanderers soon spoiled all the Houllier transfer parsimony:

the Liverpool manager simply stepped out and spent a cool £11 million on *two* new goalkeepers, the Pole Jerzy Dudek from Feyenoord and a budding young England hopeful, Chris Kirkland from Coventry City. Cup-winning hero Sander quickly packed his bags, chastened by his manager's ruthlessness.

An uneven Liverpool start to the new season – the holder Reds were soon knocked out of the League Cup at home by little Grimsby Town – was then further undermined by dreadful misfortune for Houllier himself. During a routine home league draw with Leeds United on 13 October 2001 the Frenchman complained of chest pains. At half-time he was rushed to Broadgreen Hospital in Liverpool, where he received 11 hours of emergency heart surgery on a damaged aorta. Exhaustion, more than stress, was the cause of his problems – and a football man's unwillingness to own up to his own vulnerability: 'I was reluctant to go into work, which was just not me,' he said later. 'Physically, I felt something was wrong, but I did not show that to my players. If you show you are weak, your team will be weak.' So he had soldiered on. Phil Thompson now took over, despite local calls to bring back Kenny Dalglish as stand-in manager, and immediately led Liverpool to a historic Champions League victory in Kiev.

Phil Thompson led Liverpool determinedly and astutely during his manager's absence, keeping Liverpool's defensive pragmatism alive and well in both league and European competitions. He also oversaw – while Houllier directed, of course – the controversial £12 million transfer of local hero Robbie Fowler to Championship rivals Leeds United, with Fowler reluctantly leaving behind an astonishing record of 171 goals in 329 matches for the club – quite a legacy. By this stage even Gary McAllister's trusty legs were starting to creak at last. An Arsenal December win at Anfield – with only ten men – served early notice of where the League Championship was already heading once more.

19 March 2002: a date in modern Liverpool FC folklore. The stricken Liverpool manager Houllier returned from heart surgery, a white-faced and slightly stooping touch-line presence tossed carelessly into a cauldron of noise and passion on a breathless European Anfield night set to rank with the greatest occasions at the club. Capello's mighty Roma capitulated in the face of a

Liverpool onslaught from pitch and stands and a home manager at the very peak of his inspirational and emotional bonding with the club's fans and his young team. But if this was Houllier's glorious Anfield high, then he also seemed a rather different man following his brush with death. Replacing the all-too-familiar and careful 'each game as it comes' rhetoric of last season, suddenly the Frenchman was off to the press with an unlikely 'ten games from glory' pledge about a Liverpool team he thought was 'on the verge of greatness'. Had this sudden euphoria come from the thrill of recovery? And who would not be changed by a life-shattering experience such as that which had so nearly claimed the Frenchman?

However, bitter European defeat and quarter-final elimination awaited at Leverkusen. Curiously – as it was to do, more positively, in the European Cup final three years later in Istanbul – a crucial substitution in the BayArena concerning Dietmar Hamann seemed to seal Liverpool's fate. The German was withdrawn at a critical moment with Liverpool ahead in the tie. Some Liverpool fans claimed that defeat had been snatched by Houllier from the very jaws of victory. This shock elimination produced only deflation in the league in the face of all-conquering Arsenal. But at least Liverpool were to pile up an impressive 80 points in second place, even in a truly disjointed season. It proved to be the high point of the Houllier and Thompson domestic league challenges.

## THE END OF THE BEGINNING

With a recharged manager, a first Champions League quarter-final plus more challenges in Europe ahead, and a gallant second in the league to better all those more minor placings under the unlucky Roy Evans, surely Liverpool were now only some strategic player investments away from the major prizes both at home and abroad? What could be clearer? In a World Cup summer (2002) Houllier was given his head by the Liverpool board, once more, to bring in more firepower. Ironically, it was Rafa Benítez and Valencia who were on the brink of signing Senegal's 21-year-old forward El-Hadji Diouf when Houllier stepped in to secure the Lens man for £10 million. Fast and direct, Diouf was certainly one of the early stars of Japan 2002 and Houllier claimed that he was signing 'four players in one', with the Senegalese having exactly the sort of adaptability lacking in English players, who were 'short-sighted' and inflexible by comparison. 'Diouf,' said a delighted Houllier, 'is a fighter and a warrior.'

This was a bold claim for an indisciplined player yet to make his mark in the robust and unforgiving Premiership and a man who seemed drawn to the turf by gravity's pull even when in mere sight of international defenders. We would have to wait and see how he fared. A further £5 million was invested on Diouf's Senegal teammate, the less talented but more physical midfielder Salif Diao: a poor man's Patrick Vieira, perhaps – a *very* poor man, as it turned out. From Lille Houllier brought in the little known Frenchman Bruno Cheyrou for £3.7 million, a forward-thinking midfielder who was, soon, fatally saddled by his new manager with 'the next Zidane' descriptive baggage. By mid-season most Liverpool fans would certainly have settled for the next Ray Houghton – or even the next Oyvind Leonhardsen – because Cheyrou, two-footed but peanut-hearted in the main, seemed nothing less than bemused and cowed by the sheer violence of the English game. He disappeared almost completely.

Houllier then made an audacious – perhaps reckless – bid to sign the disgraced Leeds United midfielder Lee Bowyer, a man not long cleared in court of assault and affray after a hideous street attack. Bowyer seemed to be the antithesis of the values Houllier championed for the new Anfield. But the manager, having had his own 'second chance', seemed bent on personally reforming the Londoner – and for a hefty £9 million price tag. As Reds fans protested on the club's websites, Bowyer's advisers tried to squeeze more cash out of the proposed deal and Houllier, advised by Rick Parry, pulled the plug on the bid. It was a close shave: in 2005, as Liverpool drew ever closer to the Istanbul summit, Bowyer, by now at Newcastle United, was sent off and found guilty of bringing the game into disrepute for assaulting his own teammate Kieron Dyer in front of 50,000, mainly Geordie, fans.

Liverpool began the 2002–03 season as authentic title contenders, amassing 30 points out of the first 36 contested. Initially it looked like this might be £20 million well spent by Houllier, en route at last to the title, though, to be frank, even this

2002–03 Liverpool team ground out results rather than enthralled. Then the season flipped and, again, Houllier seemed to be the catalyst. He, first, sent a capriciously defensive formation to Middlesbrough for Liverpool's first league defeat on 9 November. Psychologically this was a massive blow: it seemed like a loss of faith by the manager in his players. It had followed a positively perverse Houllier selection for the Mestalla in the Champions League in September, where three of his new young recruits – Traoré, Diao (played at centre-back) and Diouf – were completely embarrassed by Rafa Benítez's Valencia. One journalist described the contest as a 'cultural collision', one in which Liverpool lacked coherence, flair and technical expertise, or any truly creative culture of their own. They played as if a teacher had sent them into an examination with the correct answers learned by rote – and were then faced with a quite different set of questions. Liverpool escaped Spain with a 2–0 defeat, but simply looked miles behind on the top European stage, a fact confirmed when Valencia also won comfortably at Anfield in October.

Recovery in Europe was still possible, of course, but once down 3–0 to jittery Basle in the European qualification decider in November, Houllier's new Liverpool looked utterly demoralised. Even a late recovery, to a 3–3 scoreline – shades of Istanbul in 2005 – did little to hide the cracks in confidence and ability that now ran throughout the Liverpool side. These cracks certainly seemed to damage the very sinews of the deflated Steven Gerrard, whose form was now awful. The coaching staff and Liverpool players had moved, in a matter of days it seemed, from the production of a team with some title potential and European promise – 'brilliantly efficient', according to Houllier – to one that now looked incapable of winning the shallowest of contests. The wider ramifications of this slump, including the juddering effects on players' belief in the manager, were likely to be felt well beyond this campaign. This was probably the moment when Houllier's hold on the Liverpool job really began to loosen. Demoted to the UEFA Cup, Liverpool later also succumbed to a functional Glasgow Celtic under Martin O'Neill, who were on their own way to the final to face FC Porto managed by one José Mourhino. We would hear again about handsome young José.

Back home, meanwhile, Houllier's shattered team slid, from 9 November 2002 to 1 January 2003, to an unimaginable 11-match league run without a win. Troubling statistics were now mounting: in 33 out of the last 34 occasions that Houllier's team had fallen behind in a Premiership match, Liverpool had failed to recover to win. Unlike the old Bob Paisley days, his team, it seemed, could play only on the front foot: it could do little to adjust to changing circumstances on the field. It was rigid and lacked dynamism, real belief and on-field leaders, such was the manager's obsessive determination to control things from the touch-line. Get ahead of them, it was said in the game, and there seemed no way back for Houllier's Liverpool.

Out of Europe and sliding down the Premiership table, Liverpool clung on to hopes of a revival in fortunes only via progress in the Worthington Cup and an extraordinary 4–3 win in December, away to Aston Villa. This seemed to be another turning point of sorts, though the club's league form was never entirely repaired. An FA Cup fifth-round defeat at Anfield to First Division Crystal Palace in February seemed to confirm the club's problems rather than point to any possibility of a sustained recovery. What is more, Houllier's post-match assessments now seemed strangely detached from reality: individual players or, more likely, referees were routinely blamed now for losses, and blatantly poor Liverpool performances were clothed, instead, in a blizzard of meaningless data about Liverpool's 'shots on target', their 'missed chances' and their time spent controlling possession. In defeat – at least, in Gérard Houllier's world of match 'facts' and video clips – Liverpool were performing heroically but utterly without fortune. For the rest of us, things were beginning to look rather shambolic.

As Liverpool fans began to question Houllier's management skills and, critically, his judgement – none of his newest recruits in 2002 looked even close to Premier League standard – only a gritty Worthington Cup-final victory against Manchester United in Cardiff, with Dudek, Gerrard and Hamann all prominent, saved Liverpool's season from total collapse. Later on, of course, a League Cup-final appearance would also help new manager Rafa Benítez plug a growing credibility gap with Liverpool fans and critics. Back in 2003, a 4–0 league beating at Old Trafford and consecutive losses in the final two league matches to confirm Liverpool's Champions League exclusion – the last to Abramovich's rising Chelsea – was a more accurate indicator of the depths to which the Houllier project had now sunk.

Having begun the season like potential title winners, Liverpool had finished only in fifth place and a full 19 points behind Ferguson's Manchester United. It was another lost league title. Moreover, Liverpool suddenly looked as far away from major European or domestic league success as they had ever done over the last two decades. As Liverpool fans were calling for Houllier's head, the club's board decided to give their embattled manager one last chance, his fifth season in a five-year plan. Despite his many doubters, Houllier still seemed convinced he would succeed at Anfield. He later said, 'I would never consider turning away from Liverpool, because of the bond between the club and its supporters. You have to recognise it is due to Bill Shankly, and even though times have changed, that value, that bond, is still there.' Fine words, but time was fast running out on Houllier's sometimes excellent Merseyside adventure.

# Chapter Three

# THE NEW FRENCH RESISTANCE: THE FALL OF GÉRARD HOULLIER

We've agreed to part company in an amicable way. There's no war, there's no insults, there's no bitterness and no ill-feeling.

Gérard Houllier, 24 May 2004

## THE LAST TRAIN

The Liverpool board took a sharp intake of breath in the summer of 2003 and reminded its still recovering and respected French manager of the central goals of the club: with no Champions League distractions, the Premiership title *must* be a realistic target once more in 2003–04. The board was reluctant to sack Houllier, of course – a man they still liked and trusted and who had, after all, almost died at the helm of the club. Houllier talked up the trust and loyalty of his Liverpool employers in turn, thus cementing a partnership that actually seemed increasingly unsteady. Houllier was also helped here by the fact that he was generally liked in football circles, especially by the broadsheet media, who saw him, along with Wenger and Chelsea's Ranieri, as a civilised and intelligent alternative to the usual monosyllabic, back-stabbing, 'hairdryer' exponents of traditional British football management.

Surely, conventional thinking went, this decent man deserved at least one more season in full health to get Liverpool back on track? Despite their general unease, most reasonable Liverpool fans probably felt the same way.

Houllier would again have fresh talent to call upon in the new campaign. Two earlier youth 'investments' from Le Havre in 2001 – another £6 million French gamble, in effect – now arrived at L4 in the shape of youngsters Anthony Le Tallec and Florent Sinama Pongolle. Again much coveted across Europe, Le Tallec definitely had skills and heading prowess, but he lacked physical presence and real pace, a crucial absence in England. Sinama had bundles of the latter, but could find little real balance or composure in front of goal. Combined, this pair might produce one real prospect: separated, well, that looked more of a problem. The Arsenal of 2004 would later be routinely fielding outstanding Continental 17 year olds in their midfield: Liverpool's youth recruits from abroad looked like expensive schoolboys by comparison. But at least they still had time on their side.

Of more immediate interest was the arrival at Anfield in 2003 of the Australian winger Harry Kewell out of a fire-sale at troubled Leeds United. Kewell checked into L4 for a reported £5 million fee – of which at least £2 million seemed to be paid directly to Kewell's own advisers. Kewell certainly had talent – 'a signing to get you off your seat', according to Rick Parry – but he also seemed wilful and often lacking in focus. He was also accused of lacking courage, a critical absence for fans in the hard yards of the Premiership. Leeds supporters had warned that Kewell was performing only fitfully now, that he was not a player to bet your life – or your club – on. But Houllier and the Liverpool board had invested much on Harry delivering.

The Liverpool manager even promised that Kewell's arrival meant that Reds supporters would see a new Liverpool: one dedicated to a much more attacking approach. This seemed like convulsive policymaking at best, or even a sign of panic. It also raised uncomfortable questions about the apparent divide implied here between an attacking and a defensive strategy: wasn't it the job of a great coach to *integrate* these dimensions, to offer a convincing balance in a side that must compete effectively both with and without the ball? The prospects of playing Diouf, Cheyrou *and* Kewell together in some of the Premiership's hotspots just didn't add up.

Finally, the Limerick-born cockney Steve Finnan was also recruited by Houllier, from Fulham, for £4 million. At least *he* was a reliable and solid international right-back, a man seemingly more in the Anfield tradition. On paper Liverpool did look rather stretched defensively now, with Henchoz injured and apparently no longer trusted by Houllier, and with the perpetually downcast Croatian Igor Biscan seemingly now regarded by the manager as an adequate centre-back replacement. Salif Diao, also injured, had, by now, virtually disappeared from Houllier's League equation; Djimi Traoré too. With a new Houllier pledge towards offering much more in Liverpool's attack, achieving the necessary *defensive* solidity of, say, the successful 2000–01 season actually seemed a rather distant prospect from here.

## STARS BEHIND CLOUDS

It must be said, right now, that injuries posed a terrible problem for Houllier and for Liverpool right from the start of the new campaign. Due to a chronic shin injury the reliable midfield anchor Didi Hamann played his first League match for Liverpool only on 30 November, by which time he had been joined on the long-term Liverpool injured list by both Jamie Carragher and Milan Baros: each had suffered a break in an especially feisty League encounter with Graeme Souness's Blackburn Rovers in September. An earlier 3–0 Reds drubbing of Everton at Goodison Park had, however, helped ease the problems of a three-match Liverpool winless start and even convinced some early doubters about the real pedigree of Harry Kewell: the Australian scored the clinching third goal against the Reds' neighbours. But it was new captain Steven Gerrard's drive and Michael Owen's goals that were really keeping Liverpool afloat at this stage, even if Michael, more than occasionally now, looked lost and uninspired in matches.

As early as August 2003 the small band of Houllier critics in the national press could already smell blood, among them the perceptive chief sports writer James Lawton at *The Independent*. Lawton, an ingrained Liverpool fan but a trenchant Houllier critic, had no doubt that the Frenchman had the required disciplinary values to run a top club, but wondered if he had the footballing philosophy necessary to give this expensively acquired group of players the means to play. Even new man Kewell was in danger, according to Lawton, of becoming yet another Houllier 'star to put behind a cloud'. This raised a crucial question: was Houllier's general approach and his almost suffocating focus on the team ethic actually enabling, or was it really shackling his best players? Lawton also felt that Houllier, too often now, sought refuge in a 'fantasy world' of excuses and rationalisations for defeat. Was it the effects of the Frenchman's illness that had increased his caution and his growing suspicion of forces outside Anfield's gates? There is no doubt, argued Lawton with some prescience, that even at this early stage of the new season, 'Houllier's career is so plainly on the line'.

After a struggling 2–1 win at home to Leicester City in September, three Liverpool League losses soon followed: away to Charlton Athletic, unluckily to champions Arsenal at Anfield and, desperately, away at Portsmouth. 'Not for a single minute,' reported *The Guardian* darkly, 'did Liverpool appear superior to their opponents on any level, be it physically, mentally, tactically, or technically. For much of the game it did not appear as if they had received any coaching at all.'

This was the moment Houllier chose to announce the proposed Liverpool signing in the summer of 2004 of France's international forward Djibril Cissé, perhaps in an urgent attempt to galvanise the catatonic Emile Heskey or else to confirm with the Liverpool board his longer-term planning, should things go any more wildly off the rails in the meantime. It did not look hopeful, despite mundane UEFA Cup wins against poor opposition from Olimpija Ljubljana and Steaua Bucharest. By the end of October 2003 Liverpool already languished in tenth position in the Premiership, seemingly with no hope of launching any effective Championship challenge from here.

Houllier seemed unabashed. He contended that 'the players are enjoying their football and the people are enjoying watching our change of style', though there seemed little discernible sign of any real change in approach at all. And no Liverpool fan, at least not since Shankly's day, enjoyed losing *any* football match. The manager was called in to see the Liverpool board, who told him, 'Don't read the newspapers.' It was good advice. Paul Hayward, a Houllier sympathiser at the *Daily Telegraph*, had nevertheless described the Liverpool run as revealing 'the form of Nowhere Men', while others described his squad, cruelly, as 'also-rans'. Sam Wallace, also of the *Telegraph*, suggested that, 'Houllier is a brooder: a man who has come to control the corridors and boot-rooms of Anfield and the Melwood training ground more tightly than Roy Evans and Graeme Souness ever managed, but he is also a man who scrutinises every judgement passed on him.' This was true – and growing more so by the hour. 'Houllier cannot hide it when he is hurt,' continued Wallace, 'and he cannot resist the chance to put it right by arguing passionately for the beliefs that he holds so dearly.'

In short, the Liverpool manager was dangerously thin-skinned for football management and obsessed by negative media comment: not an ideal combination in the goldfish bowl of the English Premiership. This explains why Houllier was now routinely scolding the 22 ex-Liverpool players he had carefully counted working in the sports media and who were uniformly, claimed the Frenchman, bent on criticising him. Gérard Houllier, the Continental guru whose destiny was to transform Liverpool FC and return the club to its former glories, was already in deep trouble.

Houllier praised his beleaguered team for its improving ball retention and patience, even if chances continued to be spurned, and he singled out Hyypiä, Owen and Gerrard as his three 'leaders' on the pitch. Indeed, as Owen succumbed to injury, Liverpool frequently fielded teams at this time in which only Gerrard had *not* been brought to the club by the manager – and these players had usually been brought in for a stiff fee. Houllier had also been hugely influential, of course, in shaping the career of the Huyton-born man. But this issue also raised a wider debate about youth policy at Anfield under Houllier and his staff – and about his reportedly fraying relationship with Liverpool Academy director Steve Heighway.

In the early and mid-1990s the Liverpool youth system had developed a shoal of top local players for the first team –

McManaman, Fowler, Matteo, Carragher, Owen, David Thompson and Gerrard among them. Three of these were, arguably, world-class talents. Houllier's arrival at the club as a youth-development specialist seemed to coincide, strangely, with the relative drying up of local talent – though Liverpool had largely resisted the policy of recruiting very young players from abroad. Why were no new young stars now pushing to make the grade? Houllier seemed to deride Heighway's efforts to develop players of world-class potential, while the manager went shopping for young talent elsewhere, to Heighway's obvious frustration.

## THE COOLEST HEAD IN A CRISIS

By the end of November 2003, and following a poor 0–0 draw at Middlesbrough with not a single Liverpool shot on target despite Houllier's supposed new, attacking philosophy, a downcast captain, Steven Gerrard, vocalised what all Liverpool supporters were already thinking just 13 League games into the new season: 'We have dropped too many points to win the title and that is very disappointing,' he said. 'Our position in the table is not good enough for Liverpool Football Club. We started the season with real hopes and it is a real let down that we are in this position. We have to be realistic now and a top-four finish is the best we can hope for.' This was a fair assessment, if one that was hard to take, and when Liverpool lost at home to Bolton Wanderers in the Carling (League) Cup soon after, one of the manager's reliable lifelines in times of League strife – a spring visit to Cardiff – was also cut. An angry Houllier publicly threatened his players with a life 'rotting in the reserves' if their form did not improve. Diao, for one, now disappeared, almost without trace.

In December 2003 the club's annual report carried a stern message from the usually inert Liverpool chairman David Moores. It was the first real public warning-shot from the board seemingly aimed at the embattled Houllier:

> Over recent years I have stated repeatedly that the overriding objective was consistent qualification for the Champions League. While this remains the minimum acceptable target, the ambition has always been to win every competition. Last

year we finished fifth in the Premier League, won the
Worthington Cup but failed in our target for qualification for
the Champions League. While by no means a write-off, the
season must be viewed as generally disappointing, especially
when compared to year-on-year progress. We must accept
that the season-wide performance fell short of the high
standards we have set ourselves and that our fans have come
to expect.

Liverpool immediately issued a 'clarifying' statement on the club
website, saying 'There was no suggestion of the manager being
sacked and there was no ultimatum.' But here it was in black and
white: the 'minimum acceptable target' – not that many Liverpool
fans would have accepted fourth place in the League for this. In
fact, this was the sort of finish that had effectively dealt the fatal
blow to Roy Evans back in 1998. But Champions League football
now meant big cash and the prospects of recruiting top players:
Gerrard and Owen were already hinting darkly, for example, that
they could hardly be expected to stick around in L4 for another
season of UEFA Cup fare – not with Euro 2004 just around the
corner and with sponsorship cash and image rights to consider.
Chelsea's moneyed emergence had definitely made things more
difficult in this area for the Liverpool manager: now it looked like
the top three League spots were already pre-booked for Arsenal,
Manchester United and Chelsea. Liverpool had already lost at
home to all three in the new season. Could Houllier's ailing club
now at least see off the other pretenders for fourth spot?

The Liverpool AGM on 5 January 2004 was a predictably stormy
affair, showing a noticeable change in temperature and emphasis
compared to any other during Houllier's reign. The manager was
forced to sit through a string of angry shareholder criticisms about
team performances and the manager's own showing, with one
irate fan commenting that all three of the latest managerial
appointments at the club – including Houllier himself – had been
'disappointing'. Keith Evans, another shareholder, commented
that loyal fans were 'running out of patience with the team' and
that 'Over the last five years we have spent more than £100 million
and we have heard a lot of excuses and gloss from under-

performing teams. Money has been spent on foreign players, many of whom have been of questionable quality.' (Houllier's *gross* spending since 1999 actually chalked up at a cool £115 million, with another £14 million already committed.)

Confronted directly by the ambitious builder, property developer and potential investor Steve Morgan – and visibly shaken – club chairman David Moores said that he still believed in the 'values' epitomised by Gérard Houllier, but he confessed that he might have to consider his own position inside the club if performances on the pitch did not improve. 'The coolest head in the crisis,' commented pundit and TV commentator Clive Tyldsley later, 'belonged to the head man. Chairman David Moores was shaken and stirred by the dark mood at the annual meeting but stood resolutely behind the buck of final responsibility. Moores has his critics and rivals,' continued the amenable Tyldsley, 'but a chairman from the club's own fan base who provides generous personal and financial support without seeking to interfere or absorb praise is in a minority. If he does fall on his sword next summer, I can think of a few managers who may try to buy him.' There was some truth here, of course, especially concerning Moores' long-standing and loyal support for the club. But some frustrated Liverpool fans were also beginning to think that a little more *leadership* from the top table might be worth having – and from a slightly more interventionist chairman.

Houllier's own valedictory speech to the club AGM in January 2004 began, hesitantly, with a clumsy metaphor: 'I hope this speech will be like a miniskirt: short enough to grab your attention and long enough to cover the subject.' It raised few laughs. He mentioned the 'difficult period' the club had been in and also the pressures from the press, who 'have to do a job', before talking again about the importance of ethics and values at Liverpool, including the behaviour of players, and about the link between fans and the club: a timeless theme this one, but also perhaps one aimed at exposing the more consumer-driven relationships now operating more nakedly elsewhere. 'I also want this club to be loved,' said Houllier. 'We want our fans to be close to us, to be with us. We see them as supporters, not as customers. That is why this club will always retain a human dimension.'

He at least admitted, for the first time, that 'Some of the players bought in 2002 have fallen short of what they can bring to the side. They have not shown what made us buy them in the first place.' But he thought that there was still time for these stars to show their true mettle and he stressed that they all remained 'desperate' to do well for the club. On this basis, no, there were no plans for Liverpool to be active in the transfer market during the January window. 'I retain faith in my squad,' he muttered. The truth was slightly different. Although lightweight all season in defence, the club board remained unwilling to meet the terms demanded by the highly-rated French centre-back Jean-Alain Boumsong.

This was, essentially, a low-key affair: hardly a call-to-arms. It was also a carefully worded performance: notice it was the new players who had let the club down, not the judgement of the manager in recruiting them. Perhaps this is inevitable: what manager, after all, would criticise himself in the dog-eat-dog world of elite football management? The 'soft' politics of the club dominated here more than the hard business of winning football matches. It was a plea for patience, for more time, and the board and the club's fans still had a strong emotional bond to Houllier, though its hold was lessening with each depressing defeat, each piercing headline, and each public expression of denial by the man in charge. Press gossip now began to grow louder from north of the border that Celtic's Martin O'Neill was at the end of his useful time at Parkhead and was the man being primed by Liverpool to replace Houllier at Anfield. There seemed no real substance to the stories, simply more paper-selling newsprint. But Houllier clocked it, as always, and was enraged: he refused even to take O'Neill's phone calls professing his own innocence of any unlikely plot.

## GLIMMERS OF DEFIANCE

And yet, as had happened so often before for Houllier in some of his darkest hours at Anfield, 'events' – or, in this case, results – intervened once more. Three wins in a week early in January, including away at bogey club Chelsea with the exasperating Bruno Cheyrou scoring the winning goal, signalled, even then, the possibility of better times ahead. An abject League loss, at Spurs, reignited old doubts, but when Liverpool then saw off Newcastle United at Anfield in the FA Cup in a pulsating contest – this time with Cheyrou scoring *twice* – even the guys in the Centenary Stand carrying the 'Sort it out, Houllier – no more expensive mistakes. We want the title' banner must have been impressed. Plans for a major fan demonstration against the manager at the forthcoming derby game – actually always unlikely, simply not the Liverpool fans' style – suddenly seemed especially inappropriate once more. But could the club really drive on from here?

In the FA Cup fifth round Liverpool faced Portsmouth at home – an absolutely critical match in the current climate, a real chance at least for Liverpool Cup success to quell widespread League disquiet. After two minutes Michael Owen had already glided through to put Liverpool ahead, but chance after chance was then wasted to allow Matt Taylor to volley a late equaliser for a poor Portsmouth: a deadly blow. As we knew they would, a 'rotated' Liverpool then choked in the replay on the south coast, with Le Tallec, Cheyrou and Kewell all coming up way, way short. This was an abject loss. Michael Owen also looked positively semi-detached here, while his manager huddled silently on the touch-line, his overcoat raised miserably against the Hampshire sea breezes and the wrath of his travelling followers.

Houllier, now a target of Melwood graffiti artists, fled briefly to France. The Liverpool board, predictably, pledged their public support for their manager as fan anger continued to mushroom on Merseyside. Ian St John, one of Houllier's fiercest critics among the ex-players, argued the club's fans were now sitting through games like zombies. Houllier scoffed. 'There are two sorts of fans,' he remarked, gnomically, as if in reply, 'those that understand what we have been doing at this club and those who do not.' There were certainly fewer and fewer true believers now, more and more in the St John camp, and it was simple Houllier fantasising to expect otherwise. Not even the most loyal fans could offer him unconditional support. Moreover, his once-trusted assistant Phil Thompson now seemed to be effectively 'gagged' by the manager. Thommo no longer appeared in front of the media and was also less and less the agitated, directing and occasionally annoying loudmouth presence Liverpool fans had grown used to on the touch-line. Liverpool looked increasingly like an unhappy football club led by a man under siege.

And yet, an immediate, upbeat 2–0 UEFA Cup triumph at home to Levski Sofia – with all of the recent flaky Houllier signings, bar Kewell, left out of the side once more – even produced an emblematic televised touch-line hug for the manager from his goal-scoring captain Steven Gerrard. Let's face it, some modern footballers can be disloyal, self-obsessed money grabbers, and even downright cheats a lot of the time, but others can also be caring and decent human beings when they decide to be – and as Houllier, himself, would want them to be. Here, perhaps, was a case in point, though cynics might also point out that Gerrard had much to thank his manager for – the Liverpool captaincy and a fat new contract, for example. But this was a very human expression of public support for a man with whom Steven had also had his differences, and who was now facing the gallows. Even the Kop – despite themselves – managed an 'Allez, Houllier' chant, the first one for weeks. Paul Hayward of the *Daily Telegraph* captured well some of the wider significance of the moment, arguing that it reflected 'glimmers of defiance' from the club and its supporters and that, importantly, Liverpool FC remained above all 'a robust club staffed by people who understand that football is not a commodity . . . [with] a tradition of finding good youngsters whose accents match those of the fans'. Not that there had been too many of those in evidence recently.

Maybe some of this crowd response here *was* a mixture of tawdry sympathy and even hypocrisy, rather than outright affection or respect. Houllier, after all, had been a fans' target for months and, early in March 2004, he was even reported to have received death threats, investigated by the police, following the home draw against Portsmouth. Football fans can be driven to do crazy, horrible things. No manager of any football club deserves this sort of cruel madness, nor the kind of general media scrutiny someone like Gérard Houllier had been under – and certainly not a man as sensitive as Houllier had become. 'Judging from the newspapers,' Houllier twinkled in a moment's respite at this time, 'you would think my first name was "Under Pressure", not Gérard.' Fair play to him: for all his weaknesses and misjudgements, the man had taken a lot and had come back fighting. Maybe his beloved European stage would save him again, despite everything.

But Houllier's once-reliable football defences were now built on sand: first a future adversary, Marseille's Didier Drogba, adroitly cancelled out Milan Baros's UEFA Cup goal for Liverpool at Anfield in front of a group of travelling French fans who made one remember what football crowds in England *used* to be like. Then, in the return leg in the Stade Velodrome, and after Liverpool had looked in charge following Emile Heskey's early goal, Spanish referee Ibanez rightly sent off the hapless Igor Biscan for dragging back Marlet. But the referee wrongly awarded a penalty for the offence, converted by Drogba: a fatal double whammy to Liverpool's hopes. Despite Liverpool's brave resistance a second Marseille goal, an unmarked header for Meite, settled matters early in the second half. A half-committed Michael Owen then came off injured, looking less and less like a footballer whose contract was actually owned by Liverpool Football Club. And Houllier? For the first time he seemed uncertain at the last. 'Will I be here next season?' he asked journalists, rhetorically, soon after the Marseille defeat. 'It's not up to me to answer that, but in an ideal world I'd like Liverpool to be my last job. I'm not thinking of retirement but remember my role has not been questioned by the players or the board.' In an ideal world Liverpool would qualify comfortably for the Champions League. But this was not an ideal world any more, not even close to one.

## HOULLIER'S END

The Liverpool squad actually battled hard for Houllier in the League at the fag end of what had become a very poor 2003–04 Liverpool season, and even managed yet another away win at Manchester United in April. Indeed, a muscular and confident 3–0 victory at Birmingham City in May ranked as many supporters' favourite Liverpool performance of the season. All of this, and convincing home wins against Blackburn Rovers and Middlesbrough, even rendered the final Liverpool League fixture with pressing Newcastle United unimportant: the fourth Champions League spot was already secured for Anfield. But at what price? Liverpool finished on just 60 points, 15 behind the top three clubs and a crushing 30 points behind unbeaten champions Arsenal. Houllier's team had won only ten League matches at home and had finished closer in points to the relegated Leicester City in 2004 than they had to the coveted – and promised – title berth. The truth was hard to swallow: the Liverpool club had become the narrow leaders of the League's also-rans.

But with the £14.1-million player Djibril Cissé still being lined up by Houllier, Liverpool FC's close-season business seemed to be proceeding much as usual. That is until the manager's last Liverpool press briefing, on 14 May 2004. Houllier, under yet more pressure from comments made by shareholder Steve Morgan about his own performance, ordered his press officer Ian Cotton to fetch the latest statistics sheet in order to prove a point about his Liverpool team. The journalists who were gathered looked at their feet. Many of them liked Houllier and they still wanted him to succeed, but this was embarrassing. They had seen more and more of this obsession with statistics over the past few months: an obviously intelligent man dubiously wedded to what he insisted on calling 'the facts', even in the face of a competing, much more plausible, reality. A press sympathiser told the manager that resorting to these statistical crutches could not work any more at Liverpool. Houllier picked up his sheaf of football 'evidence' and walked out.

Ten days later Houllier was gone, his departure from Anfield wrapped up in amiable rhetoric about his leaving the club as a 'friend' and, above all, 'on good terms'. Whilst Houllier would, of course, 'prefer' to stay as the Liverpool manager, it was implied that he had not been sacked, but was rather being gently eased out into a new, more appropriate, position some way away from Anfield. Those noble gentlemen of the Liverpool boardroom had stuck to Houllier's much prized 'values' to the last. However, the true costs of Houllier's leaving Liverpool only came out much later in the club's balance sheets: it was to prove a very expensive business indeed, keeping on the right side of what was a discarded and, let's face it, an ultimately failing football manager. The bill for the manager and his departing staff was reported to be over £10 million. For all his virtues and his expressed devotion to Liverpool Football Club, Gérard Houllier was certainly not a man to go anywhere cheaply.

So, who saw him die? 'Not I,' said an appalled Michael Owen. 'Nor I,' said Steven Gerrard, who even described the departing Houllier as a 'father figure' for him at the club. But it seems barely believable that the Liverpool board did not 'consult' their two most saleable, their least expendable assets, before the manager was finally cast adrift. Maybe their views were not decisive, but these players would, surely, have been listened to. The stark reality is probably that the Liverpool board could no longer endure the, by now, intense pressure coming from Steve Morgan and others for change, both in the manager's chair and in the boardroom.

There was also no popular mandate for Houllier to stay among the club's fans, and, with a proposed new stadium to fund, another season of 'hide and seek' with the fourth Champions League place was simply untenable, at least under Houllier again. Why the club sanctioned the sale of Emile Heskey and the signing of Djibril Cissé when Houllier's time at the club was already all but over remains an interesting question. What was clear was that the important work of the first foreign football manager at Liverpool was now at an end. Despite his admirable cup successes – not least in the marvellous 2001 season – Houllier lacked some of the last vital ingredients that could produce League title success, and that distinguishes great football managers from talented coaches.

## THE HOULLIER LEGACY

And so, what of Houllier's lasting Liverpool legacy? There are many things that Liverpool fans should thank him for. He set the context, of course, for Rafa Benítez's reign by internationalising the club's recruitment strategies and thus dragging Liverpool into the global era. He also, famously, introduced a more disciplined and more 'scientific' approach to player preparation at Liverpool. When he arrived, the drinking and clubbing culture was still prominent at Anfield and too little at training was, by this stage, tightly geared to match preparation. With his coaches Houllier set about improving player professionalism and extending the consideration of tactics among his players; he also impressed on them – not always with positive outcomes – the importance of skills development, and of flexibility and athleticism in the modern game. A number of key Liverpool players of his time – Danny

Murphy, Carragher and Steven Gerrard among them – owe much of their success as elite footballers to Gérard Houllier's leadership and guidance. He also tried to teach his young millionaire charges the importance of respect – no simple prospect this – and of dealing with other workers in the club and with fans with due care and modesty. He curbed the Spice Boys image and stressed instead hard work and the importance of the team over the individual. He also cared deeply about the club: about its deeper meaning and importance to fans and to the city of Liverpool in an era of glitz and ballooning sports consumption. He deserves respect for that, perhaps, above all else.

On the negative side, Houllier's signings for Liverpool were no more than a mixed bag – but only as all football manager's recruits tend to be. Some of his early captures were definitely his best. Signing the defensive trio of Sami Hyypiä, Stéphane Henchoz and Dietmar Hamann in 1999 for just over £14 million was good business by any standard, with almost 800 games played between them for Liverpool. They were crucial figures in the great Liverpool triumphs of 2001 and two of them were still prominent in 2005. Netting John Arne Riise for £4 million and Milan Baros for £3.4 million in the summer of 2001 was also good work. Significantly, of the Liverpool players who made it onto the pitch in the European Cup final of 2005, no less than ten were Gérard Houllier signings. In short, without Houllier, Liverpool's 'miracle night' in Istanbul would not have been able to happen. Also some of his ultimately less successful and more expensive signings – Camara, Barmby, Ziege, Westerveld and ultimately Emile Heskey – Houllier managed to move on for (admittedly lesser) fees. And despite their many critics who still see them as 'almost men', other Houllier picks, such as Smicer, Traoré, Biscan, Dudek and Kewell, were all still around in the squad to take their Turkish bows on 25 May 2005.

# GÉRARD HOULLIER'S LIVERPOOL SIGNINGS

| 1999 | Cost (millions) |
|---|---|
| Jean Michel Ferri (Istanbulspor) | £1.5 |
| Frodde Kippe (Lillestrom) | £0.7 |
| Rigobert Song (Salernitana) | £2.7 |
| Djimi Traoré (Laval) | £0.55 |
| Sami Hyypiä (Willem II) | £2.6 |
| Titi Camara (Marseille) | £2.8 |
| Stéphane Henchoz (Blackburn Rovers) | £3.5 |
| Sander Westerveld (Vitesse Arnhem) | £4.0 |
| Dietmar Hamann (Newcastle United) | £8.0 |
| Vladimir Smicer (Lens) | £4.0 |
| Total | £30.35 |

| 2000 | Cost (millions) |
|---|---|
| Emile Heskey (Leicester City) | £11.0 |
| Bernard Diomède (Auxerre) | £3.0 |
| Nick Barmby (Everton) | £6.0 |
| Christian Ziege (Middlesbrough) | £5.5 |
| Gregory Vignal (Montpellier) | £0.5 |
| Daniel Sjoland (West Ham) | £1.0 |
| Igor Biscan (Dynamo Zagreb) | £5.5 |
| Total | £32.5 |

| 2001 | Cost (millions) |
|---|---|
| John Arne Riise (Monaco) | £4.0 |
| Milan Baros (Banik Ostrava) | £3.4 |
| Jerzy Dudek (Feyenoord) | £4.85 |
| Chris Kirkland (Coventry City) | £6.0 |
| Anthony Le Tallec and Florent Sinama Pongolle (Le Havre) | £6.0 |
| Total | £24.25 |

| 2002 | Cost (millions) |
|---|---|
| Abel Xavier (Everton) | £0.8 |
| El-Hadji Diouf (Lens) | £10.0 |
| Bruno Cheyrou (Lille) | £3.7 |
| Salif Diao (Sedan) | £5.0 |
| Total | £19.5 |

| 2003 | Cost (millions) |
|---|---|
| Steve Finnan (Fulham) | £3.5 |
| Harry Kewell (Leeds United) | £5.0 |
| Total | £8.5 |
| Total spend (1999–2003) | £115.1 |

Houllier's eventual downfall at Liverpool was strongly linked, of course, to his poor player recruitment, especially in the summer of 2002. Houllier's *release* of players – especially players from Merseyside – has also been criticised, but it is difficult to argue that any of those major ones who left for fees – Dominic Matteo, David Thompson, Stephen Wright or even Robbie Fowler – have especially flowered elsewhere. In the main these look now like rather good sales. In 2003–04 Liverpool paid £65.6 million in salaries and wages: 71 per cent of club turnover; a 21 per cent annual increase. It was the fourth-highest wage bill in the Premiership – for the fourth-finishing club. Maybe Liverpool had ended up where they could reasonably expect to be, but the coach seemed to be offering no measurable added value: not for a £115 million gross spend over five years and another questionable £14-million man who was about to appear at Anfield. Champions Arsenal, 30 points distant, had spent only £5 million more than Liverpool on salaries: a chilling thought.

Houllier's obsession with the new 'science' of football – with the reductive focus on analysing sport through computer programmes, statistics and measurement – also revealed a lack of a really intuitive feel for the game. Perhaps his own failings as a player are important here – and perhaps this is also why he was such an interventionist coach. Whatever the reasons, it was often difficult to see beyond the humdrum pragmatism even of Houllier's best Liverpool teams. They were often honest, but essentially unexciting – enlivened only, for example, by Gary McAllister's unexpected reinvention in midfield in 2000–01. Even Houllier's supposed new attacking Liverpool formation in 2003 actually searched desperately for imagination and guile, as his players struggled to express themselves within the rigid formations already laid out for them to fill. Obsession with structure can render agency – the necessary individualism needed to unlock opposing teams – impotent. Ironically, too, the season Liverpool came closest to Premiership success – 2001–02 – was the season the manager spent mainly away from the squad, recovering from illness.

All of this also revealed a deep personal flaw – or rather a simple human frailty – in Gérard Houllier, one that proved an instant disqualifier from any protracted and successful stay in English football management: he didn't enjoy, and eventually could not deal with, criticism. It can be productive, of course, for football managers to generate a sense of embattled defiance within a football club: a 'them against us' mentality designed to enhance inner commitment and team-building. But, eventually, Gérard Houllier simply became haunted by his many critics: he was hounded by their incessant chatter until he could no longer trust the evidence of his own eyes. Houllier was never short, especially later on in his reign, of excuses for failure.

He needed many fewer of these in the good Liverpool years between 2000 and 2002 when he certainly made Liverpool Football Club respected again, both at home and abroad. He has – and deserves – his place in the club's history books and will be remembered fondly much more for his triumphs than for his weaknesses. And, in the end, who could blame a man caught in the public eye in twenty-first-century Britain for developing even an unhealthy cynicism about English football and the ugly doings of the British tabloid press? After all, as his ambulance drew away from Anfield on that afternoon in October 2001 when his heart finally gave way, the Liverpool manager heard a dull thud strike the roof of the vehicle. Allegedly, a press photographer had jumped on board in search of another sporting exclusive. Maybe, for his own sanity, Gérard Houllier actually got out of the British game at just the right time. Meanwhile, in Spain, and barely a week after Houllier's departure from Liverpool, another young manager would be painfully severing his own ties with a club that Liverpool fans had come to both admire and fear. His route was already planned to end at Anfield Road, Liverpool 4. The king is dead: long live the king.

# Chapter Four

# SPANISH STEPS:
# THE LIVERPOOL 'RAFALUTION'

What Liverpool sees when it looks at Benítez is a
shrewd football operator . . . and a good man. A
man without an ego that crushes those around him;
a man who knows life as well as he knows football.

James Lawton, *The Independent*

## PLAYING THE FIELD

Gérard Houllier had left Liverpool in May 2004 in sorrow, not in
anger. He had things to be proud of, no doubt about it. He took
special pleasure in the new facilities he had created at Melwood
and the changed lifestyle of Liverpool players off the pitch. He also
identified 'four strong pictures' that he would take with him from
his time at Anfield: Michael Owen's goal 'with his left peg' to win
the FA Cup in 2001 ('we used to tease Michael that his left foot
wasn't very good'); second, the Kop mosaic, the huge display of
'G.H.' at the Liverpool v. Manchester United match that Houllier
watched from his hospital bed after heart surgery; third, his
reception at the Roma match after his illness; and fourth, Gary
McAllister receiving the Man of the Match award in Dortmund at
the 2001 UEFA Cup final.

Each of these moments has the distinctive Houllier stamp. He is centrally involved in each of them himself. And why not? Houllier also argued, in his own defence, that the unexpected 2001 Liverpool cup successes had 'raised expectations too early', which meant that Liverpool fans sought the title itself too soon afterwards, that they had unrealistic targets. Whoever took over now would have to face some of the same problems. For Liverpool fans, Houllier's departure also promised rather more rational post-match assessments of the team's strengths and problems. As a correspondent to the excellent fanzine *Through the Wind and Rain* put it, Liverpool 'managerial press conferences shouldn't be as embarrassing as watching David Brent dance'.

In Liverpool there were clear signs now of a popular backlash towards bringing another foreign coach to the club, though the real antipathy was probably towards more unknown foreign signings. A survey in England in December 2004 revealed that only 43 per cent of Premiership players were now English – there were fewer still in Liverpool's first-team squad. After mixing up his purchases early on, Houllier had more recently increasingly looked to France for players, and few of these later signings had worked out in England. It was now widely felt that the latest Houllier team lacked the go-forward and organisational heart of earlier versions and that perhaps a *British* manager might now be able to motivate the Liverpool players more reliably and bring in a few new British players to offer the squad more steel and more resolve to go with its Continental know-how. The team needed leaders, proven men who understood the British game. Perhaps a British manager was now a safer bet for Liverpool, especially as Houllier had already introduced some necessary Continental changes into the Liverpool back-room set-up.

A few favourite names were in the frame here, but for once no ex-Liverpool players: a sign of the changing times. Celtic's Martin O'Neill definitely had his Merseyside supporters. Celtic's approach on the field was uncomplicated – to be kind – but with cash to spend, perhaps O'Neill could bring some of his famed inspirational powers here, to L4. He had a proven record of sorts in the Premiership, once lifting even modest Leicester City up to sixth place. He had also had some European success – a recent UEFA Cup final with Celtic, for example. We knew his team would work hard, give its best, and that O'Neill would manage, pretty well, the important media side of things. He looked something like a return to earlier Anfield days, when managers could be humorously idiosyncratic in front of the press, as well as sternly autocratic back at base.

Martin had little time for the new science of football, so much of the Melwood number-crunching and video-scanning would go out of the window. But O'Neill could also be flaky in the public eye, and would his Liverpool simply be too much honest perspiration and not enough of all that other stuff the team now needed? After all, many of the passionate objections to Gérard Houllier from fans were about the *style* of play he favoured, almost as much as anything else. Could the Irishman deal well, and spend money wisely, in the opaque global transfer market, and could he manage 'big time' players? There were also rumours that senior Liverpool players just didn't fancy O'Neill.

A second, youngish British management name widely bandied about was that of the experienced Charlton Athletic manager Alan Curbishley. The London man had now been more than ten years at Charlton and, in that time, had successfully made bricks out of straw. He was widely talked about as future England coaching material, but he seemed to be going a little stale at The Valley, another victim of his own successes in keeping the club firmly in the Premiership. Charlton fans now wanted their day in Europe, which was perhaps a step too far. Their manager was beginning to talk about the need to redistribute TV income to give the smaller clubs a better chance of success. He needed a change. A move to a club the size of Liverpool was, arguably, exactly the sort of step-up a man like Curbishley deserved – and he might have reasonably expected an option like this one at this stage of his career. What counted against him was his little knowledge of life in the media goldfish bowl at the elite clubs and a complete lack of experience of coaching for European football. Despite his long apprenticeship, he still looked like a manager learning his trade. And he was from London: the deep south. Liverpool had barely signed a London player over the past 40 years, never mind given the club over to a London manager. It looked a risky and implausible gamble.

So, too, did the case made for Bolton's Sam Allardyce, a transformed meat-and-two-veg ex-English stopper, a man who had brought into the Reebok ageing global recruits with no transfer fees, but with big wages on short-term loans or short contracts. Despite the novel international flavour at Bolton – Sam once fielded a team with no British players involved at all – Allardyce still enjoyed the physical stuff in his teams: they were built with endurance, rather than subtlety, in mind. But Wanderers had certainly prospered under big Sam, a man who had fully embraced the new science in the game, thus offering some potential British continuity with the Houllier years of wider, positive change at Anfield. But recruiting a man like Allardyce now might be asking too much from a guy used to thinking on his feet and only on a season-to-season basis. Liverpool, after all, had to plan on a much bigger canvas – and, as we have said, Allardyce's European competition experience was slim. Moreover, part of Liverpool's problem now in making a suitable appointment was attracting a new coach who could also satisfy the ambitions of the club's key players, especially perhaps Owen and Gerrard, both of whom were giving out strong signals that they might soon have to look elsewhere for the success they felt they deserved. Asking either player to stay under Bolton's Allardyce was, clearly, something of a no-brainer. Despite the misgivings of some fans, Liverpool would have to look abroad, once more, for a suitable managerial replacement.

## THE REIGN IN SPAIN

Europe's hottest managerial property in 2004 was definitely FC Porto's José Mourinho: a young manager with looks, confidence and brio, whose unconsidered club had not only cleaned up in Portugal but had also mugged Europe's G14 elite by winning the 2004 European Cup, thrashing Monaco in the final. In March 2004 Mourinho brought Porto to Old Trafford and, to the complete satisfaction of those Reds followers at the western end of the M62, had joyfully eliminated United. The Liverpool board and its emissaries had been monitoring the performance of Mourinho and may even have made contact with the Portuguese. Mourinho was a known Anfield sympathiser and a Premiership fan, and it seemed clear that the Liverpool kingmakers were already planning to ditch Houllier, with or without a Champions League place, for the next League season. But with Mourinho apparently keen on discussing a move to Anfield, the Liverpool board were, reportedly, concerned about the exuberance of his Old Trafford celebrations. Running up the touch-line and celebrating like a wild player or a fan was not what Parry and Moores had in mind for a new Liverpool boss. In any case, as the stock of the Portuguese continued to rise with little Porto ploughing onwards and upwards, Chelsea's Abramovich later came calling. With hundreds of millions of euros at the Russian's disposal, young José's head was soon turned: he would be bound for London, not Liverpool.

Apart from Porto, the most successful football club in Europe in 2004 was arguably the Spanish club Valencia. Known as *Los Ches,* because of the club's reliance on Argentine players – the Cuban revolutionary Che Guevara had been exiled in Argentina – Valencia had made consecutive European Cup final appearances in 2000 and 2001 under their stern Argentinian coach Hector Cuper. Cuper's team was built around the uncompromising Argentinian defenders Ayala and Pellegrino, and the midfield strength of Baraja, Vicente and the skilful Mendieta. Despite this obvious success, tough-guy Cuper still had problems convincing the infamously fun-loving people of Valencia, the hedonistic home to *Las Falles* – the festival of the bonfires – that his teams were actually attractive to watch. In February 2000 they were even calling for his head – in favour of much more attacking play.

'Something is obviously missing,' said the puzzled coach. 'Valencia fans demand more risk and entertainment, but what is spectacle? I like my teams to play attacking football but I'm not going to commit suicide or give the opposition presents.'

By the spring of 2001 Cuper had had enough of the Mestalla hecklers, who might have had a point: their team finished a hefty 17 points behind Real Madrid in La Liga. He announced that he was off to join Inter Milan, where his cautionary approach was liable to be better appreciated.

The Valencia board offered their prestigious managerial vacancy to the cream of Spanish coaches – Javier Irureta, Luis Aragones, José Esnal and Victor Fernandes – but all passed up on the chance to follow Cuper. The Valencia job looked a thankless task: Cuper had over-performed in Europe and had still been hounded out. With little in the way of funds for playing reinforcements there was also a volatile home crowd to satisfy with more than mere results. To the disgust of the Mestalla faithful the board turned to a relative unknown, a new young Spanish manager called Rafael Benítez. Although his stay at the club was not always a happy one, in three seasons under Benítez Valencia were to win two La Liga titles – their last had been in 1971 – and, in 2004, added to them the UEFA Cup, defeating Liverpool's conquerors, Marseille, in the final. With Valencia's modest €90 million budget set against that of Real Madrid's €300 million, for example, the new man Benítez was nothing if not a football realist, but he was also not a man to be fazed by financial power alone: 'If you go to a tailor to buy a jacket for £10,000,' he once said, 'normally you will have a better jacket than someone who spends £1,000.' (This guy also likes his clothes.) 'But football is not like that. In Spain you have Real Madrid and Barcelona, but Valencia win. Why? Because it is football; different things can work.'

He meant, of course, that good managers, teamwork and resourceful players can always erode the effects of financial clout. Otherwise why would sport – or the coaching of top players – be interesting at all?

At 41 the youthful Rafael Benítez Maudes, like Gérard Houllier before him, was already known in his own country as a deep thinker and a serious student of the game. He was also a man with no real professional playing career to speak of, but was a frighteningly early managerial starter. He once labelled himself 'a loner with a laptop' because of his meticulous, painstaking, pre-match planning and the intensity of his match focus. Once, while managing Real Madrid's youth team, at half-time he walked right past his sister and father: he was so deep in the coaching zone he simply failed to see or hear his distressed relatives. Benítez's father was in the tourism business and was only a fair-weather follower of Real. Rafa's keen sporting interest really came from his mother, a committed Atletico fan.

As a boyhood supporter of Real Madrid, and already aware of his own playing limitations, Benítez shelved early thoughts of becoming a doctor but also said that he never dreamt of scoring the winning goal in the Bernabeu. Instead, even as a 13 year old, he spent hours alone ranking the club's players, giving them marks for performance and making detailed notes about their contribution, hoping one day he might even emulate the great Real coaches. He joined Real as a player at 14 years of age in 1974 and at 16 he often sat in the dressing-room after the club's junior matches writing about his teammates' play, chiding them about their 'poor reports' and urging them to improve. He could be a real pain in the arse – aloof, a little pedantic, a bit anal even, in his analysis of players' performances – but even then he was determined to succeed as a coach.

Benítez studied for a degree in physical education at the Polytechnic University of Madrid and at 18 he was already player–manager of the university team. Before the finals of a minor university tournament in Seville, the young coach insisted that his players get a decent night's sleep rather than party until the early hours, as was the usual student custom for this sporting weekend. His players trudged home to their beds: but they won the match the next day. In his early 20s Benítez was, briefly, a midfielder at obscure Parla in the Spanish Third Division, and he helped them to promotion in 1983. He then joined Segunda B side Linares, but a lack of real progress as a player and a succession of knee injuries meant that by 26 years of age – and rather like Liverpool's own Roy Evans – any pretence to being a serious professional footballer was already behind him.

Benítez retired as a pro player in 1986 and settled down, instead, as a coach in the Real Madrid youth system. By 1990 he was in charge of the Real Under-19s, and by 1994 had coached the Real B-team to a respectable seventh place in the Spanish second division. He regularly played chess with the head coach at Real, Raddy Antic, but it was football talk that Benítez was really after.

'I saw straight away he was a very clever lad, crazy about football,' said Antic. 'At the time he was very into studying the pressing game played by the Milan teams of Arrigo Sacchi. We used to have long discussions about it.'

Benítez would favour the 'pressing' game later at the Mestalla, but not always to his club followers' approval.

Benítez acted as number two to caretaker-coach Del Bosque for a twelve-match spell in 1993–94 during one of the Real club's familiar crises, but ambition and the lure of management soon took him away from the chessboard and out of the comfort zone of Madrid. He left for Valladolid for his first spell as a club manager in the 1995–96 La Liga season. It was a painful debut, because after six months and twenty-three games Valladolid were rock bottom of La Liga and a floundering Benítez was out of a job. Worse was to come, because his successor was eventually to guide the Spanish strugglers away from danger and later to qualification for a UEFA Cup place. This was, it seemed, a case of inexperience and early managerial uncertainty rather than a lack of sufficient club potential.

Ambitious Osasuna in the Spanish second division were, apparently, not dismayed by the Benítez flop at Valadollid – quite the contrary – and they signed the young manager immediately, believing he could pilot them right away into La Liga. But patience was in rattling short supply here. After just nine games with one win, and with Osasuna in the relegation rather than the promotion places, Benítez was shown the door once more. The young perfectionist seemed to be heading down, rather than up, the Spanish football pecking order. He next ended up, in 1997, at little Extremadura, another second division club in a rural town of just 20,000 people. But here he really started to hit his managerial stride, even getting the tiny club promoted into the Spanish elite – but it wasn't to last. In 1998–99, faced with competition and resources beyond his scope, Benítez was sacked once more, as Extremadura were immediately relegated.

For almost five years Benítez had tried – and failed – to become an established football coach in Spain. He had had four disappointing years in management and one pretty successful one, at Extremadura. But no Spanish club was now willing to risk another punt on a man with what was a mixed management CV, to say the least. He could go back to the training pitch, of course: Real would definitely have him back on youth-player coaching, if he wanted it. But Benítez still believed he could become a successful coach/manager and when faced with a spell of enforced unemployment in Spain – he needed some time, anyway, to distance himself from the Extremadura relegation fiasco – he decided to try to extend his football knowledge by visiting other clubs around Europe and studying their coaching systems. This was no luxury option, no series of gold-standard invitations; Benítez was barely known outside Spain and not much known in it. He had to plead with administrators and coaches to be allowed access to foreign clubs and he paid his own way, budget flights, poxy hotels and all. He went to all the right places, though – to see Capello at Milan, Lippi at Juventus and Ranieri at Fiorentina, along with later stops in England, including at Old Trafford – but it was a gruelling, depressing time for a man who would bounce back later to the very top of the European game.

Benítez was now fortunate – and how much in this managerial game is actually about luck? – that Tenerife, another Spanish second division club, recognised his, by now seriously scarred, potential for the 2000–2001 league season. They gave him another chance after his 'learning' year in the coaching wilderness. As Gérard Houllier was wowing the Liverpool faithful over at Anfield with cups galore, so Rafael Benítez was driving Tenerife on to promotion in Spain, earning his own rave reviews in the process for the club's organisation and attacking prowess. It was an amazing turnaround for a young coach that no top Spanish club had seemed to want. And it would get better. As the coach, Cuper, left Valencia bound for Italy in 2001, it was Benítez who stepped up to the top job at the Mestalla, where other, more experienced, coaches had feared to tread. As some British journalists later rightly pointed out, Benítez had actually had to do considerably less in Spain to get a chance at a major club than an English coach, such as Alan Curbishley, had had to do in England. But now the Spaniard took that chance with both hands.

What, exactly, had turned things around for the young coach Benítez? Had he really discovered the elusive secret of football club management during his European coaching sabbatical? It seemed unlikely. 'The answer,' argued journalist Gabriel Marcotti, 'is probably that, while he had failed as a manager he was not a failed manager. He was a manager who had tasted defeat but learnt from it, analysing where he went wrong and studying the game. He was written off, but returned as a better manager.' And, of course, he was the right man at the right time to find a top Spanish football club willing to take a gamble on a rising talent.

For all the local difficulties at Valencia that had seen off Cuper, Benítez had taken charge of a Spanish club that was in rude good health. Although he had failed by miles to secure the Spanish title, Cuper had been headhunted because of the European achievements of the club under his charge. Valencia had lost only on penalties to Bayern Munich in the 2001 European Cup final and the defensive core of this team remained: the reliable 'punk' keeper Canizares in goal; the experienced defensive strength of Frenchman Angloma and the tough-tackling and ageless Carboni; the Argentinian centre-back pillars Ayala and Pellegrino; the brilliant Albelda, Baraja and the left-sided Vicente in midfield; and the beanpole Carew and dangerous Kily Gonzales up-front. There was also little Pablo Aimar, *El Payoso* (The Clown), to consider: a thrilling Argentine midfield schemer. Surely Benítez needed only to tinker with, rather than reform, Cuper's impressive side for more international *and* domestic success?

Out went the veteran Frenchman Deschamps and the talismanic, but unsettled, Mendieta – for a miserable stay in Barcelona before ending up on the British East Coast Riviera in Middlesbrough. In came a wide attacking midfielder, Rufete. The hard-running midfielder Angulo often became a lone 'striker' in a favoured 4–2–3–1 counter-attack Benítez formation we would later see at Anfield. There were also intimations here of Steven Gerrard's more advanced forward role for Liverpool. Under Benítez, this team was not always the prettiest to watch – that pressing Sacchi game again – and after 15 matches Valencia had scored a paltry 15 goals. Not only were the local fans complaining but so, publicly, were some of the club's players, the influential Kily Gonzales and Angulo among them. At Espanyol in December 2001 Benítez survived a real crisis moment – a preparation, of sorts, for Istanbul in 2005. With fans, and some Valencia players, openly calling for his head, and the club's board reputed to be ready to act, *Los Ches* recovered from a desperate 0–2 half-time deficit to win 3–2. Benítez survived, by the skin of his teeth.

Benítez's Valencia worked hard for each other, kept the ball and ground out results: they were pragmatic – and hugely effective.

'TEAM – with capital letters,' Benítez stressed to the Spanish press. 'This is what my team stands for.'

With two games still to play, and with Barca and Real in chaos, Valencia were already Spanish champions. But for some Benítez critics – and there were plenty – this was a pyrrhic victory. Baraja top-scored with just 7 goals, and Valencia scored only 51 goals in 38 matches, the lowest in Spanish championship history. Benítez's approach was described, by some commentators, as 'risible' for championship aspirers, especially when he seemed almost to eschew goal-scoring entirely by fielding a team with no genuine forwards at all at lowly Tenerife. The Mestalla was often bored. Kily Gonzales claimed publicly that, in any case, the title-winning team was not forged by Benítez at all, but was Hector Cuper's. The championship was certainly built on the Argentinian's carefully assembled defence: Canizares kept an astonishing 17 clean sheets.

So the Benítez–Valencia camp was not a happy one, even in the glow of winning La Liga. In August 2002, as Valencia prepared for a Spanish Supercup clash, the manager even sent all of his players home from training for not working hard enough, before savaging them in the local press. Nevertheless, in November that year his Valencia squad utterly outplayed – and out-muscled – Houllier's Liverpool in the Champions League, and it was the lumbering Carew who later scuppered Arsenal's hopes in the competition by scoring twice in a decisive European contest at the Mestalla. Ironically, it was Cuper's Inter Milan who were later just too strong for Valencia in the quarter-final, winning the tie on away goals.

In 2002–03, after a strong start to the season, Valencia slumped to fifth position in La Liga, failing even to qualify for the 2003–04 Champions League. They were frequently accused in Spain now of being cynical – even dirty – and the Mestalla natives became restless once more. Benítez, who had already lost his club president and supporter Pedro Cortes because of board in-fighting, now found his new president, Jaime Orti, at loggerheads with the club's major shareholder, Paco Roig. With this ugly unrest at board level, Benítez was also having real problems seeing eye to eye with his technical director – and player-recruiter – Jesus García Pitarch. According to one source the pair 'shared the kind of relationship you'd get if you put a pit bull and a wolf in a three-foot cage'. But without Champions League pressures, and by moving his defensive line 10 or 15 yards forward, in 2003–04 Valencia won the UEFA Cup and La Liga title instead. With Mista now a key forward, and playing the defence much higher up the pitch, Valencia also played rather more free-flowing, attacking football in both. The Benítez full commitment to policies of player rotation – again in evidence at Liverpool later – also began to be seen in productive sharp relief now, with his squad being much stronger than those of both the *galacticos*-constrained Real Madrid or of Barcelona.

But despite this extraordinary success in just three seasons in charge, there were still Mestalla crowd murmurs about the alleged 'overly conservative' approach of Benítez on the field. The club delivered too little excitement but, instead, a highly organised 'bloody-minded consistency', in the eyes of one observer. There were also some suggestions from inside the Valencia boardroom that this high-minded young coach, Benítez, was receiving far too much acclaim for achievements that had actually been shaped by the previous manager. Benítez was obviously successful at Valencia – but he didn't feel much loved, or respected.

Moreover, Benítez now began to struggle, more openly, with the management systems inside Spanish clubs. It is the owners, or directors of football, at clubs who select players for signing, while the coach has the, sometimes thankless, task of integrating the signings into his team. A powerful and wanted manager can make his influence tell strongly here: he has much more of his own way on signings. As a two-times La Liga title-winner Benítez might have reasonably expected some slack now on his own transfer dealings, but he felt things were actually slipping the other way. For a proud man so devoted to the importance of systems of play and to team tactics, this situation, in which someone else did the shopping for players, was now becoming intolerable. When, earlier, a little known Uruguayan winger, Nestor Canobbio, was bought for him by Pitarch – a little hint about the crab-like style of football it was alleged Benítez was delivering and how a change was needed – he began to talk about this development in a language that he expected all supporters might understand. Imagine you are furnishing your home, he said, and you need a sofa but someone else decides that you should have a lamp. (What, a lamp? On the wing?) This strange analogy might have got the message home, but the Valencia board still seemed bent on a bout of brinkmanship with their manager. Benítez even suspected that the Valencia managing director, Manuel Llorente, was already negotiating with his eventual replacement, the old Valencia and ex-Chelsea boss Claudio Ranieri. Something had to give.

## MEET THE NEW BOSS

Top coaches or football managers generally leave football clubs because they are perceived failures, or else they are so successful that other, bigger, clubs come calling with big money. Very occasionally, serious personal differences intervene. This was an unusual case indeed: newly crowned league champions unable to agree a working relationship with their successful coach. Although there was now some frantic boardroom back-pedalling as Benítez showed his own intransigence, the Valencia directors seemed to be publicly challenging their title-winning manager: either leave the club, change your policies or simply submit to our control. What they almost certainly did not know was that, with their increasingly semi-detached coach now in very public turmoil about his job, managerless Liverpool Football Club from England was busy oiling the Spanish wheels for an early Benítez departure.

Benítez left Valencia on 1 June almost exactly a week after Gérard Houllier had vacated his post at Liverpool. It was probably just too much of a coincidence to ignore. But, let's also be straight about this: this was no craven opting for a better offer elsewhere. Liverpool had approached Benítez, certainly. But it was a highly emotional, a tearful Spaniard who faced a press conference in Valencia to announce that there could be no agreement with the club board on a new two-year deal, that, most regrettably, he was being forced out of a football club that he loved and, no, he had no arrangements to go to any other club.

Benítez was certainly glad to be putting his struggles with the Valencia board, club officials and even sections of the Mestalla fans behind him. He thought he was undervalued and shackled at Valencia and he wanted the freedom to sign whom he wanted when he wanted them. But this last bit of his public statement about having no plans elsewhere was, for some, a little hard to accept. You don't leave a champion club with only the dole office in mind. Although nothing was yet signed, Liverpool were confident that they had already secured their man on a five-year contract.

In June Liverpool unveiled Benítez at a simple press conference at Anfield hosted by Rick Parry. The new manager was, clearly, here for the duration: he had moved to Liverpool with his wife, Montse, and their children – and most of his Spanish football staff. Parry emphasised the enthusiasm and youthfulness of the new manager – 'just look at him' – but he also stressed the European managerial achievements and experience of the man. In fact Benítez had not really built on the Champions League pedigree of Hector Cuper at Valencia at all, but he had done pretty much everything else that could be expected of him in his short stay at the Mestalla. This was a considerable coup for Rick Parry: a really top European coach secured from a very small field. The Liverpool players could also be expected to be impressed by Benítez's capture: after all, they had drooled over Valencia at Anfield in 2002, over the precision and order of the Spaniards' play and the economy with which they had kept and used the ball. They had also noticed Valencia's physical toughness and their necessary cynicism. This guy was hard-boiled, knew something about the game and had been a winner in Spain. Although there may have been dressing-room doubters, he probably deserved a shot.

Benítez made it clear later why he had decided to come to Anfield, and why he felt his short stay at Valencia had to come to an end. 'My history with Valencia was really nice,' he said, 'but the in-house fighting went on for three years. The chairman didn't have many shares and the main shareholder was not on the board. I had problems with the directors in the club, because some of them did not respect me. At Liverpool they gave me the freedom to do my job.'

He went on: 'Here, I am the manager, not the coach. I am allowed to make decisions and if they are the wrong ones then the fault is mine. The job is harder here because you have a lot more responsibility, but I don't mind that because I prefer to make the decisions myself. In Spain the chairman and the sporting director make the decisions and you can be sacked if they are the wrong ones.'

In England he would certainly be in control of his own destiny a little more than in Spain – though, as Gérard Houllier found to his cost, the British press can offer a different set of agendas for a manager struggling to get to grips with an aggressive, new football culture.

For the Liverpool fans, OK, it was another foreign coach, but it was a top-notch one: no one doubted that. And if the new manager did eventually bring over with him some Spanish stars, well, the Spanish League looked decent quality, and nothing could be as frustrating, could it, as what they had ended up watching under Houllier? As James Lawton put it in *The Independent,* Liverpool supporters 'know he is a football man to the last inch of his gently rotund body, and that his achievements in Spain and Europe were deeply impressive'. Hmmm. No one was yet talking, publicly, about the fact that Benítez had favoured player rotation and a similar sort of pragmatism at Valencia to the kind that Houllier had been so pilloried for at Liverpool. But the Spaniard also seemed less flaky, more secure, psychologically, than the Frenchman. His judgement and management of players was likely to be the key here, as with all football managers, and he had done relatively little big-money transfer trading in his career so far.

Moreover, no Valencia players would follow Benítez immediately to Anfield: that was soon made clear. In fact Liverpool and Valencia did not seem to be speaking at all. Benítez now said a few words to the gathered press boys, in faltering English, about the proud history of the Liverpool club and about 'doing the right things' and 'making people proud of the team, of the manager and of the players'. It was hardly Bill Shankly quality – or even Bob Paisley – but it would have to do for now. Benítez's limited English would prove a problem from time to time: he talked much later about once warning a Liverpool player in training about being careful about dealing with the 'wine' – what, more Spice Boys action? He had actually meant to say *wind.* 'You are a foreigner in a foreign country with players you do not really know and it is hard to explain things in the way you really want to,' he said. 'I can explain in Spanish everything that I have in my head but if you are losing a game and you need to say something, it is hard.'

Benítez would have plenty of depressing practice on this latter score during the 2004–05 Liverpool League season. On occasions, not having good English could also help in dealings with the British media, but this fella would be judged on the field, not in the classroom or in the press box. In any case, he could learn all the English he would need around L4 from Jamie Carragher.

Benítez brought with him from Spain, as assistant manager, Francisco (Pako) Ayesteran, a man he had worked alongside for over ten years, and also two new Spanish coaches: Paco Herrera, an assessor of opposing teams and possible signings, and José Ochotorena, a goalkeeping coach. Sammy Lee left his Liverpool coaching role to join the England set-up, which meant that Melwood now had no ex-Liverpool players on the coaching or management staff at the club for the first time in 50 years. This was a real break from the Anfield past, with the boot room – or, latterly, Houllier's Melwood 'bunker' – finally discarded. The club's director of scouting, the Scot Alex Miller, was recruited onto the first-team coaching side and onto the Liverpool bench for his vital knowledge of the English scene. This could, after all, be a sharp learning curve for the new staff from Spain. And Rafa Benítez and his advisers had a few little problems to deal with the instant they got their feet under the table at Melwood. Apart from understanding the Scouse dialect, and all its foreign variants – he would need his own translators – Benítez's star English players were not at all sure they wanted to be a part of his new, still embryonic, Liverpool project any more.

## STEVEN AND MICHAEL – AND DANNY: SHOULD I STAY OR SHOULD I GO?

Since Bosman in 1995, top European football players and their agents have pretty much held sway in the global game. They decide where and when they want to play their football. OK, players still have contracts, but if they don't like the direction taken by a club or a new manager, or if they start to feel another club might offer more money or better opportunities, then top players can engineer a move soon enough. The contract is but a local difficulty to be overcome. The increased flow of international players across Europe has also diluted the place ties and the loyalty of players to specific clubs or coaches. Moving clubs today seems like a standard business decision. Milan Baros wondered aloud in 2004, for example, about his next move after Anfield, arguing that 'no player stays for more than five years at any club these days'. He seemed completely oblivious to Liverpool fans' responses to this expression of the new football 'professionalism'. And try telling an Ian Callaghan – or even a Jamie Carragher – that five years is the optimum stay at any football club. You might get a rather different reaction.

Nevertheless, Bosman helped arm players in this contest because clubs soon began to get fretful about their stars running down their contracts and moving on at its end for no fee. This meant that even eighteen months into a four-year deal, for example, as a football manager you were already beginning to ask what happens next to a valued player. Instability was the new stability inside clubs. Agents were happy to move their clients on as often as possible, of course – more fees, more coverage, more clients. For them the new era offered a virtuous, and lucrative, circle. Champions League participation had also increasingly marked out the elite clubs to top players and their advisers: such players, these days, seemed to believe that playing outside this higher loop meant inevitable international ostracism. Sven, and his international manager mates, for example, were even now busily *advising* their England players to join clubs in this exclusive group. Failure to do so might mean you fall by the international selection wayside.

With player earnings by now astronomical at most top clubs, key players were also beginning to return to other, more familiar methods of measuring career success: medals, titles, trophies. But unlike the position of earlier players, or the poor, benighted football fan, they also felt that it was now their personal duty – no, their *right* – to be able to tie up now with a club that could pretty much be guaranteed to deliver for them on this front. It was the new rules of the sports marketplace. The traditional place for this sort of destabilising, sifting work to be done is the national-team arena. Here, young millionaires can get the low-down on which manager might be keen to attract which player – and at what price – without the embarrassing suggestion that you are actually being 'tapped-up': a disciplinary offence. Throw in the sort of money a Roman Abramovich, say, might want to spend on a player these days and the international football camp is a hot ticket for some fortunate footballers. Liverpool's long-term-contracted Steven Gerrard was one who was specifically targeted at Euro 2004 in Portugal, where the Chelsea contingent soon got to work.

News that Gerrard was now 'considering' his position at Liverpool was no simple case of the future of a single – albeit vitally important – Liverpool footballer. It also signalled a potential sea change in the shape of the English game and of Liverpool's place in it. No top Liverpool player in the past 50 years or more had ever voluntarily chosen to leave the club for another English club in order to try to *better* his career. In earlier periods, under Shankly, Paisley and Fagan, this would have seemed positively perverse. Here was an international-class footballer, raised from childhood by the club, an inveterate Scouser and a near spiritual leader, the team's captain, who now no longer believed in Liverpool FC's capacity to compete domestically with the top three clubs in the country. Worse, he was preparing to reinforce the ranks of a club liable to be a major player in the 2005 title chase, and even a possible European Cup rival to Liverpool. As Paul Hayward of the *Daily Telegraph* described it: 'It would turn England's most successful club into the West Ham of the north: a nursery club for the Premiership's three real heavy-hitters.'

All this hysterical 'northern West Ham' talk and the howls down the lines of local and national football radio phone-in shows added to the sense of impending crisis as Rick Parry was urgently despatched by the Liverpool board to talk to Gerrard in Portugal. Chairman David Moores also rang Gerrard constantly and, according to the player, the genial Scouser Moores was 'definitely one of the main reasons why I stayed at Liverpool . . . reassuring me and doing everything possible to keep me here'.

The club also got the player's family strongly behind the case for staying: they needed little encouragement. In interviews Gerrard himself looked torn and tormented – and sounded it. Amidst press stories alleging Liverpool gangland threats – could any of *these* guys cover in midfield? – eventually the player was wheeled out for yet another Liverpool press conference. Rick Parry said, sardonically – if not in so many words – that it was unusual to call a conference to announce that a player who had recently signed a new long-term contract for the club was actually *staying* to honour it. Stevie, himself, hardly looked over the moon about things – more like a kidnap victim: 'I've gone with a decision that's in my heart.' But Liverpool fans were ritually assured that there had been no arm-twisting by the club and that there were no conditions – that it was Gerrard's unconditional love for Liverpool and for its fans that had made up his mind to stay after all.

Few intelligent Liverpool supporters really believed all this subterfuge, presuming that Steven was still here on an agreed 'see how it goes' ticket. Others already felt Gerrard had burned his bridges with the club by threatening to leave. Unless the new manager produced a miracle transformation, the January 2005 transfer window still looked to be a likely departure point for the Liverpool captain. Little of what followed in the season pointed in any other direction, with Gerrard routinely issuing statements about 'reviewing' things later and not being willing to 'wait for ever' until Liverpool turned themselves, once more, into authentic title contenders. All of this made life pretty tough for new manager Benítez, who had to issue his own reassuring statements for fans while watching as his own captain, periodically and publicly, threatened the club with his imminent departure.

For the British sporting press, at least, the Liverpool League season now became a bit of a joke: a Gerrard soap opera. It became a tiresome case of wheeling out the 'Gerrard rejects speculation' headlines for any Reds wins, and 'Gerrard ultimatum' or 'Gerrard at the crossroads' for every awful Liverpool loss. Had Liverpool simply indulged their young captain too much by asking him about his preferred managers and by listening, uncomplainingly, to all his public pronouncements on what the club had to do to meet his own high expectations? Rick Parry could do little else but repeat his mantra that 'Steven's ambitions only match our own.' The problem for the Anfield hierarchy was that Gerrard was crucial to Liverpool's revival, and holding on to him now would confirm, at least in the short term, the club's wider standing in the game. But was this one player now dangerously close to being allowed to carry on as if he was bigger than the football club itself? Some fans began to think this way. It was significant as the season wore on that it was the rooted and committed Jamie Carragher, rather than

Gerrard, who began to carry the fans' mantle as the local Liverpool hero and leader. Carragher was going nowhere.

The situation with Michael Owen was rather more clear-cut for Benítez. Owen had been, inexplicably, allowed by Houllier and Parry to evade, or delay, discussions about a contract renewal, and now Michael was approaching his final contracted year at the club. The striker publicly reassured the club that he had no plans to leave 'on a Bosman' but there seemed no move towards agreement on a new contract. Michael's Liverpool form and attitude had been questionable for some time – if not the continuing value of his goal-scoring for the club. This potential £25 million asset for Liverpool had now been allowed to shrink, considerably, in saleable value, with Liverpool at the mercy of any potential suitor perhaps with as little as £10 million to spend, especially if they were from abroad. Owen played on the Liverpool pre-season tour in the USA, alongside new man Djibril Cissé, but nothing seemed to be resolved. The beans were well and truly spilled, however, when Liverpool opened their competitive campaign on 10 August with a crucial Champions League qualifier in Graz, with Michael sitting on the bench, thus avoiding being cup-tied. Predictably, Real Madrid proved to be his not-so-mysterious captors, but for a miserly £8 million. Also predictably, his new club seemed to have little real idea on how to use the England man. Early on, at least, Owen seemed to be perpetually on the bench at the Bernabeu – and coming off it to score goals seemed to do little to impress the Real coaches.

Back at Anfield, meanwhile, Rafa Benítez had almost certainly planned his season without the little England striker, but he still had precious little time to replace him. Real cleverly fielded striker Fernando Morientes in their own European qualifier, thus ensuring that he was unlikely to be used in any exchange deal for Michael, as Benítez had hoped. Instead, Benítez had to accept an obscure attacking reserve right midfielder, Antonio Núñez, who promptly seriously damaged knee ligaments in his very first Anfield training session. So, for the best striker of his generation, a man raised and developed by Liverpool FC from a boy, the Anfield club had now seemingly acquired a crocked Spanish midfield journeyman of little reputation and a few million quid. It was poor business, badly managed, and it left the new Liverpool manager in an early hole, but one not of his own digging.

Most Liverpool fans were disappointed, sure, but probably philosophical about Owen's departure. They certainly feared the effects of the lost goals that would result from Owen's leaving. But as the Liverpool fanzine *Through the Wind and Rain* put it at the time, Owen had been largely admired by Liverpool fans as a technician and professional, as Kevin Keegan had been at Liverpool, rather than loved by them as a Dalglish or a Robbie Fowler. Michael's incredibly anodyne autobiography published in 2004 revealed, in fact, what most Liverpool supporters already knew about him: that Michael saw himself essentially as a national figure, an England player first and foremost. Liverpool FC just happened to be the football club where he filled up most of his time between international fixtures. None of this, however, should be allowed to detract from the fantastic service offered by Owen at Liverpool, especially perhaps between 1998 and 2002, when his enthusiasm, pace and finishing was, arguably, unmatched anywhere in Europe.

Another departure from Anfield – one rather less expected and less mourned by many – was that of midfield man Danny Murphy to Charlton Athletic. This may have been a case of bringing in the cash to fund new signings, sheer weight of midfield numbers following some new arrivals, or else problems moving other unwanted players on – there were few obvious buyers for the Senegalese Salif Diao, for example. Surprisingly, Benítez seemed to rate the Croatian outcast Igor Biscan more highly than Murphy and wanted to keep him. He told Murphy he would have only 'limited' chances if he stayed. Danny, a Liverpool fan, certainly did not want to leave Liverpool and he seemed genuinely shocked by the push to a move, which also surprised and disappointed many of his fans. Murphy had his faults, of course, especially his lack of basic pace and a killer pass, but he seemed exactly the sort of reliable and solid midfielder – an intelligent player who could keep the ball – that all Premiership squads need. He was also a deadly penalty-kick taker and a decent dead-ball technician. As injuries hit Liverpool during the early part of the League season, his sale looked increasingly like a managerial error, though the wounded departee did little to endear himself back at Anfield when he claimed, bitterly, that the team spirit at divided, multinational Liverpool was poor and that he relished the chance of working once again with an *English* club manager. It was a low shot, but it looked like Benítez might have had some Liverpool players still to convince back at Melwood.

## THE SPANISH ARE COMING

The relatively late arrival at Anfield of Benítez and the confusing and disrupting developments around Owen (going) and Gerrard (staying – for now) meant there was little time for the new manager to add to and shape his squad as he might have liked. He gave some early indications of what he wanted, however: and it didn't include El-Hadji Diouf, who was banished to Bolton Wanderers on a season-long loan, nor Bruno Cheyrou, who returned on loan to France; nor did it include the immature Anthony Le Tallec, who complained publicly about a lack of opportunities for first-team play and was immediately despatched on loan to St Etienne. Full-backs Traoré and Finnan *were* staying, despite transfer interest from Everton, and Benítez brought in his predicted Spanish recruits. They included right full-back Josemi from Malaga, a tough-tackling but occasionally crude defender, not unlike Rigobert Song in playing style. A more interesting buy was Luis García, a 26 year old from the heart of the Barcelona reserve team, for £6 million – a diminutive, skilful 'hole' player and a reputed goal-scorer. He might light up dismal Anfield afternoons, it was reasoned, but could he do the same away from L4 in the belly of the brutal English Premiership?

The final Benítez signing – at least for now – was the pick, the 22-year-old international midfielder Xabi Alonso, a Basque from Real Sociedad. The silky Alonso had many suitors, but Benítez and the prospects of playing in England – Alonso's English was excellent – had sold the Liverpool transfer to the player. Alonso's strengths were his intelligence and toughness, his passing – a neo-Jan Molby treat – and his overall management of the game, even for a young man. Alonso had turned up late for his first ever professional match in Spain in 1999, but he was actually something of a football student, clean-living and a fast learner. At

21 his buy-out clause at Real Sociedad was already £21.5 million – which saw off Alex Ferguson's interest – and it was assumed he was set for Real Madrid. Now Benítez had stepped in and signed him for half that fee: a steal. Xabi was also Benítez's 'insurance', of course, in case Steven Gerrard decided he should leave Anfield now or later. Here was a ready-made replacement leader and a reliable game manager, a coach's representative on the pitch. More intriguing now was the question of how Liverpool would try to accommodate *both* of these midfield talents, each of whom enjoyed the universe of the game revolving around their shoulders; and also, who, on Merseyside, would step up to buy Alonso the sea bass he loved and had received in San Sebastian for every goal he had scored for Sociedad?

## A HAPPY HOME – STORM CLOUDS AWAY

Only Josemi arrived in time for Liverpool's first League outing, away at Tottenham. He did well, too, as did Djibril Cissé on debut, grabbing a first-half opportunist striker's goal near the Spurs six-yard box. A Defoe equaliser – with Dudek possibly at fault at his near post – spoiled the afternoon for Liverpool, and Benítez also seemed to withdraw into his managerial shell after half-time, pulling off both Baros and Cissé and getting his defenders to try hammering the ball over the top to the fast, but chaotic, young Frenchman Sinama Pongolle. Shades already of early Valencia-style caution? But a draw was a reasonable enough first away return, especially as it was soon followed by an entertaining and energetic 2–1 win at Anfield over Manchester City. Gerrard and Baros were the second-half scorers, after Dudek (again) had gifted Nicolas Anelka City's early lead.

Clearly no one told Rafa that away at the Reebok Stadium was a dark and risky place to start the English education of all three Spanish newcomers combined – and so it proved. Josemi had, even now, started to show some alarmingly early signs of positional misjudgement and pace problems when attacked directly. Little Luis García, played wide on the right and then on the left, found it difficult to get into the game and to deal with the physical challenge of the Bolton defence – though he did have a 'goal' disallowed late on for a dubious offside. Alonso showed decent touches, but got caught in possession and struggled with the pace of the game, which Liverpool began with only Baros playing forward – another early sign of the innate Benítez caution.

When he finally came on, a rather depressed-looking Cissé revealed distinct attitude problems and little real appetite for hard work up-front in adversity. He may have looked strong, willing and fast in France, as Houllier had described him, but that may not exactly be the case over here, even for a hefty £14 million fee. The Bolton goal, the winner, came from Josemi's right flank but was actually another Dudek error, the goalkeeper allowing a low cross to reach Kevin Davies, who scored easily. There were audible murmurings in the Liverpool crowd about how little things had really changed from the frequently barren Houllier away performances. But it was early days: the manager needed time to turn things round.

At home Liverpool were off to an altogether brighter start. Under Houllier Liverpool had begun to struggle at Anfield, even against the lowliest opposition, his teams unable to carve out openings when any visitors came to defend in numbers. It was torture to watch. But against promoted victims West Bromwich Albion and Norwich City in September, Benítez's new Liverpool positively bloomed – as they should, of course. Against the Albion, the impish García was the star, with terrific movement, deft flicks and a first goal. Press comparisons with Kenny Dalglish were grotesquely premature – and frankly daft – but this was already much better from García. He was also starting to link up well with Steven Gerrard, who was now scoring goals for Liverpool by playing much higher up the pitch.

Norwich arrived at L4 all sprightly and keen, but dressed in a horrible dark green outfit, and they were simply passed to death by the quite brilliant Alonso, who seemed to have the time and space to do what he liked. Cissé, García and Baros all scored, with the visitors never threatening. We remembered afternoons like this one under Roy Evans – free-flowing football, goals and the opposition subdued and then crushed – but not often since. Anfield purred, despite Didi Hamann's gross and high challenge on Damien Francis, which was late meat and drink for the TV football high court. No one in Liverpool cared: watching the Reds at home just might be pleasurable again.

Things were, predictably, more difficult away to Manchester United, where Liverpool were soon under siege, with Ronaldo and Giggs running the Reds' defence ragged. But this 2–1 setback was more notable for three other things: first, the weaknesses and unfamiliarity of the new Benítez zonal-marking system – Liverpool conceded both goals by Silvestre to headers from dead-ball situations, and the Liverpool defence looked confused and quite at sea with the new arrangements; second, a depressing long-term injury to Steven Gerrard – a stress fracture to the foot meant he would be missing from now until 20 November, a crucial blow and a cruel one for Benítez; third, Cissé's poor showing as a lone Liverpool striker, the Frenchman putting no pressure at all on the returning – and strolling – Rio Ferdinand.

'Football is not like business,' Benítez was fond of pointing out. 'In football you have two games a week, two chances to change people's minds. The key is hard work and not listening too much.'

But a routine Liverpool away defeat at League leaders Chelsea, from a single, late deflection by Joe Cole after a free-kick – with Chris Kirkland now in goal for the error-prone Dudek – did little to raise League spirits. Liverpool looked way off the Premiership title race already.

So it was a fragile Liverpool that travelled to an equally fragile and out-of-form Fulham on 16 October. The Reds' away record was already a dismal four defeats in all competitions. At half-time it looked like becoming five. Liverpool were trailing 0–2 to two Boa Morte goals, and were being horribly outplayed, with Josemi – in again for Finnan – unhappy and shredded at right-back, and on the way to a deserved sending off. Salif Diao was laughed off the pitch by some Liverpool fans at half-time and never reappeared. This was already a mini-crisis in the making for Rafa Benítez.

With no Gerrard, and with Xabi Alonso inexplicably left on the bench until the interval, Liverpool lacked control and direction from midfield. When the Spaniard came on at half-time to replace the anonymous Diao, the game turned – thrillingly so. Liverpool scored four unanswered second-half goals as the match became an open, pretty much structure-free assault on the Fulham goal.

Home confidence clearly drained as soon as Liverpool scored – a fortunate deflection off defender Knight – but the visitors pressed home their advantage, including a classic Alonso free-kick for 3–2, and a sumptuous late counter-attack move between Warnock, Cissé and the perpetually bemused Liverpool sub and icon, Igor Biscan, for the Croatian to score for ten-man Liverpool. This was a case of a journey from half-time despair to full-time ecstasy for the travelling faithful, as they trooped, bubbling, back along the Thames. It was shades of Espanyol for Rafa Benítez: and it would not be the last time this season that Liverpool fans would experience this volatile shift in emotions between two halves of football.

A few things now seemed clearer. The new Liverpool could be expansive and destructive at home but often vulnerable away, where the manager was cautious and often unambitious. Of the new signings, Josemi showed real defensive problems, while García could be wonderful at home but frequently miserable away. Cissé was struggling to settle and lacked real guile and also the heart needed to battle alone away from home. He was also an uncertain finisher, one-on-one, for the huge money Liverpool had invested. But he had pace and could produce the unexpected. Alonso looked sublime, though when he tired he could occasionally give the ball away in dangerous parts of the pitch: a quibble at most.

The manager had already made some strange choices, selected some weak formations away from home: Josemi preferred to Finnan at right-back; one up-front at places where Liverpool should really dominate and win; Alonso on the bench when we needed him off it. But he had also produced some good signs: Riise revitalised and back in midfield; and Carragher a dominant force at centre-back. Some familiar problems also remained: Kewell looked peripheral and Dudek increasingly vulnerable; Baros was his usual frustrating mix of hard work, self-made goals and head-down wastefulness. But Stephen Warnock seemed to be emerging from the younger players at Melwood as a potential squad member. He could cover at full-back or in midfield, and was doing well while he stayed fit. But how long would this last?

At home to Danny Murphy's Charlton in October, with *both* Baros and Cissé involved again, Liverpool poured forward and were unlucky to be goalless at half-time. After the break Riise scored – astonishingly, his first League goal for Liverpool since Middlesbrough in February 2003 – and García scored an even better goal to seal the match. Luis García was a conundrum, indeed. He frequently looked lightweight and peripheral, but with his team on the front foot and at home he could also be lethal. He packed a real clout on his left side. He would need to, because away at Blackburn Rovers resulted in more Liverpool injury woes. A coruscating 2–2 draw – Josemi and Hyypiä gruesomely weak at the back; Riise scoring *again* from midfield – was more notable for a terrible injury to Cissé, a horrible double break to the leg, graphically captured by slow motion TV replays. It was a season-long injury for sure, perhaps a career threatening one for a man who had shown only flashes of what he might be capable of here. It also meant that, with Baros also missing, Liverpool started next at home to Birmingham City with no recognised striker, Kewell and García 'leading' the home line.

Despite overwhelming dominance against Birmingham, perhaps predictably there were no home goals. The geriatric Darren Anderton scored, instead, for City. When Baros returned to play against Crystal Palace at Anfield, he weighed in with all three goals for Liverpool, but only in a worryingly shaky 3–2 win. Away at rugged Middlesbrough it was full-scale Liverpool misery, with Alonso, Josemi and Núñez all tellingly substituted: a sure tale of lack of suitable Spanish resistance in a comprehensive 2–0 setback on a familiar Reds bogey ground. Returning substitute Steven Gerrard could do little to turn the tide here and he looked downcast and disillusioned, as was the Liverpool end at the Riverside. Even worse news was to come: Milan Baros was soon injured playing for the Czech Republic and Luis García was also out of League action with hamstring trouble, picked up in Liverpool Champions League action. Arsenal at home now loomed in the League, with Rafa Benítez still struggling with the shape of his side and even to field a convincing Liverpool team at all.

## 'GERD' MELLOR AND THE GOODISON BLUES

Manchester-born 22-year-old Neil 'Gerd' Mellor had made just three League appearances for Liverpool since turning professional in 2001, including one start, against Aston Villa, in January 2002.

The son of loping ex-Manchester City winger Ian, Mellor was best known to Liverpool fans for a Worthington Cup semi-final first-leg goal at Sheffield United in 2002, but had since disappeared from the Liverpool first-team League scene, eventually going on loan, but not impressing, at West Ham United in 2003–04. Under the rotation-favouring Benítez, he had played as part of the 2004 Liverpool 'kids' Carling Cup campaign and, *in extremis,* he had also filled in for the Reds in the recent Champions League tie in Monaco, but had looked out of his depth.

But the 'Gerd' moniker was more than just an ironic joke at Melwood and among some Liverpool fans – it was after Gerd Muller, of course, the lethal German striker. Mellor could finish all right; he just lacked pace and the real aggression and desire required to play at the highest level. He could score for fun in the Liverpool reserves, but found the speed and physicality of the Premiership just too difficult to handle. But his time was now coming in a Liverpool shirt. Whatever happened from now on in his career at Anfield, or anywhere else in football, he would have at least one glowing memory to tell his own kids about: and even to take to his grave.

Wenger's current Arsenal were fearsome opponents at the best of times, and they were challenging again at the top of the Premiership: a side full of tough professionals and seasoned internationals. Benítez had few enough forward options at this stage and so he selected the young Sinama Pongolle for his first seasonal League start, but to play mainly wide right, in order to keep the dangerous, attacking Ashley Cole fully occupied. Mellor would lead up-front for Liverpool, but this time with a returning Steven Gerrard playing a high, pressing role just behind the young Liverpool striker. Alonso and Hamann would take the deeper midfield berths, with Riise at full-back and Kewell wide left. A fit-again Antonio Núñez made his Liverpool debut on the bench. This looked like a familiar 4–2–3–1 formation from Benítez's years at Valencia, with Steven Gerrard playing the Angulo role. It also looked like a major challenge for a wafer-thin and confidence-lacking Liverpool home squad that had little in common with the Mestalla thoroughbreds.

This was the first authentic tactical innovation from Benítez we had seen at Anfield, and a brave one: a formation chosen precisely to disturb and attack Arsenal at the back but also to stop at source the supply to their vaunted strikers. It even began to work, Gerrard winning the ball high up the pitch and starting to get at both Campbell and Toure, with Liverpool also looking reasonably solid on the flanks. Arsenal were being choked, and when Xabi Alonso drove forward, linking with Gerrard as Mellor drew the Arsenal defence to score a thunderous first-half goal for Liverpool, there were even dreams on the Kop of a famous victory for a much depleted squad. But that would be just too easy, wouldn't it? Arsenal came back – naturally – Henry and Pires constructing for Patrick Vieira an almost walked-in, exquisite second-half equaliser around Jamie Carragher and Kirkland. The match appeared to be meandering to a deserved and honourable draw for Benítez and his team: that is until Gerd's Great Liverpool Moment.

With injury-time now leaking away, Kirkland launched one last clearance downfield for Liverpool, one that the usually reliable Arsenal defence, surprisingly, allowed to bounce. As Campbell and Kewell competed in the air for the loose ball, it fell to the advancing, slightly padded Neil Mellor. He seemed miles away from the Arsenal goal, but hit the ball instantly on the volley anyway, his shot curving around the startled Toure and bouncing before, and beyond, the flailing Lehmann, low into the goalkeeper's right-hand corner. The Arsenal players looked on disbelievingly as the Kop exploded, the early leavers now scurrying back up the steps to rejoin the frantic Liverpool celebrations on and off the field. There was barely time for the restart. It was a famous victory, both dramatic and timely, with Liverpool already a troubling 13 points behind leaders Chelsea, and still back in seventh place in the League on 23 points. This was now five home Liverpool wins under Benítez, with only four goals conceded: the beginning, perhaps, of a return to the days of the old Anfield League 'fortress'.

The confidence drawn by Liverpool from the Arsenal win was still apparent in a week's time at Aston Villa, where a still depleted Liverpool side, with Núñez starting at last, played brilliantly and was utterly dominant for an hour, Harry Kewell scoring with a header from a well-rehearsed free-kick involving Jamie Carragher.

With Gerrard again playing in front of the ball and completely terrifying Villa on the Liverpool left, a second goal looked a formality – but just refused to come. When ex-Bluenose midfielder McCann stole a late first-half free-kick from Jamie Carragher, it was the moment for Nolberto Solano to place a curling shot *over* the gigantic Kirkland: an unlikely and worrying equaliser, and one that was totally undeserved. This easy submission of two points meant that Liverpool were now comfortably trailing their neighbours Everton in the League table, and it was a trip to the inhospitable Goodison Park that was coming right up.

For this vital fixture – and was the manager properly alerted to this fact? – Rafa Benítez confounded his supporters, once again, by omitting the in-form Alonso and Finnan from the Liverpool starting line-up, with Mellor and Sinama both getting another chance up-front and Josemi starting – surely an unnecessary risk. Where was the old-fashioned Liverpool credo of fielding our strongest possible side when playing our neighbours and closest rivals from across the park? It looked like a visiting Liverpool team without conviction or goals, wrongly selected for what we knew would be a battle. It was a no-brainer, for sure. Mellor was off the pace, Sinama marginalised and Núñez alarmed by it when he came on. The shaven-headed Blues 'male model' Lee Carsley scored a second-half winner for a strangely passionless, but ultimately smug, Everton, thus breaking Liverpool's derby-day stranglehold established under Houllier. This Everton goal raised further questions about Chris Kirkland, who seemed to be clumsily wrong-footed by a gentle shot that crept home in front of the Gwladys Street faithful. The guy looked the part of a decent goalkeeper, but he seemed to make precious few saves and looked generally meek and unsure in the Liverpool first team. His footing looked woefully suspect. And does the Liverpool goalkeeper, these days, ever *talk* to his defenders? Both Dudek and Kirkland seemed mute.

The general approach of manager Benítez to the derby match also raised questions among some Liverpool fans. His seemed to be a coldly professional eye, one which took too little account of the wider significance of fixtures to the Liverpool *fans*. He blamed the midweek European drama against Olympiakos for draining his players for this League encounter. But why 'rest' Alonso and play Diao now, for one of the biggest fixtures of the season? Why fill this side for Goodison Park – of all of his away-match selections – with obviously weaker 'squad' picks, with too many men who were yet to go through the fire? It made no sense, and it had cost Liverpool three points to a bitter local rival and competitor, not to mention all those important local status and bragging rights we love to talk about up here. The Blues, needless to say, were annoyingly ecstatic: and still ahead of Liverpool in the League.

Without Baros, Cissé and García, Liverpool's League goals had now threatened to dry up. Even with Baros returning, only one came at Anfield against lowly Portsmouth – Gerrard again – but enough only for a disappointing home draw, following another Dudek error. Newcastle United offered easier pickings, with Mellor and Baros actually working surprisingly well together for a goal apiece in a comfortable 3–1 Anfield win. The televised Boxing Day Liverpool visit to relegation-threatened West Bromwich Albion, who were boasting a new manager in Bryan Robson, produced an early home sending off and then a goal rush for the visitors: a 5–0 rout, one almost to match the 6–0 from May 2003. Then, it had been Baros and Owen to the fore; now it was a couple for Riise and further goals for Luis García, Gerrard and Sinama, as Albion – and their grizzled manager – wilted. All that was left in the League now for Liverpool in 2004 was a scratchy 1–0 home win, against Southampton, with Sinama converting a glorious Alonso pass through a square Saints defence. 'Pongy' had seemed a little calmer in front of goal this season and this was his fourth League goal: he just might prove to be a real Liverpool asset after all.

## A REDS RAFALUTION?

So how had the new man, Benítez, fared in the League in the first half of his new assignment at Liverpool? Well, it had been a start of decidedly mixed fortunes all right, and one plagued by serious injury problems. At various points, Baros, Cissé, Gerrard, García and Núñez had all succumbed to serious fitness problems. Cissé would be absent for some time yet and Vladimir Smicer was still to kick a ball in anger for Liverpool this season – or for Benítez. So the manager could offer some mitigating circumstances for his patchy

League start – and it had been desperately uneven at times. At home in the League Liverpool had looked more convincing and more exciting than for some time, winning eight matches out of ten and scoring twenty goals, a decent return, conceding only seven. At home both García and especially Xabi Alonso looked top-class signings and Liverpool were, occasionally, playing with a freedom and dynamism rarely seen under Houllier, at least not since the early weeks of the ultimately gloomy 2002–03 season. The home defeat of Arsenal, especially, had shown both the Liverpool spirit and some welcome tactical nous. This was the good news.

Away from home there was, clearly, much still to learn. Liverpool had managed just two wins from ten League matches under Benítez: a home collapse by Fulham and a virtual surrender by a poor West Bromwich Albion side. There were already five defeats to report on here – some in difficult places – but defeats nevertheless. The manager looked overly cautious away from Anfield, and the men he had added to the squad – Alonso excepted – had found it impossibly hard to function away from L4 when pressured in a typical, high tempo British contest. Benítez had started to risk playing Steven Gerrard ahead of the ball away from home when we really needed him behind it, controlling the play and bullying the opposition. The new players would learn about the Premiership and the weekly challenges it posed, of course, as would their rookie manager. But could they adapt to it?

Benítez had, occasionally, added to these problems away from Anfield by trying to rotate the squad in places where rotation was simply asking more questions than providing answers. By now, too, his preferred right full-back Josemi had confirmed all the fears that had surfaced early on about him: he played square on at the back and was caught by men running wide and beyond him. He was also crude, offering too many free-kicks against. He had a lot to prove. Núñez could cross the ball and had a decent header on him, but he was also slow and lacked real guile. He would also need plenty of hard work to improve. Benítez had definitely improved Riise's game and added to his confidence: the 'confidence' of players and the importance of a 'strong mentality' was something the manager kept coming back to in his still-stilted interviews and press conferences. Benítez had got Riise scoring again, from midfield, and he had also helped to produce more goals from an advanced Steven Gerrard. But Harry Kewell was still struggling – and not scoring.

Sinama's game was developing a little, and Benítez had begun to include Mellor and Stephen Warnock, mainly from the substitutes' bench, and had even part-rehabilitated the previously lost Igor Biscan into occasional first-team League and European action. Benítez liked to dance and direct his team from the touch-line, a welcome change from Phil Thompson's bawling, and from the latter-day Houllier's touch-line inertia and gloom. But what had really changed was the post-match Liverpool back-room performance. At the bitter end, Gérard Houllier had been offering what one *Through the Wind and Rain* correspondent had memorably called delusional 'metaphorical Potemkin-style villages around the club and the team': a rosy picture quite at odds with what most fans were registering with their own eyes. Benítez's limited English meant his press conferences were very different: short and to the point. If Liverpool had played badly, he was usually willing to admit the fact. And he said nothing at all about the raft of injuries that had ambushed his arrival in the Premiership.

At the turn of 2004 Liverpool were just squeezed into the Premiership top six – way too low and behind Everton, and a thumping fifteen points behind Chelsea. Things would have to get better, and fast. The leaders, the money-bags men from Stamford Bridge and their full-of-himself manager José Mourhino, were due at Anfield for League action on 1 January 2005. Happy New Year. It was, potentially, a great way to start 2005, though it was to prove decidedly otherwise for Liverpool. He didn't know it yet, but Rafa Benítez had more injury worries and more horribly indecisive Liverpool League form looming just around the corner.

## Chapter Five

# A TALE OF TWO CUPS

## UP FOR THE CUPS?

Liverpool supporters are notoriously dismissive of clubs that are considered 'cup sides': those that have no real stomach for the long, hard slog involved in winning League titles. Yet, it is now 16 years since the last League triumph for the Red men, and as Jamie Carragher recognised about Liverpudlians in December 2004, 'Everyone is desperate to win the League. The supporters are so used to it but once it's gone it is so hard to get back. I think they realise now. They appreciate what the club did a few years ago even more. They are desperate to win the championship – it's all anyone talks about. It does get people down.'

Still, the club and its supporters have to wrestle with a deep, but hopefully not impossible, problem: all associated with Liverpool FC are rightly proud of a past that deserves to be celebrated, but building for a successful future, and constructing a team capable of returning the League title to Anfield, requires a recognition that the game has undergone dramatic changes since 1990. One part of these changes involves the major clubs' increasing disdain for the domestic cup competitions in England – especially the League Cup, but also the FA Cup. The scorn that many Liverpool fans feel for those teams that are traditionally considered as pretenders and occasional cup specialists (Spurs are a convenient target here) is heartfelt. But, aside from the odd exceptional season over the course of the last 15 years, in the absence of a team that can truly expect, year in year out, to compete for the big prize domestically, then Kopites have had to take their comfort where they can find it. Winning cup competitions does not have the same deep satisfaction as sitting atop the League at the end of May, but it definitely helps to ease the pain. It also usually involves a bloody good day out for the Anfield community singers and flag-makers!

In this sense, the drama and luck involved in cup football have become increasingly significant ingredients in the 'average' Liverpool season. For Liverpool managers, cup success has become a crucial means of buying some breathing space. And yet, serious fans could still, even *after* Houllier's 2001 team had achieved a magnificent Treble of cup wins, draw up a balance sheet that saw real disagreement about whether that season could be considered as paving the way for long-term success. In other words, was that team really heading in the right direction: was Houllier building a Liverpool team that could provide an authentic challenge for the League? It might seem uncharitable, particularly for fans of clubs who loyally support their team throughout year after barren year – where 'standing tall on the Town Hall balcony is about as likely as hen's teeth' (to borrow from the Tranmere Rovers stalwarts Half Man Half Biscuit) – and for whom the open-top bus ride is merely the stuff of dreams.

If it is true that the League campaign is the real benchmark by which to judge Liverpool teams and managers, then that is not the same thing as saying that the domestic cups are unimportant; nor does it mean buying into the cynical commercialism that has taken a tight grip on the football administrators, and too many among the football public, in England in recent years. This has resulted in a crass and, frankly, disgraceful view that footballing success on the pitch is somehow secondary to the state of a club's bank balance. Even some Liverpool fans have been infected by this sort of thinking. Despite the fact that the club and the fans had just enjoyed one of the most thrilling (and draining) weeks for many years, with the improbable 2001 FA Cup victory in Cardiff over Arsenal, followed on the Wednesday by an unscriptable 5–4 defeat of Alaves in Dortmund, some Liverpool fans, and some among the board of directors (and even perhaps among the playing staff) argued, oddly, that finishing fourth in the League in that season was of greater significance than these triumphs.

In order to justify the unjustifiable, some invoked Liverpool's historical concentration upon the League at the expense of 'mere' cup competitions. This was a sham. It was a transparent effort to deflect attention from the perceived financial necessity of qualification for the potentially lucrative group stages of the Champions League. In the end, while the club's administrators might be expected to think in such terms, for fans to adopt such a mentality was a negation of the club's historical code of 'just run on the pitch and win'. For any real fan, commerce and business must always be secondary to winning football matches, even if the two are not necessarily mutually exclusive. But, in all honesty, the glory of Cardiff and Dortmund in May 2001 surpassed by a massively long chalk reaching the heights of fourth place in the Premiership! Although another League Cup win was secured by Houllier in 2003 (over Manchester United, which helped magnify the achievement), this time, unlike 2001, many fans saw it as papering over the cracks: a palliative rather than a sign of regeneration. Welcome as this trophy was, it did not appear to be an authentic expression of a team on the up.

Rafael Benítez arrived at Liverpool in 2004 with some knowledge of the English game, and of Liverpool in particular. Soon after he had taken over at Valencia, Benítez's new side played Liverpool in a pre-season tournament in Amsterdam. While Liverpool came out on top, Gérard Houllier acknowledged that the Reds had been 'a bit lucky . . . the Spaniards were passing the ball around and making us look ordinary on occasions'. The following season, in competitive matches in the Champions League in autumn 2002, Valencia displayed their real mettle; they comprehensively defeated Liverpool home and away, the modest scorelines not reflecting the gulf in class that existed between the sides. There is also a good argument to suggest that the lesson in possession football handed out by Benítez's team in those two games helped to fatally undermine Liverpool's sense of confidence during that season.

Valencia had come to Anfield as La Liga champions, for the first time since 1971–72, and when Rafa Benítez arrived at the Mestalla, this was clearly a club with very high expectations. But these expectations did not extend to the domestic Spanish Cup, the Copa del Rey. For Benítez, arriving in England would require some cultural adjustment. He was warned by one Kenny Dalglish that 'English football would be an all-new beast for him because every game is a cup final in this country.' In late October, Benítez began his Liverpool career in domestic cup competition with what could fairly be described as a baptism of fire: Millwall away in the League Cup third round.

## WELCOME . . . TO THE NEW DEN

The trip to Millwall was to prove a stern test for Liverpool, both on and off the pitch. For supporters, this was a journey backwards in time to the 1970s or early 1980s, when away trips to London were often fraught with the risk of violence. In the past decade or longer, these risks have been considerably diminished. Here, though, the Reds were facing a hostile and provocative home crowd, some of whom were prepared to goad Liverpool's fans with ugly chants about the Hillsborough disaster (as no other opposition supporters have done collectively in the years since 1989). But, strangely, this was also a glimpse of a possible future for Reds followers, and it was a pity that much of the reaction to the match inevitably focused on the chanting from some elements among the Millwall crowd, and some Liverpool fans' justifiably angry reaction, rather than the events on the pitch. In terms of team selection, Benítez was thought to be either bold or foolhardy by fans nervously awaiting kick-off. His intention to use the League Cup for experimental purposes, and to gauge the strength of his large squad, was laudable, but perhaps he had not fully anticipated the likely physical battle that playing in the Lions' Den would entail.

Jerzy Dudek was back in goal, having been dropped for four games after the away defeat to Olympiakos in late September. The back four consisted of Stéphane Henchoz, largely frozen out in terms of first-team opportunities; Zak Whitbread, a tall and lean young Texan (who was already a US Under-21 international) making his first start; Benítez's first signing, the right-back Josemi, who had already attracted some muttered criticism from fans; and Djimi Traoré. In midfield, two of Houllier's highly criticised signings, Salif Diao and Igor Biscan, were given a chance to stake another claim. Diao had been jeered and mocked by sections of Liverpool's away support at Fulham when he was substituted at half-time with the Reds facing possible painful and humiliating defeat. There was more support for, and interest in, the other midfielders, both of whom had come through the ranks of the Kirkby Academy. On the left side was combative local lad Stephen Warnock, who could be guaranteed to stand up and be counted in any physical confrontation. On the right, Irish Under-21 prospect Darren Potter, who had already made a couple of starts against Graz in the Liverpool Champions League qualifying games. Potter looked talented on the ball, could see a pass, but was also worryingly slight and perhaps lacking self-belief. This was not a midfield line-up that was likely to strike terror into the hearts of Millwall's hardened pros. Up-front, Florent Sinama Pongolle would have the pace to frighten Millwall, but there was little evidence that he possessed a real goal-scoring threat. Almost exactly the opposite applied to Neil 'Gerd' Mellor, making his first appearance of the season; he had scored liberally for the reserves, but was still noticeably short of pace and aggression.

The local fans created an intimidating atmosphere for the Reds youngsters, but the truth was that Millwall, having lost a couple of key players from the team that made it to the 2004 FA Cup final, looked bereft of ideas and real menace. The Reds manager had hedged his bets somewhat, with experienced first-teamers on the bench, in the shape of Carragher, Riise, Finnan and Baros, so there was at least an insurance policy if Liverpool did fall behind. The last-named was to have a major influence on the outcome, coming on soon after half-time to replace an injured Sinama, and scoring twice to seal Liverpool's victory. Liverpool already led 1–0 at half-time, with Diao, who put away a half-volley after a corner, an appropriate scorer at Senegal Fields. Of the new boys, Whitbread had looked composed and positionally sound, but maybe could do with filling out a little before he could be risked in the physical maelstrom of the Premiership. In truth, Millwall had shown very little up-front, but this still represented good work from the young defender. Warnock was solid and committed, but there are question marks over his ability to contribute in the attacking third, and full-back looks a more natural position for him. Potter received the plaudits for a lovely pass for Baros's second goal, after he had moved inside, when Steve Finnan had replaced the tiring Mellor with 25 minutes to go. Earlier, though, his contribution from the right flank had been limited. All in all, though, as Chris Bascombe in the *Liverpool Echo* noted, 'for those of us who have watched the Reds closely over the last few years, this was one of the most satisfying wins for a long time'.

## MOST DON'T MIND US, AND WE DO CARE

Kept in the ground for an hour after the match, and thanked for our patience and understanding by the PA announcer, there was plenty of time to discuss Benítez's babes, and the prospects for a very different approach to the League Cup than had been offered by the *ancien régime*. However, the earlier crowd disturbances involving some Liverpool supporters in the lower tier had distracted attention, and there was still considerable anger in the away end. The ramifications of these incidents described, with customary hyperbole, as a 'riot' by some news broadcasts and papers would rumble on for months and months. There is no doubt at all that a fairly substantial group of Millwall supporters did chant provocatively from the lower tier of the West Stand about both the Hillsborough disaster and the murder of Ken Bigley (a Liverpudlian hostage killed in Iraq a few days previously). It was clearly audible to those of us in the North Stand upper tier, towards the corner with the West Stand. Some Liverpool supporters rose to the bait, and missiles and a few seats were thrown from the away sections, but in the circumstances, as Chris Bascombe reported in the *Echo,* 'it is a fair argument to say the Liverpool supporters were restrained in the face of the strongest provocation'. In the aftermath, the then Millwall chairman, Theo Paphitis, and Joe Broadfoot of the Lions' official supporters club, both denied hearing the chanting, and Paphitis said, 'We are not prepared to be scapegoats again after doing so much to put our house in order.'

There had been bigoted and inaccurate comments about Hillsborough, and Liverpool more generally, in an editorial in *The Spectator* magazine, where Liverpool as a city was accused of failing to acknowledge 'the part played in the disaster by drunken fans at the back of the crowd who mindlessly tried to fight their way into the ground that Saturday afternoon'. *The Spectator* went on: 'The police became a convenient scapegoat, and the *Sun* newspaper a whipping-boy for daring, albeit in a tasteless fashion, to hint at the wider causes of the incident.' Boris Johnson, Tory politician and editor of *The Spectator,* was moved to visit Liverpool and apologise, disowning the content of the editorial. Followers of Liverpool were, and remain, understandably sensitive to any perceived backsliding over what *really* happened in Sheffield on 15 April 1989. Many of those Reds at the New Den had been at that FA Cup semi-final, or had friends and family who were injured or worse, and many more will have played a role in the ongoing grass-roots campaign (lead by the Hillsborough Family Support Group and the Hillsborough Justice Campaign) for the truth about the disaster to be acknowledged, particularly by the football and policing authorities, but also in sections of the media and among fans more generally.

This campaign has played an important political and social role in underlining the refusal of ordinary people to bow to arbitrary authority, especially when those authorities have systematically lied to them. It is in this context that the high emotions roused by the Millwall provocation need to be understood. As a club, Millwall, by all accounts, have worked very hard over recent years to tackle the club's minority of racist and antisocial supporters, and progressive fans of other clubs applaud those efforts. These steps are likely to be undermined, however, if the officials and some supporters of Millwall continue to deny that some of their supporters were the catalyst for the anger of Liverpool fans. In a typically snide piece of journalism, the *London Evening Standard* began: 'After their notable success against Liverpool, Millwall fans will be polishing their terrace chants. "There's only one Boris Johnson" must rate as one of the wittiest – and most politically incorrect – chants heard in a football ground for years.' It's not called the gutter press for nothing.

In a frankly bizarre coda to these incidents, the FA duly charged Millwall, but for alleged racial abuse by some fans aimed towards Djimi Traoré. This had certainly played no part in the disturbance that led to the original inquiry, and neither club had mentioned it in their submissions, but it was apparently picked up when the FA studied video evidence from the match. Liverpool were astonished and perplexed when the Merseyside club was also charged with 'failing to prevent their fans conducting themselves with threatening and/or violent and/or provocative behaviour'. Paphitis described the charges against Millwall as 'completely ridiculous', while Liverpool played a straight bat in public, expressing merely 'disappointment' with the charge. Finally, after a three-day hearing in April, where chief executive Rick Parry gave evidence for Liverpool, it was reported in June that the FA panel investigating the events had found Liverpool FC not guilty of the charge of failing to control their fans, but had found Millwall guilty of 'failing to ensure that their spectators refrained from racist and/or abusive behaviour'. They were fined £25,000, plus a further £7,500 for 'failure to prevent spectators throwing missiles onto the pitch'.

Millwall then appealed against these rulings. Paphitis described the verdict as 'flying in the face of all the evidence' and said that 'Liverpool have supported us in this. We couldn't have asked for more from them and they are as astonished as we are.'

Perhaps predictably, professional controversialist and Millwall supporter Rod Liddle took up the cudgels to bemoan the FA's alleged 'political correctness' and favouritism towards Liverpool in *The Spectator*, which was clearly quite happy to open another front in its offensive against the 'flawed psychological state' of Liverpudlians. He couldn't resist a couple of gratuitous digs at Liverpool, the city and Reds fans, and although he couldn't quite bring himself to say that chanting about Hillsborough was fair game, he almost managed it. All in all, a very sorry tale.

## BORO BURIED

Rafael Benítez, meanwhile, had certainly made it absolutely plain that he intended to use the League Cup to test the limits of his new club's strength in depth. Whether for good or ill, this was a policy that he would stick to consistently in the domestic cups, at least up until the semi-final of the League Cup. Some Liverpool supporters applauded this audacious approach, especially as it gave an opportunity to local youth-team products, and they contrasted it with the caution or even conservatism of the previous management. However, there were also concerns that Benítez might test this theory to breaking point and beyond, and that he had imported a view of domestic cup competition as essentially superfluous. This could prove dangerous, but after Millwall, attention turned to a more severe test: Middlesbrough at home in the fourth round.

The Boro game came only a fortnight after Millwall, but the Reds had managed to squeeze in three matches in the meantime, and they could be viewed as a microcosm of the season so far. These three were a frustrating 2–2 draw away at relegation candidates Blackburn; a battling, unexpected 1–0 victory in La Coruña against Deportivo; and Liverpool's first scoreless game at Anfield in the League, where Birmingham City stole all the points with their only shot on target. Consistency is difficult to achieve for any side, but with so many enforced changes, and a manager who was still coming to terms with the squad at his disposal, Liverpool's inconsistency was to become an enduring feature of the autumn and winter.

For the Boro meeting the goalkeeper and back four replicated the Millwall game, except that Steve Finnan came in for Josemi. In midfield, the same four started, and up-front once again were the tyros Sinama Pongolle and Mellor. By contrast, Boro looked to be taking the task of defending their first trophy for 128 years seriously. They fielded a strong side, with experience as its spine, in the shape of Colin Cooper, Bolo Zenden and Mark Viduka. Benítez had got to know Steve McClaren during his sabbatical in England in 1999, when he visited Manchester United for a week to study their coaching. McClaren was a 'good friend', said Rafa. On paper, this fixture looked to be a severe test for Liverpool. Benítez had few options up-front, but kept faith with his second-string midfield and back line.

## THE STORY OF EMLYN HUGHES (NICE ONE, WYLIE!)

Before kick-off, there was a minute's silence for Emlyn Hughes, who had died the previous day of a brain tumour, aged 57. Signed by Bill Shankly in 1967 from Blackpool as a nineteen year old, Hughes had been an inspirational figure over a twelve-year period at Anfield, winning four League Championship medals, two European Cups, two UEFA Cups and the FA Cup. Hughes was a galloping, bullocking presence on the pitch, a talented footballer, but, perhaps above all, a leader. As journalist Rob Hughes put it, in a heartfelt appreciation, 'Skill was a factor, but it was secondary to the self-belief and unceasing physical energy. Emlyn Hughes was an extension of his manager's personality on the pitch.'

He played 665 games for Liverpool, initially at left-back, but later on as a centre-half and midfielder, where his sheer enthusiasm and will to win often pulled the team through. He played for England for more than a decade, winning 62 caps, 23 of them as captain. Steve Kelly, editor of *Through the Wind and Rain*, summed Hughes up as 'a magnificent player who embodied everything that made us great in that era. Ability. Heart. Passion. Energy. A winner. He could be a pain in the arse, of course, but if there were 11 players in our current team with a fraction of what he had we would rule the game again.'

Nicknamed 'Crazy Horse', Hughes's dominance, drive and stamina made him formidable, and this dynamism was particularly evident when he made lung-bursting forward surges, brushing aside opponents with vigour. And when he scored, there were few who celebrated with as much gusto as the mighty Emlyn. Never universally popular in the Liverpool dressing-room (take a bow, Tommy Smith!), Hughes, nevertheless, is acknowledged as a true Liverpool great, and his early death represented a sad blow to all Reds supporters, especially those who vividly remember him lifting the European Cup, for the first time, in Rome in 1977. John Barnwell, who signed him from Liverpool, said, 'The greatest thing Emlyn had was enthusiasm. He would make a cup of tea better than anyone; he could play snooker better than anyone; his opinion was always better than yours – that was the character of Emlyn.'

Liverpudlians don't remember Emlyn Hughes for his gut-churning, post-playing celebrity, but, as Rob Hughes put it, 'as a man who played for the shirt', and there is no higher praise amongst Liverpool football aficionados.

## GERD MAKES HIS MARK

Liverpool began brightly, with Igor Biscan and Djimi Traoré maintaining their good form, and Whitbread (on his Anfield debut) and Henchoz dealing in relative comfort with the heavy Viduka and gangly Joseph-Desiré Job. The game developed as an enjoyable, but not passionate, affair, with few chances in front of a desultory 28,000 crowd. Middlesbrough had what looked a good goal by Zenden chalked off for offside just before half-time, and, as Chris Bascombe pointed out, 'on such strokes of luck, names are carved on silver'. Potter again featured only intermittently on the flank, and it was difficult to see from where Liverpool might conjure a goal. Unlike the Millwall game, Benítez did not appear to have too many options on the bench. Riise was there again, but the other regular first-teamers looked on from the Main Stand. Sinama, who had toiled without much real service, was replaced after picking up a knock, and on came diminutive winger Richie Partridge. Partridge is routinely described as an Irish Under-21 international, as if he were still a teenage prospect. However, he is 24, and serious injury has restricted his first-team opportunities; indeed, his last appearance in the first XI had come fully four years earlier in another League Cup tie at Stoke City, an 8–0 Reds win. Partridge was another Anfield youth-team product who looked talented, but perhaps was just not physically capable of competing at the very highest level.

A Boro goal seemed inevitable in the second period, but a combination of luck (Job hit the post), a couple of decent saves and some profligate finishing kept the tie goalless. That is, until the last ten minutes, and with thoughts turning to extra-time the Reds put together a rare passing movement, involving Potter (again more effective after moving inside) and Partridge. Mellor ran on to the through ball and lifted it over keeper Carlo Nash for an unexpected, and probably undeserved, breakthrough. The *coup de grâce* was delivered, again by Mellor, in the final minute, with a smart turn and finish under the keeper. Whatever Mellor's limitations, he wasn't afraid of taking the responsibility. As Chris Bascombe pointed out, 'The Reds don't get at least one enquiry a month about this lad for nothing.'

Liverpool's young side had shown a willingness to overcome

adversity, and they had presented Benítez with a significant dilemma: in the quarter-final the Reds had been paired with Tottenham at White Hart Lane, and any manager could be forgiven, in their first season at a club, for prioritising a possible final appearance over keeping faith with the reserves and young squad members who had battled through to this stage.

## TRIAL BY PENALTIES

There were four Liverpool matches before the tie against Spurs: two wins and two defeats. The inconsistency was becoming predictable. A poor, injury-plagued performance in Monaco in the Champions League left the Reds with an uphill struggle to qualify for that competition's knockout stages. However, there was a massive injection of belief just prior to the Spurs game when Liverpool defeated Arsenal in the League. The high-tempo attacking verve on show left the Anfield crowd both euphoric and admiring. Still, in its own way the midweek game three days later would match, or even exceed, the joy generated by beating the misfiring Gunners.

Sticking to his reserves and youth policy at Spurs, Benítez again picked an experimental side, with nine changes from the Arsenal match. Faced with a Tottenham at virtually full-strength, with Robbie Keane and Freddie Kanouté up-front (and Defoe on the bench), the Liverpool manager again preferred his 'League Cup' back four: Dudek was back in goal, Henchoz and Whitbread re-formed their reserve-team partnership at centre-half, with Warnock coming in at left-back, and a full debut for local teenager and England youth-team captain David Raven at right-back. In midfield, there was yet another debutant, in the shape of Antonio Núñez, the Spaniard who had arrived as the makeweight in the Michael Owen transfer to Real Madrid. Salif Diao and Igor Biscan once again formed a solid, but not highly creative, central partnership, with Potter once more consigned to the flank. Mellor and Sinama started up-front.

It must be said that, although history is always written from the victor's perspective, it should also be written forwards and not backwards. If we put ourselves back at White Hart Lane before kick-off, and perhaps especially at the end of a first half in which only a combination of excellent Dudek saves and poor Spurs finishing conspired to keep the tie scoreless, then the prevailing mood was pessimism. There was the real danger of a morale-sapping exit from the competition. Although it may have been fourth and last in the club's priorities at the beginning of the season, the League Cup was probably the best remaining chance for Liverpool to win a trophy. In truth there was also some questioning of the manager's apparently wilful disregard for a competition that, at the least, offered the potential for silverware. Not everybody was afflicted by a sense of foreboding, however. A fair number of the travelling support appeared and sounded more interested in perfecting their new Rafa Benítez–Spanish players song (a clever, but convoluted, take on Tex-Mex classic 'La Bamba') than worrying too much about the fate of the team, which had been under the cosh almost from the first whistle.

Crucially, though, these young Reds would not give up without a fight, and maybe the determinedly upbeat message from the stands did filter down. Fans like to think their collective efforts really can affect the outcome on the pitch: maybe it was happening here. Blind optimism and faith have got something to recommend them, for in the second half Liverpool gradually began to get a foothold in the game. More prosaically, the replacement of Mellor (drained after his heroics against Arsenal) with combative midfielder John Welsh stiffened the backbone of the side and allowed Liverpool to retain a greater proportion of possession. Twenty-one-year-old Welsh had featured as a late sub against Boro in the previous round, but otherwise had languished in the reserves (albeit as captain), and he certainly seemed desperate to impress. The Reds had not forced Spurs keeper Paul Robinson into significant action in the first three-quarters of the match, but at least now the torrent of chances at the other end had begun to slow. Sinama Pongolle was discomforting the huge centre-half Anthony Gardner, who should really have been sent off for hauling down the flyer from Réunion. Yet another diminutive home-grown Liverpool teenager, Mark Smyth, came on for his debut, replacing the ineffective Núñez, as the match edged towards extra-time.

By now the Reds fans banked behind the goal had become gripped and fascinated by the match; it had been exhilarating to watch this young side grow into the game. The ovation that greeted the players at full-time was heartfelt. They had given a good account of themselves and had improved their footballing education against seasoned League professionals. Reds fans were keen to acknowledge their bravery and their readiness to battle for the cause. For many clubs and their supporters – and this is important to the story of not just this match but to the way that the whole season unfolded – 'heroic defeat' might present itself as an option, though an unwanted one at this point. But faced with extra-time and the 'dreaded' penalties, for Liverpool fans it became even more critical that this deserving side should now see the job through, and make certain they got their reward by *winning*.

This was no longer simply just an enjoyable opportunity to take pride in the high-spirited performance of the team and the fans, but a critical chance to reassert Liverpool's self-proclaimed identity as single-minded winners. With a new team and under a new manager, the fans could sense that here was a significant chance to grasp a connection and some continuity with the glorious past. Of course, all of this remained unspoken, but it was intensely felt. One of the most impressive characteristics that Rafael Benítez embodied, and which he mentioned regularly in interviews, concerned the requirement for players to have the right, winning mentality – to refuse to settle for talent alone. As extra-time wore on at White Hart Lane, experienced supporters realised they were witnessing one of those defining passages of play when reputations would be forged. Welsh curled a shot marginally wide from the edge of the box, but the key element of this first period was a goal-saving tackle by Raven on England international Defoe. This last-ditch heroic effort had all the hallmarks of that winning mentality, and the Reds fans greeted it with howled exclamations of appreciation, clenched fists and the sort of celebration that usually accompanies goals scored.

Still, it looked as if this script was going to end in deep frustration and anti-climax when Defoe turned in a Kanouté cross from close range just after half-time in extra-time. A last throw of the dice saw Benítez introduce Partridge for Diao, but time was ebbing away, and belief was draining away in the stands as well. Ultimately, it looked as though we would have to make do with 'heroic defeat' after all: a bitter finale to a warming story. Then, inexplicably, Kanouté handled from a Potter corner, and Liverpool had a lifeline. Suddenly the script was back at the production stage and in the hands of the writers. Sinama Pongolle, Liverpool's dominant, at times only, attacking force in this match, volunteered for duty, although a good number of supporters would have preferred the no-nonsense Welsh or the cultured Potter, or even the bludgeoning Warnock to have a go from the spot. At least if Warnock hit it, it would stay hit. Sinama's balance and shooting were not always in synch, and, as with many players of real pace (think Craig Bellamy, Julian Joachim or any of the Wallace brothers), he could not be guaranteed to get his coordination right in front of goal. When given time to think, with this kind of player the result could be embarrassing. As it transpired, Flo side-footed the ball coolly home, having sent Robinson the wrong way: a composed and apparently nerveless finish. And that was it: one apiece after 120 minutes of exhausting endeavour. Not for the last time in this tumultuous season, penalties would be the decider.

As the Reds gathered in the centre circle to await their fate, a Gospel version of 'You'll Never Walk Alone' gradually gained momentum among Liverpool's revivalist followers and filled the away end. The kicks would be taken in front of the home fans, at the Paxton Road end, and Spurs would go first. Bad news, on both counts. After Defoe had scored, there was some consternation – and even some excitement – as Stéphane Henchoz made the long walk from the centre circle. Henchoz was widely expected to leave the club in the January transfer window, having been almost completely overlooked by Benítez. In over 200 games for the Reds, Henchoz had never scored. With his last ever kick for the Reds, he did so for the first and only time! Partridge made it 2–2 after Carrick had beaten Dudek, and then Kanouté compounded his penalty sins as the Pole saved his kick. Potter was next for the Reds, but Robinson guessed right, and so it remained all square. The advantage swung back to Spurs, but the narky Michael Brown blasted well over the bar, and Welsh scored to put Liverpool ahead for the first time all night. Ziegler took Tottenham's final spot-kick, and levelled it up at 3–3. It was left to Sinama Pongolle, the man of the match, to stroke home his second penalty with the same authority and maturity as the first, and the Reds were through to the semis.

Most Reds fans rushed for the exits, with trains and buses to catch, but with a real spring in their step. As we filed out, the texts came through: Watford rather than Man United or Chelsea in the two-legged semi-final. Cardiff looked tantalisingly close from north London as we weaved in and out of disconsolate and bemused Spurs followers, trying to make it to our 'away' pub on Scotland Green before closing time. 'Going out to the Scousers is bad enough,' grumbled one old Tottenham fella, 'but to lose to their Under-12s, well, it's takin' the piss!'

We rested our aching limbs, soothed our hoarse throats and cajoled the barman into a couple just after time; mostly, though, we beamed and drank deeply from our pints, savouring an intoxicating night.

## TURFED OUT AT BURNLEY

In terms of domestic cup competition, attention could now be turned to the League Cup's much more prestigious forebear, the FA Cup. As it turned out, the game with Burnley, due to be played on a Friday evening (for television) at the historic Turf Moor ground, was postponed only 45 minutes before kick-off, and after both sets of supporters had struggled to make it along the north-west's clogged arteries. With inconvenience to travelling fans par for the course in this brave new world of the television paymaster, the tie was rescheduled for the following Tuesday week, and we reverted once more to the League Cup. Watford fans took over the Anfield Road end lower tier. Rafa Benítez had decided to pick almost the strongest side available to him, but yet more injuries intervened. Having picked up three wins from four in the League over Christmas and the New Year, Liverpool morale was high, but the loss to injury of Xabi Alonso, the classy Basque, was a real blow to our prospects. Benítez had said that, 'I was planning to use youngsters at Burnley and then look at their level after that. We can mix with the senior players [against Watford] but we will use strong players.'

With the postponement, the whole squad had effectively had a week's break. Dudek continued in goal. Some doubters had begun

ABOVE: The 1998 Roy and Gérard Show: Paisley tradition meets Continental drift. Despite the smiles, this was not a football marriage made in heaven.

BELOW: Signing on at Liverpool in 2004: the Spaniard Rafa Benítez humours the British press in time-honoured fashion. But could he humour the demanding Liverpool fans?

ABOVE: A hostile League Cup baptism at The Den: but Liverpool's youngsters and their fans come through the fire. Scorer Salif Diao is congratulated by young guns Whitbread, Potter, Sinama and 'Gerd' Mellor.

BELOW: Djimi Traoré gets tangled up at Burnley for a comic third-round FA Cup own goal. Manager Benítez hits his first Anfield crisis.

ABOVE: The first European meeting of Liverpool and Juventus since Heysel – close to the 20th anniversary of the disaster. The Kop offers words of sorrow and friendship; some Juve fans resisted its overtures.

BELOW: Fear and loathing in Turin: a comical turn from Juve ultras, on a hot night, but Liverpool – and their fans – survived the test.

YOU ARE MORE UGLY THAN CAMILLA

ABOVE: José Mourinho, the 'master of provocation', tried to keep Rafa Benítez in the background throughout the 2004–05 season. In the end each man would have his triumphs – but Benítez would be the more content.

BELOW: Luis García, 5 ft 7 in., brings joy by scoring the disputed Anfield goal that took Liverpool past Mourhinho's Chelsea and into the 2005 European Cup final.

ABOVE: The great unwashed: the magnificent Liverpool fans, abused and initially devastated in Istanbul, rise to the occasion and prepare to drag their team to victory in Turkey.

BELOW: The perplexing Milan Baros wrestles the sublime Xabi Alonso to the ground to celebrate the Basque's penalty equaliser in Istanbul. It was 3–3 – and we'd only just begun.

ABOVE: The condemned men: Liverpool players await their turn at the Istanbul penalty shoot-out. Steven Gerrard would be excused his final duty by Milan's misses.

BELOW: The Miracle of Istanbul: Liverpool forces from on-high scupper Shevchenko's spot kick, easily saved by Jerzy Dudek, to give an extraordinary victory to the Reds.

ABOVE: The blissful moment when Liverpool's players realise they are 2005 European Cup winners. Willing foot-soldiers and heroes, Carragher, Hamann and Riise, are all deservedly to the fore.

BELOW: Manager Benítez gets his own deserved moment of glory with his captain. Domestic uncertainty is erased – for now – but Liverpool fans will soon demand the Premiership title.

Sometimes a grim Steven Gerrard was too much the 'Liverpool story' in 2004–05. Here he seems at peace at last – and now promises more trophies for Anfield.

to speculate that the injured Chris Kirkland might simply be one of those unlucky footballers who would never manage to fulfil their early promise; others cautioned that the club should persevere with him, that goalkeepers only mature considerably older than Kirkland's 24 years. Only time would tell.

Of the back four that had defended so stoutly against Spurs, a frustrated Henchoz was now in the process of finalising a move to Celtic, Whitbread and Raven were unfortunate to be left out of the sixteen, and Warnock started on the bench. In their place, Traoré was moved inside to play alongside Jamie Carragher at centre-half, with Steve Finnan at right-back and Riise on the left. In midfield, García, Gerrard and Hamann all started their first League Cup games of the season, while Núñez was given a renewed opportunity to win over his L4 doubters. Biscan and Potter, League Cup stalwarts, were relegated to the bench, while Diao had been shipped out to Birmingham on loan. Fans were generally sorry to see Henchoz leave, but by contrast Diao's departure went unlamented. With Diouf out on loan, and already causing aggravation elsewhere in Lancashire, Houllier's expensive (and personally costly in terms of his Liverpool future) African experiment was coming to a close. Up-front, Benítez chose Mellor and Sinama Pongolle ahead of Baros. The latter had had a stop–start season, but had bagged 11 goals from 16 starts. He worked relentlessly, often ran himself (and his marker) ragged, and his directness could sometimes pay dividends, but he also consistently played with his head down, rarely even looking to link up with colleagues, and he needed three or four clear-cut chances for every one he put away. In the second half of the season, Benítez would signal his growing frustration with the Czech, often leaving him out or hauling him off.

The match was played in difficult, windy conditions, but still the standard of passing was poor, and Watford showed the resilience that had helped them to overcome Premiership opposition in the previous two rounds (Southampton and Portsmouth). Nonetheless, Liverpool were undeniably lacklustre; indeed, it was Watford who looked more dangerous in the opening half, although that wasn't saying a great deal. Veteran keeper Paul Jones, who had enjoyed a very brief loan spell with Liverpool, had almost nothing to do, and the fewer than 30,000 Reds fans in the 36,000 crowd were growing restless. Baros now replaced the ineffectual Mellor, and his run down the right flank and his swerving cross, which Jones could only parry towards the penalty spot, led to Liverpool's breakthrough, as Steven Gerrard side-footed a precise shot that was helped in by a deflection. And that was pretty well that in this first leg. The Hornets rightly believed themselves to be in with a decent shout back at Vicarage Road. As home fans trudged out, moaning and mithering, the mood could hardly have been more different than that at White Hart Lane. Before that second leg, however, things were about to take a real turn for the worse, unleashing Rafa's first authentic Anfield 'crisis'.

After a damaging home defeat at the hands of Manchester United the Reds needed a rapid pick-me-up. Instead, what appeared to some as a wilfully below-strength team selection at Burnley, and a performance characterised in various quarters as 'scandalous', 'shockingly inept' and 'embarrassing', left the manager facing a concerted backlash for the first time. Some of the youngsters who had brought such pride during the earlier rounds of the League Cup were thrown into the fray again, but this time foundered. In the *Daily Post,* Andy Hunter correctly pointed out that there had been, earlier in the season, a sense of 'Russian roulette attached to the brave selection policy' in the League Cup. This time Benítez 'found the loaded chamber, and Liverpool's FA Cup aspirations took one right in the temple'. Whitbread, Warnock, Raven, Welsh and Potter all made their Liverpool FA Cup debuts and, aside from the tireless Warnock, they were all below par. However, they escaped the worst of the vitriol.

The real opprobrium was reserved for a manager who was accused of taking the opposition lightly, even of wanting to make a point to the board that the resources he had at his disposal were simply too meagre to compete in four competitions. The usually measured Chris Bascombe in the *Liverpool Echo* reflected a groundswell of local opinion, arguing that Benítez had made a 'gruesome misjudgement . . . believing the FA Cup could be treated with the same gung-ho attitude as the Carling Cup, wrongly thinking a "forgiving" Anfield public would tolerate failure'. In allegedly treating the FA Cup 'maliciously', the manager had made a 'cataclysmic error', and 'got his priorities horribly confused'. And if he did not realise the importance of the competition, then the board had erred in not pointing out that in England these things are done differently.

Equally culpable, according to many fans, were the more established, or at least the older, players on show, such as Sami Hyypiä, Igor Biscan and Djimi Traoré. The latter two were singled out, along with Antonio Núñez, as not being 'worthy of the Liverpool jersey'; there is no greater insult on the Red half of Merseyside. If Traoré was understandably pilloried for the sheer stupidity of the own goal that proved to be Burnley's winner, then he was not the only one occupying an overcrowded doghouse. Antonio Núñez had looked, at various times during the season, hapless and unready for the physicality of the English game, but here he was simply dreadful. He compounded a terrible night by being sent off for throwing an elbow five minutes from the end, as Liverpool's wretched performance degenerated. In some eyes, the ambling, disinterested midfield stroll of Biscan was, if anything, even more shameful. He really seemed *not* to be trying, a cardinal sin in the view of any group of supporters. Biscan, of all people, could not afford to coast along, as if this type of Reds fixture was simply beneath him.

Liverpool had given away possession cheaply, and the experiment of playing Sinama Pongolle with Potter just behind proved to be a singular failure. The introduction of Baros with twenty-five minutes remaining, and then Mellor ten minutes later, did little to improve matters, and (Núñez apart) the Reds subsided without a whimper. In truth Burnley had not even had to raise their game. And yet, Liverpool had lost ignominiously before in the FA Cup to lower-league opposition (or, in the infamous case of Worcester City in 1959, to *non-league* opposition), including several times at Anfield in the course of the previous decade (e.g. Bristol City, Bolton Wanderers and Crystal Palace), so this was not a completely unprecedented capitulation. A sense of proportion was needed in the media storm that engulfed Liverpool and Benítez in the following days. Predictably, however, the press reaction here was strong on hyperbole, and, in some cases, on hypocrisy. This is not to say that the anger of fans was not genuine, but there were certainly efforts made to manipulate this reaction.

For instance, many of the journalists who accused Benítez of devaluing the FA Cup by playing home-grown locally recruited reserve-team players and leaving out expensive, largely foreign first-teamers were the same scribblers who had been first in line earlier in the season to pick up on Danny Murphy's ill-judged comments about Liverpool allegedly sacrificing the English heart of the club. Then, the Liverpool board and the new manager had been berated for signing too many foreign players, and denying English (never Scouse!) talent a fair crack of the whip. Six months later and it was all change. Equally, as Steve Kelly pointed out in *Through the Wind and Rain*, a large part of the media peddled the line that 'plucky' Conference side Exeter City had upheld the essential romance of the FA Cup with their fighting 0–0 draw at mighty Manchester United in the third round. That United and their manager had also been guilty of devaluing the competition (not for the first time) by fielding a hugely under-strength side was not part of the narrative this time.

Other supporters were less forgiving, and Dave Houlgate, in the same issue of *Through the Wind and Rain*, summed up the depth of anger:

> The FA Cup is not some tin-pot trinket; its importance to our club and our fans should NEVER be underestimated. It took the club 73 years to finally win it [after defeat in the final to Burnley in 1914 and Arsenal in 1950]. For many Reds 1 May 1965 is our greatest day.

He went on to remind readers of the pain and suffering involved after the 1989 FA Cup semi-final, and that this memory should ensure that Liverpool, of all clubs, must do all in their power to honour the competition. Efforts to 'batten down the hatches' and allow the storm to blow itself out were comprehensively wrecked by the supine performance from the 'first team' at Southampton in the League the following weekend. As Harold Macmillan might have said if he'd been a football manager, rather than prime minister, 'Results, dear boy, results!'

'Crisis' did not seem too strong a word, even for those who had been preaching a sense of perspective after the Burnley debacle. While it would be neither rational nor logical to contemplate *removing* Benítez and his staff less than a year into the job, another loss at Vicarage Road would almost certainly lead to logic and rationality being in short supply. The reaction to the loss on the south coast (and the cumulative effect of the week) from fans, journalists and the ubiquitous ex-Liverpool players plying their trade in local and national media showed how hysterical things could get: Liverpool had either produced their worst performance in '14 years', 'a generation' or '40 years', depending upon your taste. Suddenly, whatever the long-term preferences of our Spanish coach, the League Cup must have seemed to him like the Holy Grail!

## A NIGHT AT THE VICARAGE

On a freezing night in late January Reds fans made their way to homely Vicarage Road with trepidation. True, Watford had not shown a great deal in the first leg, but by the same token, no one could honestly say where Liverpool's next goal was likely to come from. A 0–0 draw would see us through, but surely that ought not to be the limit of Liverpool's ambition? Well, tonight it was. An early goal for the Reds, deflating the home side, and a comfortable passage with no calamities at the back or from the keeper – that was what we silently hoped for. But, in the circumstances, just getting through, no matter how, would represent something to cling on to. At the back Traoré was moved across to left-back, with Finnan returning to the right. The Limerick man had missed the three defeats since the first leg, and, given his excellent form, the Reds' downturn in his absence seemed no coincidence.

The ever-reliable Carragher was partnered in the centre by a new man, the Argentinian Mauricio Pellegrino. Now, Pellegrino was remembered among Reds as an archetypal South American defender, who had been solid and intelligent on the ball and cynical off it during his triumph at Anfield with Valencia in October 2002. *'No Pasaran!'* ('You shall not pass') was his watchword. However, despite Pellegrino's two appearances in European Cup finals, eyebrows had been raised when the thirty-three year old arrived on a six-month contract, having hardly played at all since Ranieri had taken over from Benítez at the Mestalla. These eyebrows were not lowered after a couple of shaky League performances. One 30-year-old central defender (Henchoz) had been waved on his way, apparently considered too old and slow by the management, and his replacement, in the short term at any rate, seemed even more pedestrian.

The midfield was complicated, with Hamann and Biscan (who barely deserved his recall) both occupying what many fans felt should be only one defensive 'holding' berth, Riise back on the left and Baros, a proverbial square peg in a round hole, out wide on the right. Steven Gerrard was asked in this system to play high up the pitch in a roving forward role. The problem with this was that Gerrard could not 'invent' the game from this position; indeed, he often went for longish periods without seeing the ball, which was an understandable frustration. Here, he played just behind another new man, classy Spanish striker Fernando Morientes. The Morientes pedigree could hardly have been better, with three winning European Cup appearances with Real Madrid and a defeat in the final while on loan the previous season at Monaco. But Morientes had not played a great deal for Real this season, and he would need time to adjust to the frenetic pace and physicality of the game as it was played in England. In the current malaise, he wasn't going to be given a lot of leeway. In the first half Morientes almost scored after a neat one–two with Gerrard, and, in general, Liverpool showed desire and discipline, with the hugely underrated Hamann controlling the middle and rarely permitting the limited Watford side into threatening areas of the pitch. But there was still not enough Liverpool goal threat, and it remained 0–0 at the half.

The second half was more of the same, and although nerves were not exactly on edge as Liverpool continued to dominate possession, it was not until the 77th minute that Gerrard burst through and scuffed a reverse-angled shot beyond Jones, putting the tie beyond Watford. Even then there was still scope for things to run into trouble. Sinama Pongolle, only moments after coming on as a sub for Baros, suffered a serious knee ligament injury that would end his involvement for the rest of the season. The worst ten days by far of Benítez's fledgling Anfield career finished up with his team pulling together and securing a tenth League Cup final appearance for the club. Relief was the dominant emotion in the stands, but at least thoughts could turn to brighter vistas.

Perhaps predictably, Steven Gerrard was highly praised after this victory, some reporters going far too far in suggesting that Liverpool were a 'one-man band'. Arguably, the goal apart, Gerrard had not had a particularly effective night, and his influence on the side did not match that of Carragher, Finnan or, indeed, Hamann. He had been troubled by a hamstring strain, so perhaps judgement needed to be suspended, but tactically, the jury was still out on Gerrard's forward role. Increasingly some fans were fed up with the idea, peddled assiduously in the London press especially, that *all* of our waking thoughts revolved around the future of the captain. The earth revolves around the sun, and not the other way around! Still, the circus was up and running again and Gerrard himself seemed unwilling to stop it, supposedly making ambiguous statements to the press about 'assessing' his future at the end of the year.

## BREAD OF HEAVEN?

This narrative was picked up with renewed vigour after Chelsea had overcome Manchester United in the other semi-final and set up what was billed as the nouveau riche rouble-fuelled Johnny-come-latelys of west London, marching serenely towards their first Championship for 50 years (count them!), against Merseyside's penurious footballing aristocrats, who were strapped for cash and were looking a little dishevelled in the League. Arriving in Mumbles, just outside Swansea, on the day before the match, this group of Liverpool Reds ran straight into another set of impassioned Reds. Everyone in the town was a Welsh rugby supporter, dreaming not just of competing in a one-off against the top sides in the world (and England!), but of actually winning the Six Nations Championship and rugby's Grand Slam. By half-time in Paris Wales had been battered, but somehow were still in the game at 15–6 down; the mood in the pub was quiet, but not deflated. Two rapid tries by flanker Martyn Williams at the beginning of the second half, and Wales were, implausibly, ahead. The final 20 minutes saw what must rank as among the most heroic sporting rearguard actions in many a long year. The Welsh pub erupted as stand-off Stephen Jones booted the ball away behind his own goal-line to end the contest.

For the Liverpool supporters present, there were several pertinent messages here: pride and passion were still the greatest and most attractive sporting values. This Welsh team had not only won in Paris, giving themselves a realistic chance of winning the Grand Slam for the first time since 1978, but they had done so by playing 'the Welsh way', conforming to the historical cultural identity established over generations and kept alive through the dark years by Welsh rugby's grass-roots. That was why the success was greeted with such euphoria. As the French international fly-half Thomas Castaignède observed, Wales played 'with total brio, sparkling, enterprising rugby and indomitable spirit'. Something essential had been recaptured, and the legends of the golden era of the 1970s (Mervyn Davies, Barry John, Gareth Edwards, Phil Bennett) lined up to welcome a new generation of gods to the pantheon.

Not all of Liverpool's supporters might have appreciated this great popular rugby reawakening happening under their noses, but they could certainly understand the idea that the crowd could act as the guardians of a sporting culture and identity: the Liverpool Way was not unchanging, but it did continue to enshrine a certain ethos of collectivism and self-organisation. The new Chelsea were perceived by many to represent the antithesis of these values, most evidently off the pitch, but also on it. For this reason, above all others, this League Cup final was freighted with political symbolism. The Reds fans who paraded through the streets of Cardiff a couple of hours before kick-off with a huge gold-framed portrait of a steely-looking Rafael Benítez, whilst being wildly applauded by fellow Reds, looked for all the world like an impassioned *political* demonstration in Beirut or Buenos Aires. This was only partly an expression of faith in the new manager, and optimism regarding our prospects; it was just as much a sign of *defiance*. The Liverpool crowd instinctively understood the club's historical culture, of which it is a living part, and could see that this culture was under real threat from the new direction in English football, represented by a Russian billionaire's takeover of Chelsea.

If part of the Liverpool Way entailed that 'Liverpool Football

Club only exists to win trophies' (as chief executive Rick Parry had correctly stated), then the obvious question in the contemporary era was: would Liverpool and its supporters ever accept significant investment or even a takeover by a billionaire outsider, if that was the only way of maintaining the club's ability to compete for the sport's major prizes? This was not merely a theoretical question, of course, as the pre-season link with raising investment from Thailand's prime minister, Thaksin Shinawatra, had underlined. Many agreed with the *Daily Post*: 'Liverpool must be certain of the background of anyone they deal with or the club's famous name could be sullied.' Some fans did argue that Liverpool had to operate in the prevailing conditions, and if this kind of financial deal was necessary to compete, then so be it. For others, if the Reds sold out to the highest bidder in a last-ditch effort to match Chelsea and Manchester United, this would besmirch the integrity and 'golden' heritage of the club and would make a sad mockery of the vaunted commitment to its communal values. The argument was not resolved at this time of asking, but it was unlikely to go away for long.

## 'THE WORST DAY OF MY LIFE'

The League Cup final seemed, ironically, to have become critical to the judgements that would be made about Rafael Benítez's first season at Anfield. Equally, and also ironically, the match had taken on a huge importance to José Mourinho, the flamboyant Chelsea coach. As Chelsea were comfortably clear at the top of the League, this may have seemed perverse, but two Chelsea defeats in a week (first to Newcastle United in the FA Cup and then in Barcelona in the first leg of the Champions League last-16) had left the Portuguese self-proclaimed 'special one' looking as though he might have feet of clay after all. Mourinho not only seemed fallible, but he had the unsavoury knack of becoming the 'story': in defeat, this was maybe not such a bad thing but, as would transpire again in Cardiff, he was capable of taking some of the lustre away from his players even when they won matches. In 2004 Mourinho had taken his Porto team to Old Trafford, and he had again usurped his players. After a last-minute away goal that effectively put United out, and Porto through to the next round,

Mourinho engaged in a mad celebratory dash along the touch-line, almost from the dugout at halfway to the corner flag. It was clear that the contrast between Mourinho's self-aggrandising antics and Benítez's undemonstrative and methodical approach could hardly have been starker.

The managers of the previous year's European Cup winners (Porto) and the UEFA Cup winners (Valencia) found themselves face to face, battling for the English League Cup, and the game would not be short of talking points. Benítez stuck with what was rapidly becoming his first-choice back five: Dudek in goal, Carragher and Hyypiä as the defensive heart of the side, with Traoré and Finnan at full-back. Two crucial questions presented themselves here: first, how would Djimi and Steve cope with the threat from the Irish winger Duff? At least Chelsea were deprived by injury of Arjen Robben, the Dutch winger who had made a big impact in his first season in England, so if we could bottle up the dangerous Duff, then Chelsea might be forced to narrow their game. Second, how would Hyypiä cope with the aerial threat of Didier Drogba? The Ivory Coast forward, bought for a fantastic £26 million, had dominated Sami physically at Anfield in the previous year's UEFA Cup, while he was still at Marseille. Drogba had not been an unqualified success at Chelsea, but Hyypiä would need to banish those painful memories. In midfield Steven Gerrard started with Dietmar Hamann in the centre, our strongest available pairing, with Riise in his familiar role on the left flank. Harry Kewell was given an unfamiliar berth wide on the right. Benítez had probably his most difficult decision to make up-front: whether to start with Morientes *and* Baros, or just one of them, plus Luis García in the hole. In the event, Baros was again the unfortunate bench-warmer, and Morientes started what one paper claimed was the 17th major final of his career!

Liverpool's fans were again housed in the Millennium Stadium's North End, from where we had disbelievingly watched Michael Owen snatch the FA Cup final from Arsenal in 2001. As usual there was a sea of red flags and banners, some proclaiming allegiance to specific districts and alehouses in the city, some reminding the watching millions of Liverpool's historic status, and some barbed slogans reflecting the Reds' disdain and scorn for these newly moneyed pretenders, a team constructed on the back of Soviet cash. 'Money can't buy history, heart, soul' was one among many similar offerings. By contrast, and it is an inescapable and politically significant contrast, the Chelsea fans presented us with row after row of St George's flags, with 'CFC' or 'Blues' etched carelessly across them, but few, if any, original slogans. As we were still taking in the scene, and digesting Mourinho's decision to start with the little-used Jarosik in midfield, referee Steve Bennett got us under way, and immediately Benítez's team selection looked inspired: Morientes turned neatly away from William Gallas on the edge of Chelsea's box on the right flank, put in a deep cross to Liverpool's only other player anywhere near the vicinity, and John Arne Riise, enjoying by far his most consistent spell at Anfield and a possible candidate for Liverpool player of the year, arrowed a vicious volley back across the stranded keeper. Cue pandemonium. The 'unbeatable' Cech in Chelsea's goal, who had only conceded eight League goals in the first two-thirds of the season, had been comprehensively beaten after just forty-five seconds.

What followed in the next 78 minutes was excruciating, but almost delivered the Cup for Liverpool. The Reds fought a brave, but ultimately doomed, rearguard action. Chelsea dominated possession, and Liverpool were careless on the ball, giving their skilled opponents the initiative almost throughout. The Liverpool team adopted – whether by accident or design would be the subject of bitter dispute later – a siege mentality, very rarely breaking into the Chelsea half. To borrow from the Orange lexicon familiar to the founder of the club, John Houlding, the slogans that come to mind are: 'No Surrender!', 'Not an Inch' and 'What we have, we hold.' Liverpool under Gérard Houllier had often displayed these characteristics, and it was no real surprise that they were in evidence here, given the continuity of personnel, and especially with Carragher, Hyypiä and Hamann all genuinely relishing this type of contest. Indeed, there was something heroic and even noble about the dogged resistance and the defiance on display, but nobody could pretend that this was 'pass and move', or a style of football that conformed to Liverpool's self-proclaimed tradition. But, as Houllier had proved on more than one occasion, it *could* be successful.

Rafa Benítez, nothing if not pragmatic, would later point to two opportunities in the second half to seal the win on the counter-attack for Liverpool; one for Hamann, after a flowing move, that was well-saved by Cech, and one for Gerrard that probably should have resulted in a goal. Even at 1–0, and despite Mourinho's substitutions of Gudjohnsen (for Jarosik at half-time) and Kezman (for Gallas after 73), the Reds looked as though they might hold out. Traoré had gone off injured on sixty-six minutes (freeing up the dangerous Duff), replaced by Biscan, and ten minutes earlier Núñez had come on for Kewell. The key problem for Liverpool was that they couldn't hold the ball high up the pitch and relieve the pressure. Morientes was ineffectual and clearly tiring, and Baros came on with 15 minutes to go, but despite his customary energy, we still couldn't get or keep the ball. Dudek, though, had dealt well with all that Chelsea had thrown at him.

Then, the killer blow, and a self-inflicted one at that. The excellent Hamann was rightly booked for a necessary 'professional' foul on Lampard on the halfway line. The free-kick was aimless, and a clutch of Liverpool players rose, with no Blue head among them. The ball skimmed off Steven Gerrard's head, curved agonisingly towards the Liverpool goal and dropped in off Dudek's left-hand post. An unsaveable and savage piece of ill-fortune. The balance of forces shifted inexorably from then on; the Reds held on for extra-time, but at the start of the second period an innocuous long throw from right-back Johnson was missed by the otherwise impeccable Hyypiä. Drogba poked the loose ball in from no more than a couple of yards out. It was a soft goal, and an unworthy way to lose, especially given the defiance that had gone before. Within another three minutes Kezman scored from similar range, and we could no longer see a way back. This was cruel, but having been pinned back for so long, it was hard to make a legitimate case that Liverpool had been hard done by. Only a minute later, though, Liverpool had cause for renewed hope: another long throw was poorly dealt with by the Chelsea defence, and Cech was slow to come off his line. The much-maligned Núñez bravely looped a header gently into the unguarded net (his only goal of the season), and we had another seven minutes of gut-wrenching, imploring, prayerful wishing. It was not to be. There was no generous Liverpool applause for the winners, just bitter emptiness.

In the media fallout from the match, two tiresome elements were repeated ad nauseam: first, it turned out that Mourinho had been sent from the dugout after goading the Liverpool supporters when Chelsea equalised. This was something and nothing, but again confirmed Mourinho's unerring ability to upstage his players. Second, and of more consequence for Liverpool, a fierce argument raged about Steven Gerrard's role in the defeat. Of course, there was a great deal of nonsense talked on the radio phone-ins (is there ever anything else?) regarding Stevie's commitment during the match and his apparent embrace of Lampard and Mourinho in the aftermath. The truth is that Gerrard had not played well; he had been put firmly in the shade, for example, by the magnificent Hamann. But he was evidently distraught at the outcome and his inadvertent part in Chelsea's breakthrough. Beneath the surface, though, some fans were all too ready to vent their frustration at the club's captain, who had so nearly joined Chelsea the previous summer. By so publicly contemplating the possibility of leaving Anfield for Chelsea, of all places, Gerrard had sacrificed a good deal of the huge pride and loyalty he had previously commanded from Liverpool fans.

While most Liverpool fans were certainly pleased that Gerrard eventually decided to stay, they had inevitably stored up some resentment towards him, and his position remained ambivalent throughout the year. Steve Kelly, as usual, accurately summed up the position of one group of supporters:

> Steven Gerrard is a very good footballer – he is NOT, nor will he ever be, Liverpool Football Club. If he dares move to Chelsea and says a single word about supporters playing a part in his decision, he'll trash any last vestige of respect we had for him. There is no smear or stance or smokescreen or manipulation that will ever make that decision palatable to us.

Harsh? Perhaps. But at times during the season it seemed as though the collectivism inherent in the Liverpool Way was quite foreign to our captain. On the eve of a crucial European first-leg tie against Leverkusen, from which Gerrard was suspended, he was reported as saying that 'it probably isn't our year [to win the European Cup]' and, more damagingly, that 'hopefully the lads can pull a result out of the bag and keep me involved for the second leg'. Rightly or wrongly, the impression was sometimes given that the rest of the team and squad, as well as the fans, existed to satisfy *his* ambitions, and that if they were unrealisable, he would be perfectly within his rights to seek to fulfil these ambitions away from Liverpool. It was almost as if Gerrard believed that none of the other players or supporters had the same determination or drive to bring trophies back to Anfield. Understandably, this was seen by many supporters as simply insulting.

Others, both inside and outside the city, took a different view. Ex-assistant manager Phil Thompson argued that Liverpool supporters needed to recognise that Steven Gerrard had 'carried the club this year', while Henry Winter in the *Telegraph* argued that Gerrard could 'take his leave of Liverpool without any guilt'. Those doubters who suggested that the club should contemplate selling Gerrard should 'beware what you wish for; it may come true'. But the point here was that Steven had come close to leaving Liverpool the previous summer. It was *his* loyalty that was in question, and it was up to him to keep his feet on the ground, knuckle down and show his renewed commitment to the club and value to the *team*. In the end, the proof of the pudding would be played out on the pitch, and Gerrard had not, since the turn of the year, performed at his high standards consistently enough. Certainly, this was true in Cardiff.

As we headed mournfully home from South Wales, a venue that had been so good to Liverpool in the past, we digested all of these elements, and, as all fans do, we looked forward to keeping our season going as a meaningful venture into April and May. That meant pushing to finish as high as possible in the League, but it also meant getting through to the quarter-finals, and hopefully beyond, in the European Cup. With his determination apparently undimmed by this painful defeat, Steven Gerrard gave us renewed hope, with an interview in the *Echo*: 'It's going to be a tough ask to win anything this year, but we'll give it our best shot in the Champions League. If we get through and Chelsea get through, I'd like us to meet them again because I'd fancy our chances.' Fighting talk. Beware what you wish for! But this was the kind of battle cry we wanted now from our captain. There was a lot still to play for.

# Chapter Six

# EUROPE CALLING

## QUALIFYING – BUT NOT IN STYLE

After qualification for the 2004–05 edition of the Champions League had been unconvincingly secured by Gérard Houllier's squad, the Liverpool board knew that any new manager's first task would be a potentially tricky one: to make sure in his first competitive matches that the team got through the third qualifying round and into the group stage of the competition. This might not be the formality that some imagined, particularly given that failure would cast a long shadow over the new boss's early days in charge, as well as having serious financial implications for the club. Rafael Benítez knew that he had a crucial opening to his new career, and that some of the teams that Liverpool could draw would provide a stern test, especially as they might well be further on in their pre-season preparations than the Reds.

There was some relief when Liverpool were paired with Austrian league and cup Double winners Grazer AK. Without taking anything for granted, Liverpool supporters knew that a trip to the wonderfully named Arnold Schwarzenegger Stadium was not too onerous, and that Austrian football, at one time so strong, had been in the doldrums for several years. This looked to be an eminently winnable tie.

With only four pre-season friendlies under their belt, Liverpool's squad set off on their European Cup odyssey in early August, when many of the fans were still only half-concentrating on football, preferring to indulge in the quaint but outdated custom of a 'close season'.

With the Steven Gerrard transfer saga up and running almost as soon as the old season had ended, the notion of a summer break was all but lost to a good number of fans. As Liverpool headed for Graz, they included only one new Benítez signing, the full-back Josemi, but the team-sheet was more notable for who was left out than who was actually in the starting XI. Michael Owen, the talismanic forward and Liverpool's all-time record goal-scorer in European competitions (and all by his mid-20s), was on the verge of moving to Spain to join Real Madrid, and the Spanish club was insistent that Owen should not be cup-tied for what they assumed would be a long run in the competition. The TV cameras spent a good deal of the first half focused upon a stony-faced Michael, and it was clear that he was on his way out. There was some bitterness expressed by fans at Owen, who had spent a good deal of the previous year saying that he had hoped to sort out a new contract and was keen to stay with the club (terrain also to be explored later with Steven Gerrard). Given that Owen had only a year left on his contract and, in the end, faced with a concrete offer from Real (that paltry £8 million), Liverpool's board had little realistic choice but to sanction the transfer. Steve Kelly commented, 'Maybe I am being unnecessarily bitter after all he's done for us, but if this is a player with Liverpool "in his blood", I'd hate to watch a mercenary.' Some mischievous reporters argued that Benítez had not 'fancied' Owen at all, and that it was the new manager who had instigated the deal, but this seemed fanciful in the extreme.

The match itself resulted in a comfortable victory, 2–0, against moderate opposition. Both goals were scored, in typically explosive style, by Steven Gerrard. Djibril Cissé, our new French signing up-front, who would have to shoulder a lot of the Liverpool goal-scoring responsibility now that Michael was out of the picture, showed up pretty well. He played just in front of Baros, with Kewell and Gerrard pushing forward in support. If this was indicative of Benítez's approach away from home, we could expect more of an attacking threat. Cissé's position at the club was interesting: he was pursued and signed for a record £14 million by a manager (Gérard

Houllier) who was sacked soon afterwards, so this was not an easy situation either for the striker or for the new manager, Benítez. We must presume that Benítez liked what he had seen of the Frenchman, and this was certainly a sound debut. Riise began at left-back, and Finnan on the right, but in midfield. In time Benítez would decide that Riise was the genuine midfielder, and the Irishman a more natural full-back.

There was a full house at Anfield for the home leg and, despite the usual noises to the contrary, it certainly felt as though the players and the fans felt the job had been done in Graz. There was to be a real scare at L4, as Liverpool couldn't get going at all, and Graz took the lead on 55 minutes with a well-struck volley from the edge of the box after the Reds had failed to clear a corner. As the ball dropped, Kewell fatally turned his back on Tokic, the centre-half, in a feeble challenge; two minutes later the Australian was yanked off by Benítez, the manager displaying an early ruthlessness that was certainly applauded by Kewell's many vocal detractors in L4. The management also showed their desire to give some reserve-team prospects an authentic chance to impress: Darren Potter played the full 90 minutes on the right flank, Warnock enjoyed a run-out as sub for the hapless Kewell, and Sinama Pongolle was given 15 minutes at the end. The experience no doubt did them all some good, but it was something of a gamble, and one that nearly backfired. This was deeply disappointing fare, with very few efforts on goal, and it could even have been worse. Salif Diao had started with Gerrard, rather than the tried and trusted Hamann, and both central midfielders had uninspiring nights, outshone by the Grazer captain, Aufhauser (who managed to get booked twice in the space of seven second-half minutes, with the Spanish referee forgetting to send him off!). All in all, an amateurish – and almost a costly – European night at Anfield, but Liverpool had scraped unceremoniously into the group stage.

## GROUP OF GOOD HOPE
In the draw for the group stage Liverpool dodged the most difficult potential opponents, or so it seemed. Even although Monaco had made it into the previous year's final (disposing of Real Madrid and

Chelsea along the way), Deportivo La Coruña had shown a fine pedigree in this competition under the guidance of Javier Irureta, and Olympiakos were dangerous customers (in Athens, at any rate). Nonetheless this draw looked negotiable for the Reds – so long as they performed better than against Graz at Anfield. In contrast other groups looked to be significantly stronger: Juventus, Bayern Munich and Ajax were paired together, while poor Celtic faced a hugely problematic assignment, with AC Milan, Barcelona and Shakhtar Donetsk to tackle. There is a perennial debate among fans regarding the merits of the old knockout format of the European Cup versus the League-and-knockout palace of varieties known as the Champions League. No less a figure than Kenny Dalglish added his thoughts to this argument in the run-up to the group stage. Kenny's typically pragmatic opinion was that the Cup is hard to win in any era, but that 'the competition is far more forgiving now in its current format than it ever was when I was a player'. Even after losing 3–8 to Monaco in 2003–04, Deportivo La Coruña still managed to qualify from their group and go on to the knockout stage. There is a safety net in place here that wasn't there under the old format, when a single bad night could mean the end of the European road for another year.

In front of a disappointing crowd of only 33,517 Liverpool took on Didier Deschamps' Monaco. Some Reds fans clearly showed a pragmatic and price-sensitive approach to the Champions League; at £28 or £30 for a ticket to a game where nothing would be decided on the night, there were many who thought better of it, and either watched at home or decamped to their local alehouse. Monaco brought with them the grand total of six supporters! They didn't always get very many more at the Stade Louis II, but Monte Carlo, it can safely be said, is not a hotbed of football – yachting, perhaps. Still, this team were no mugs. Monaco were in a transitional phase after losing several key players from the side that unexpectedly reached the 2004 final. They had also had some early-season injury problems, particularly to front-man Saviola, so were considerably under-strength. Liverpool began with García and Cissé up-front, and Baros relegated to the bench. In central midfield our new Basque arrival Xabi Alonso started only his second game for the Reds alongside Gerrard, with Finnan and

Kewell out wide. The back four and keeper were the same as started the away leg in Austria: Riise, Hyypiä, Carra and Josemi, with Jerzy in goal. Sami Hyypiä, our granite rock at the back, passed a major milestone in this match, becoming only the 13th Liverpool player to play 50 games in European competition for the Reds. Of the current squad only Jamie Carragher had also reached this exalted company, while later in the season Steven Gerrard and Dietmar Hamann (in the final in Istanbul) would join the 'Legends Club'. This kind of experience is a critical factor for success in the rarefied atmosphere at the summit of the European game. Still, Liverpool had no one that could get even close to the top 40 list of player appearances in the European Cup/Champions League competition, led by Raúl with 95 appearances for Real Madrid.

Liverpool took the lead with a goal founded on quick, accurate inter-passing involving Gerrard, Alonso and García, and a strong run and firm finish by Cissé – his first Anfield goal. The Reds played with a high tempo, passed the ball early and at pace and pinned the *Monegasques* back. If it was slightly over-egging things to describe the central midfield Liverpool pairing as a 'partnership crafted by the gods' (as the *Echo*'s Chris Bascombe did), it was certainly true that fans were left optimistic about the tidy, accurate work of Alonso being a winning complement to the strong running and vision of the skipper. Frustratingly, the Gerrard–Alonso combination would not be seen again in the group stage until the final match at home against the Greeks.

There were several other encouraging features in this first test, and Liverpool's supporters were appreciative of what appeared a considerably more attacking philosophy at Anfield from the new management. Bascombe perceptively commented that Hamann would be required for the sterner examinations that would face the Reds later in the competition, especially abroad. At home, however, against teams with 'no ambition except to defend in depth, a traditional anchorman isn't needed'. All that was missing was a second goal to make the game safe, and Liverpool squandered several clear-cut chances before substitute Baros engaged in a typically blinkered run in the right-sided channel, refused to even contemplate a simple pass into the box and instead lifted a cool finish from an acute angle over keeper Roma. This was a satisfying and bright night's work from the Red men, and although there was some discussion in the Flat Iron later about the quality of the Deschamps side, most preferred to dwell upon Liverpool's own lively showing.

Two weeks later Liverpool travelled to Athens for the testing visit to Olympiakos without Steven Gerrard, who had broken his foot at Old Trafford. Hamann came into the side, with Baros winning the vote ahead of Cissé, and Warnock being given a start ahead of Kewell (but surely he ought to have been at full-back, and Riise higher up the pitch?). The first half saw a surprisingly ill-at-ease Reds performance, with Olympiakos quicker to the ball and more committed in the physical confrontations. The Benítez zonal-marking system that had already come in for some early-season criticism was again blamed for Stoltidis's opening goal after 17 minutes, from a deflected free-kick taken by the Chaplinesque bow-legged Brazilian conjuror Rivaldo. But there were problems for Liverpool all over the pitch.

The Reds found real difficulty in keeping possession up-front, and none of the midfield four were very comfortable in pushing forward to support the isolated front two. Also, Luis García was busy cementing his Liverpool reputation as a talented maverick but something of a luxury item away from home, a man who could also cause danger to his own team with his casual surrendering of possession around the halfway line. Young Warnock, desperate to make his mark, thundered into a couple of rash challenges, was inevitably cautioned and was sensibly withdrawn at half-time. Liverpool improved a little after the break, but that did not say much, and they still could not muster a decent effort on Nikopolidis's goal. Cissé was thrown on for Josemi for the last quarter, but far from building an understanding, Baros and the Frenchman often seemed to be operating in entirely different theatres. A night of few redeeming features was made only slightly more bearable by the news that Monaco had beaten Deportivo. The Reds faced back-to-back fixtures with Depor that would go a long way to deciding the outcome of this European season.

We now knew everything there was to know about Spanish opposition, so when La Coruña arrived on Merseyside for 'Match-day 3', there was informed discussion in the pub concerning the merits of Irureta's team. They had made it into the European Cup semi-final the previous year, after a thrilling 4–0 demolition of the mighty AC Milan at the Riazor in the home leg of the quarters led to an unlikely 5–4 aggregate win. But in this season's qualifying round Depor had struggled to overcome Irish champions Shelbourne. There was no shortage of technical ability here, with Valeron, Victor and Brazilian World Cup-winner (in 1994) Mauro Silva all highly skilled. Valeron, in particular, was singled out as a beautifully balanced midfielder, always unruffled, with a languid style and a lovely range of passing. On these European nights seeing some of these technically gifted players in the flesh was an authentic treat; just so long as Liverpool were not overawed at the prospect. Our last two Spanish opponents at Anfield (Barca and Valencia) had outclassed the Reds. Up-front for Depor, Diego Tristan was still feeling his way into the season after injury, and was left on the bench by Irureta, to our relief. Walter Pandiani, the Uruguayan 'Rifle', started as the lone front-runner, supported by Luque from the left flank, but this team selection did not suggest the Galicians intended an all-out assault.

Rafael Benítez chose to use both his main strikers, and García from the right flank, so this was a bold Liverpool formation. Alonso and Hamann resumed in midfield, but there was a notable switch, with Riise pushed further forward and Djimi Traoré coming in for his first European start of the year. Chris Kirkland replaced Dudek in goal. In front of a close-to-full house Liverpool began at a high tempo, hustling and harrying the Depor artists, and generally the Reds were well on top. Three excellent chances went begging, however, and although Depor had threatened only rarely, there was a feeling at half-time that the Reds may be made to pay for their profligacy. Depor played on the counter-attack, and even then created very little. In the second half Liverpool continued to huff and puff, but gradually ran out of steam, and, despite an imploring crowd, Molina in goal was relatively comfortable. Defences ended up in the ascendant, with Duscher and Manuel Pablo excelling for Depor, and Carragher and Hyypiä impassable for the Red men. Benítez had stressed the paramount importance of winning your home games in the Champions League, and Liverpool had failed, but there were still encouraging signs if you were willing to look for them. Equally, though, the Reds now faced two tough-looking trips to Spain and France, knowing that they might well require a win (or, at any rate, two draws). The front-runners, Baros and Cissé, were no nearer an effective understanding. When the Czech was asked 'How do you think the partnership is doing?' his reply was, in its own way, eloquent: 'Ask the manager!' After Cissé's appalling double fracture at Ewood Park, this conundrum was left to one side for virtually the remainder of the season.

## IGOR! IGOR!

Liverpool travelled to Galicia without their injured forward and, understandably, approached the Riazor with respect. Benítez played Baros as the lone workhorse, supported by Kewell and García, but the surprise came in the decision to leave out Alonso in favour of the Croat Igor Biscan, who partnered Hamann in the Liverpool engine room. It was claimed later that Alonso was suffering from a calf strain, but he had finished the previous game at Blackburn, started the following match against Birmingham and even came on for the last few minutes here. The back five remained the same as at Anfield, at least providing some important continuity. It seemed to some fans as though the manager was running scared: his overly conservative judgement was now questioned openly.

On paper this now looked like a makeshift Liverpool side, and one that could not be expected to trouble the scorers. A glance at Deportivo's record in Europe at the Riazor was enough to frighten the life out of travelling Reds; they had not conceded a single goal from open play in the last 11 home games in the competition! Perhaps Liverpool's players had not read the stats, though their meticulous manager would certainly have been all too aware of Depor's fearsome home record, for they started with confidence and, God forbid, a certain panache. The home side again began with Tristan warming his arse on the sidelines, and the Rifle was significantly short of ammo, although Victor was playing higher up the pitch than a fortnight previously.

Biscan, awkward and self-effacing, was often the recipient of a certain mocking humour from Liverpool fans. Some of this was gentle and essentially supportive, but on occasion it could be sharp and cruel. Sam Wallace, in the *Telegraph*, had bizarrely described Biscan as 'that great wrecking ball of a midfielder'. Making his first start in a European tie since he had been risked as a centre-half by Houllier in the previous year's UEFA Cup quarter-final defeat in Marseille, where he had been sent off after looking like a fish out of water, Biscan proceeded here to produce a towering performance alongside Hamann. As well as some composed defending, Igor found time to skip, purposefully, through the centre circle after a quarter of an hour, brushing aside a couple of challenges, before feeding Riise on the Liverpool left flank with a beautifully weighted pass. The Norwegian fired a low cross into the box, almost impossible to defend, and Jorge Andrade, with Milan Baros racing in behind him, was only able to steer the ball beyond Molina and in at the near post. The Reds had several other good chances to extend the lead, but again Baros and García were frustratingly indecisive or wasteful.

In the second half Liverpool's control was less evident, and Tristan finally came on to provide a real test for the Reds' back four, who coped admirably, with Carra, Sami and Traoré all playing out of their skins. This was not a siege, however, and this unheralded Benítez side saw out the last 20 minutes in some comfort to bring home the Reds' first victory in Spain since the 1983 1–0 win against Athletic Bilbao. Perhaps there was some artistic licence in Chris Bascombe's claim that this European victory could 'sit proudly alongside some of the club's most inspirational', particularly given the strangely off-colour display by Depor, but still this was genuinely heartening and hopefully a portent of future achievement. Liverpool were joint top of the group with seven points, along with Olympiakos, and one above Monaco. La Coruña had two points, and no goals, and were surely out of contention.

## BOUND BY WILD DESIRE

Frankly, in late November and with the English winter beginning to extend its cold and damp embrace, it was not too difficult to see why generations of upper-class parasites had decamped to Nice's Bay of Angels, or Antibes, or any of the other haunts of the Côte d'Azur, to see out these dark days in the warmth and sophistication of the south of France. Thankfully, from the point of view of travelling Reds, the advent of low-budget airlines meant that three thousand or so of hoi polloi had availed themselves of the easyJet from Speke (or other points of origin) and could gatecrash the aristocrats' party. Arriving at the harbour in Monte Carlo on the afternoon of the match, the presence of the great unwashed was already evident: the ocean-going boats, worth several millions each, were liberally plastered with the ubiquitous 'Don't Buy *The Sun*' and 'Hillsborough Justice Campaign' stickers!

If the Liverpool supporters arrived in typically insubordinate style, then the team was in less robust shape, after yet another morale-sapping away defeat in the League, this time on Teesside. Baros had aggravated a hamstring strain while playing for the Czech Republic and would miss the next three weeks. So, Liverpool were reduced to two fit strikers: the twenty-year-old Sinama Pongolle and the twenty-two-year-old Mellor, plus the out-of-sorts Kewell and the capricious García. Benítez did not complain about his terrible injury blight ('If you are too busy crying, you are wasting time') but remained calm and focused. This is what we wanted from the manager, and it was a boost to hear it. He knew that a win would confirm that Liverpool would qualify from the group, but a draw would give the Reds a better-than-even-money chance. Even a defeat would not rule out qualification, but it would complicate things considerably.

There was also some astonishing good news. After sixty-two days on the sidelines Steven Gerrard was fit to start, in a five-man midfield along with Hamann, Biscan, Riise and García. Finnan replaced Josemi at right-back. Otherwise, the defence picked itself again. Mellor was asked to play as a lone ranger up-front. Perhaps, we hoped, the Reds might sneak a goal and be able to defend it. Monaco, once more, had their own problems: they had been on a winless eight-game run in the Championnat, and for their last home match (a 3–1 defeat against Sochaux) only 2,000 hardy souls had bothered to turn out. It's a safe bet that the six who had made it to Anfield in September had not deserted their team, but many others clearly had! Tonight, at least, a full house of 15,000 was guaranteed. This lack of passion for the game was reflected in ticket prices as well: €10 (about £6.50, or less than a quarter of the price of a Kop ticket) to stand behind the goal in the *Populaires* worked out significantly less than the price of a pint in Monte Carlo. Still ruminating on this, we turned our attention to the Monaco side. In a completely overhauled front-line Adebayor and Kallon were missing, and diminutive Argentinian Saviola (nickname 'The Rabbit') came in as the focal point of a three-man attack, including Chevanton and the Congolese Nonda.

*Le Monde,* in its report on the match, characterised it as 'poor, played on a poor pitch, and overseen by a poor referee . . . but with a good outcome'. The pitch, never the best as a result of the car park beneath the surface, was truly awful; it was described variously as a 'potato field' or as 'concrete'. It certainly didn't allow for any kind of passing game, and both sides searched desperately for any kind of meaningful attacking movements. It was 0–0 at the half, and largely uneventful. Now, this suited Liverpool after a fashion, but it was still a long way to safety, and misfortune, never far away from the Reds, it seemed, had already struck, as early as the second minute. García pulled up with what was clearly a hamstring problem, to be replaced by Josemi, with Finnan pushing up into midfield. In the second half Josemi himself would be carried off, requiring 20 stitches in a head wound. By then, Saviola had scored the game's only goal, after a neat one–two *and* one of the clearest handballs you're ever likely to see: except the Danish referee missed it – or at least refused to give it. Apart from a Hyypiä header, well saved, the Reds could not muster any serious response. Mellor had run his proverbial socks off, but in truth a harsh judge would say that he lacked the necessary sharpness and class at this level. Kewell had come on after an hour but was again ineffective.

We, the fans, made a sorry, dejected bunch as we waited in total silence on the platform at Monte Carlo for the midnight train back to Nice. But, at our lowest ebb, in one of those moments that makes being a football fan worthwhile and encapsulates the spirit of the travelling Liverpudlians, once we got back to Nice and found the obligatory 'Irish' bar at one in the morning, we found ourselves gloriously caught up in a boisterous and rousing session of singing (and drinking). The 'craic was mighty' (to be sure!) and the singing of genuine quality, with the highlight undoubtedly the massed choral version, word perfect, of Johnny Cash's 'Ring of Fire'. We slept soundly, and woke with dry throats and feverish heads, but we had purged our disappointment. After all, we could still go through. All that was needed was a two-goal margin of victory over Olympiakos in the final game; even 1–0 might be enough, or 2–1 if Depor could only find a goal from somewhere and beat Monaco, although nobody could be fully sure of UEFA's labyrinthine regulations.

## THREE-GOAL SECOND-HALF COMEBACKS (PART ONE)

After morale-boosting wins against Arsenal in the League and Spurs in the League Cup, there was a positive mood ahead of the group-stage decider. This was a critical game for the future of the season: if the Reds could get through, it guaranteed a last-16 place and, with a kind draw, a potential quarter-final against one of the 'big guns' in late February and into March. The season would be alive at least until the spring. Even defeat, though unpalatable, would not mean the end of the European adventure. With Deportivo out of the running, third place in the group would mean that the Reds dropped down into the UEFA Cup, an ugly device dreamed up by UEFA for financial reasons, but if necessary we would hang on to it.

Still, the portents bode well. Olympiakos were notoriously poor on their travels in Europe: they had not won a single Champions League fixture outside Greece in twenty-four attempts and had only drawn four. Against Juventus the previous season they had lost 7–0 in Turin. They had never even scored in England in five attempts. And Liverpool had shown in 2002 that they could produce a two-goal margin of victory if required, and against Roma, who were certainly a tougher proposition than the Greek champions. These types of statistics tend to make some fans nervous but, beyond the history, the pre-match pub-talk in the Flat Iron was about tactics rather than pedigree.

Rafa Benítez faced some tricky decisions, both in terms of personnel and approach. Tactically, some argued for a high-tempo, high-energy approach that would knock the fragile Greek side out of its stride and hammer them psychologically. If the Reds managed to score early, according to this view, any heart and fight would drain from the visitors, and Liverpool could ease to the required victory. Another, more cautious opinion argued against too gung-ho an assault, as Olympiakos could be dangerous on the counter, especially with Rivaldo shooting from distance; we didn't need to go out all guns blazing, but should adopt a patient, disciplined mindset, at least until half-time.

Hamann, Liverpool's great midfield enforcer, was suspended after two previous bookings, but for the first time since Monaco at Anfield, Gerrard and Alonso could start a match together. The key, unknown factor was whether Baros would be available, having missed five games with his hamstring; in the event, he played, lacking match fitness, for seventy-eight minutes. Kewell was asked to play in the 'hole' behind Baros, with Riise on the left flank and the unknown quantity of Núñez on the right. This looked to be a significant gamble, as the Spaniard had only played a couple of times since overcoming his knee injury and was still feeling his way into the side. At the back we had begun to have a look of permanency, with the same back four and Kirkland beginning his fourth consecutive European match.

Liverpool started like a train, forcing three corners in the opening minutes, with a Baros header cleared off the line and a Hyypiä header just wide at the near post. Steven Gerrard hit the post with a flick from around the penalty spot, and the Reds were clearly dominant. Gerrard had, yet again, been the subject of intense argument among supporters, after his comments on the eve of the match that 'if things aren't looking good [in terms of the team's League and European position, presumably], I will have to see in the summer'. The captain of Liverpool Football Club appeared to be holding the board to ransom. This was a regular occurrence by now, and the Sword of Damocles was constantly looming in and out of sight. Some fans were losing patience with this circus, along with the 'reassurances' from the club: the mistake had been for Liverpool to prostrate itself at the feet of the captain the previous summer. To get embroiled in this ridiculous carry-on just before a crucial match was simply embarrassing, and deeply dispiriting. At least once the game had kicked off, Gerrard (and the rest of us) could concentrate on actually playing and trying to win, rather than worrying about what might happen if we didn't!

Liverpool were well on top here, so perhaps Gerrard's 'concerns' could be assuaged – until the next Liverpool defeat, at least. Out of the blue, though, Olympiakos went ahead, and we were facing elimination. Rivaldo, the wily old campaigner, had 'bought' a free-kick from Spanish referee Manuel Mejuto González (who would play a major role later on in the Reds' European adventure, as it transpired). Just on the edge of the box, at the Kop end, we waited with trepidation, knowing that now Rivaldo could no longer run, he basically spent the game trying to engineer just these kinds of free-kicks. And so it came to pass. The Liverpool wall broke, the onrushing Núñez didn't get anything on it, and Kirkland, positioned poorly, directly behind the wall so he couldn't see the shape of the kick, remained motionless as the ball gently rolled in at his far post. A sucker punch. With news coming through of Deportivo's capitulation at home to Monaco (it would eventually end up 0–5, and still somehow Irureta wasn't sacked), Liverpool now required three unanswered goals. We surely needed at least one before half-time, but it failed to arrive, even though the Reds continued to press. The Greek side, winless away in Europe, scented an unlikely and heroic victory.

At the interval we felt that Liverpool were not absolutely dead and buried, but to have a realistic chance of pulling this off, we *had* to score in the first ten minutes. Benítez rolled the selection dice, and, if not exactly his last throw, it was necessarily a hefty wager: off went left-back Traoré, replaced by Sinama Pongolle, who would provide energy and an extra body up-front. This was a calculated risk, with three at the back offering Olympiakos the possibility of killing Liverpool off with a second goal on the break. Immediately, the manager got his dividend for this bravery: Kewell, having an unusually active game on the left wing, beat his man and got to the byline. With the Kop bellowing at him from a couple of yards away to get it in the box, the Aussie delayed his cross and then *picked out* the darting run of Sinama, whose sharpness took him away from the marker, and who converted at the near post from two yards. This was a proper goal, with excellent wing play followed by a genuine striker's movement in the congested box. More importantly, it gave the Kop and Liverpool some belief, and planted the seed of doubt in the opposition's mind.

The question now was one of momentum. The Reds thought they had scored again on the hour, as Gerrard's speculative 25-yarder had squirmed under Nikopolidis's body. But the referee, despite howls of protest, had correctly whistled for a foul by Baros, who was constantly 'backing in' and playing the man before (and instead of) the ball. Baros is usually far too blatant in his fouling, wrestling and grappling with his marker while the ball is still nowhere in the vicinity. It simply makes the referee's job easy. Maybe his coaches have told him over the years that he should try to continue to get away with this brazen approach, or maybe they simply haven't picked up on how *obvious* it is, and how regularly he is penalised.

Time was running out, and though the Reds were enjoying endless possession, Olympiakos knew they were edging ever closer, minute by accelerating minute. Benítez threw his dice one last time, with the poacher Mellor coming on to replace the knackered Baros on 78 minutes. Again, the effect was almost immediate: after Carragher had gone down in the area and had decent claims for a penalty turned down, Sinama did well to float a cross towards the far post, where Núñez used his surprising strength in the air to climb above the defender, only to see the keeper palm away his effort. The loose ball was despatched into the top corner by young Mellor, showing, once again, a real striker's finish. Mellor might not have the required pace in general play, but here he reacted instantaneously and instinctively: the kind of forward play, in fact, that just cannot be taught or learned.

## SATURNALIA n., pl. –lia or –lias 1. An ancient Roman festival celebrated in December, renowned for its general merrymaking. 2. A period or occasion of wild revelry

Now it was the Kop (in fact, the whole of the ground) that scented the potential for a dramatic climax. The sheer convulsive *frenzy* of the crowd at special moments like these must put the fear of God into the players (not just the opposition, but all of them, ours as well), and particularly the officials, which is the point, of course. If you think about it later, coldly and rationally, it can also be rather unsettling personally, as well as exhilarating in a way that is hard to fathom or compare. The power of the crowd is literally unnerving. When people talk about the alleged 'lack of atmosphere' in the Liverpool ground since it became all-seated, what they forget is that atmosphere ultimately depends on context. This intensity of reaction is not dependent on the stadium, and cannot be manufactured inside the stadium; it only ever occurs very rarely. The last ten minutes of this game fit the bill, and will be remembered in L4 circles in the very same breath as Inter Milan '65, Saint Etienne '77, Roma '02 and perhaps a handful of others (including another couple of candidates from this year). Despite Benítez's calm exterior, surely he too was caught up in this maelstrom? His constant signalling and chivvying of the players from his technical area probably does not make any odds to them at critical times like these.

The pitch now resembled a bear garden, with no apparent order or schema; players ran helter-skelter, with tactical discipline abandoned for wild improvisation. To illustrate, with three minutes left on the clock, our stalwart centre-half, Carragher, turned a neat pirouette out on the *left-wing,* and delivered a short cross to the front of the box, where Mellor, trying to make something out of this with his back to goal, twisted in mid-air and directed a header back towards the central zone, five yards outside the box. Did he see Steven Gerrard prowling, or was this simply another instinctive (but nonetheless perfect) reaction? Who knows, or cares: probably not Mellor himself. The ball sat up beautifully for Gerrard, who, head down and weight over the ball, struck it in classical pose with his right foot. This was a half-volley from the Graeme Souness copybook: check the video from the Reds' European Cup quarter-final first leg against CSKA Sofia in March 1981. In the tenth of a second after the ball had been struck, we knew, the massed ranks of the Kop, that, unless this shot flew directly at the goalkeeper, Nikopolidis had not a prayer of saving this cannonball. It hit the net as he was still unveiling his dive.

Gerrard flew off towards the corner flag, arms pumping, knocking Mellor out of the way in the process. But for the small gate at the edge of the pitch, in front of the gangway leading out of the ground at the junction of the Kop and the Lower Kemlyn stand, he would probably have simply carried on, away out onto the Walton Breck Road, and maybe ended up in the Sandon or Sam Dodd's. In the stands there was now violent and deranged celebration. We were still trying to find our bearings as the game restarted – in truth, the crowd was still seething uncontrollably – when Josemi conceded a dangerous free-kick in injury-time. A sudden sharp shock of sobriety gripped us: Rivaldo could yet change everything utterly. But the kick was harmless, and we were through; home clear. Exhausted, still slightly unhinged, we saluted the Liverpool team and headed for the Flattie, ears ringing. A traditional winter festival, our Saturnalia, had been observed, faithfully, by the Anfield Red men.

## GERMANY CALLING

The fallout from Steven Gerrard's Greek goal and his earlier comments would continue to be played out over the coming months, but for now, at least, our captain had become the story on the pitch. The draw, in the week before Christmas, presented us with some tough potential assignments. Most supporters were relieved when Bayer Leverkusen came out of the hat, but they were quickly reminded that we had said as much last time in 2001–02, and they had eliminated us at the quarter-final stage, after a defensive shambles in Germany. Much had changed in the intervening years, but we would approach this task with due care and attention.

The first leg was at Anfield in late February, during the week before the League Cup final in Cardiff: a defining week, again. And there was more déjà vu in the person of captain Gerrard – who was suspended for the first game with Leverkusen after picking up a caution in the Olympiakos turmoil – sticking his oar in once more by virtually ruling out the Reds' chances of making substantial progress towards a fifth European Cup. This was getting beyond the joke. Leverkusen, under the guidance of Claus Augenthaler, were a much-changed side from the one that had dealt us such a painful blow when led by the mop-headed Toppmöller. They still had Hans-Jörg Butt in goal, captain and centre-half Jens Nowotny, the talented midfielder or full-back Bernd Schneider, as well as the defensive shield Ramelow and the Argentinian defender Placente. But, gone were Michael Ballack, the Brazilians Ze Roberto and

Lucio, and the powerful little Turk Bastürk. For Liverpool, in the absence of Gerrard and the long-term-injury victim Alonso, Benítez was forced into yet another shuffling of the midfield pack: Hamann, keen to impress against his fellow countrymen, and in the run-up to the 2006 World Cup in Germany, would work with Biscan, the restored García and the fixture on the left, Riise. Baros was pushed up-front and Kewell just behind. Thankfully, the back four remained absolutely solid, but Dudek was back in goal, with Kirkland's back once more playing up. Spirits were not high in the Reds camp: a desperate showing against the Birmingham yard-dogs had culminated in yet another away defeat. There was pessimism in the air, and some of us would have settled for any score that didn't involve an away goal: even 0–0 would leave us in with a shout. We had some fortune in the build-up, when Nowotny twisted knee ligaments and was ruled out. He was replaced by a real rookie: Callsen-Bracker. Suddenly, Bayer looked a little vulnerable.

In fact, as Chris Bascombe reported, 'Liverpool put on their best face and delivered . . . from the first whistle, the red shirts sprinted, harried and chased lost causes', helped by a noisy crowd, and a Greek referee who was something of a 'homer'. Biscan, who most fans wanted to discard forthwith after the Burnley FA Cup debacle, again played a central part; he strode purposefully forward on the quarter-hour and slipped a lovely pass directly into García's run. For once, in a one-on-one with the keeper, the little fella didn't panic but gently rolled it under the big Butt for the sort of cool finish that a high-class move such as this one deserved. The Reds got away with a couple of hairy moments at the back, especially when the Bulgarian Berbatov missed when clean through on Dudek. Liverpool were then awarded a dubious free-kick on 35, at the angle of the penalty area. Riise proceeded to curve the ball over the wall and beyond the late-diving keeper. On the balance of play, 2–0 was probably more than the Reds deserved, and Dudek still had to produce a couple of good tip-overs in the second half to maintain this advantage.

Liverpool were now slowly edging towards a very respectable result, and in the last ten minutes Benítez introduced a couple of subs, neither of whom had played a European role up until this point. Anthony Le Tallec, who had been recalled from his loan spell in France in January, hopefully a wiser, more patient man, came on for Kewell, and Vladimir Smicer, with three substitute appearances behind him in the League, was also back in harness. As injury-time loomed, there was a massive bonus for the Reds in the shape of Hamann's expertly flighted free-kick, but this was immediately more than cancelled out by Dudek's fumble, and Franca's tap-in at the Anfield Road end. Although we would certainly have taken 3–1 before the match, this late concession, and the soft manner of it, left us deflated. The tie was still alive, when it ought to have been stone dead. After all, teams don't come back from 0–3 in Europe. Do they?

## 'GET THE ALE IN WILL YER, RAFA, LA'

Any thoughts we might have had that the Reds were now odds-on for the quarter-finals were dispelled by a quick look at Leverkusen's home record earlier in the year. In the group stage they had comfortably beaten Real Madrid, Roma and Dynamo Kiev, scoring three on each occasion and conceding only once against the Italians. They had also defeated Bayern Munich 4–1 in the Bundesliga. This was unlikely to be a jaunt. We expected a tough assignment, with plenty of defensive grit required, and we were thankful for the two-goal cushion. Still, Nowotny remained out of action, and Ramelow was also missing, so if Liverpool were brave enough to really get at the German back four, we might nick an away goal, which would mean they would need four to win. That didn't feel so bad.

On the eve, spirits were raised among the small band of travelling fans (the BayArena only held 22,500) by the impromptu appearance among the Reds supporters of Rafael Benítez himself. Sneaking into the inevitable Irish bar in Cologne, where Reds fans were cheering on AC Milan (as they comfortably disposed of Man United, 2–0 on aggregate), Rafa, who had been wandering around with Pako Ayesteran seeking out a bar showing Chelsea's match with Barcelona, said to the first Kopite who recognised him: 'Sssh . . . be quiet.' Soon, of course, the place was in uproarious delight that the boss had joined them: 'I was in there for 50 minutes. I couldn't see the game – it was impossible because of the supporters. They were round me, kissing me. It was different. It was fantastic – a nice experience.' It's probably just as well that his wife Montse wasn't with him!

## ROCKIN' ALL OVER THE WORLD!

Kewell and Traoré were both ruled out of the second leg, so Warnock was handed his first start for six weeks at left-back, while Gerrard came in as the support to front-runner Baros. Otherwise, the Reds were unchanged. Liverpool began brightly, signalling an attacking intent, and should have had a penalty after Callsen-Bracker tripped Baros. No matter. Although Leverkusen had created a couple of half-chances, it was Liverpool who scored first, on 28 minutes, through a delicate flick by García from Gerrard's cross. Within five minutes the little Spaniard had scored again, with an even more delicate touch, helping in a header from Biscan almost from the goal-line. At 5–1 on aggregate the contest was surely over. Leverkusen knew their hopes were kaput, and as Berbatov limped off, they might as well have thrown in the towel. After the break, and with Reds fans enjoying themselves with a full run-through of the Anfield songbook, Baros volleyed only his second goal since before Christmas. Benítez now used the remaining 20 minutes to rest some of his key men: John Welsh came on for his first European appearance of the year, and Carragher was withdrawn, with Biscan moving to centre-half. These were the only 20 minutes of Liverpool's entire European season that Carra missed: it was probably no coincidence that Krzynowek scored a late consolation for Leverkusen while he was out of commission. Hyypiä, the other linchpin at the back, missed not a minute of the 1,380 played (plus 6 extra against Chelsea) that took the Reds from Graz to Istanbul: a remarkable achievement.

The Leverkusen supporters, we remembered from 2002, were an odd bunch. They seemed really not to mind that much whether they won or lost in that topsy-turvy game, which somehow made our anguish all the more painful at the end. Here, on the back of a humiliating home defeat, and a 6–2 aggregate drubbing, they still celebrated in unison when their consolation went in with a couple of minutes left, singing along with gusto to the disastrously retro Status Quo number from the late 1970s, 'Rockin' All Over the World'! There was no spitting defiance, no ironic applause and no berating their own players. Reds fans don't need music blasting from a public address system in order to celebrate a goal, but they weren't about to look a gift horse in the mouth here; immediately, and in a spirit of bonhomie but also condescension, the Reds joined in with this bizarre Germanic ritual and proceeded to adopt the song for the rest of their travels. There was a serious point here: these German fans simply didn't *care* about what happened to their team anything like as much as we did. This passion, and the memories of what can happen when it is allowed to spiral out of control, were about to come flooding back.

## MEMORIA E AMICIZIA

In the *Echo,* Chris Bascombe now dared to ask 'At what point do we start believing Liverpool can actually win this thing? In truth, only if they're leading in the last minute of the final. Even then the most avid fans won't believe it's happening.' Prophetic words, although, of course, the Reds didn't quite manage to get ahead in the last minute in Istanbul. For now there were important issues other than winning the competition to be addressed. Liverpool had been drawn against Juventus of Turin in the quarter-final. This would be the first meeting between the two clubs since the 1985 final in Brussels, a match tragically scarred by rioting and the deaths of 39 Juve supporters. Although the clubs had maintained friendly, but low-key, relations in the years since, and there had been some talk, a few years earlier, about staging a match between the two clubs, possibly in the United States, nothing had come of it. Even before the draw, in both Italy and in Britain there were plans to mark the 20th anniversary of Heysel, with several publications and TV documentaries already in production. In Liverpool, at the club and among the fans, there were also similar plans afoot, and chief executive Rick Parry had met with fans to discuss the most appropriate means of commemoration. There would now have to be a rethink.

Liverpool were drawn at home in the first leg, on 5 April, which at least offered the club a chance to set the right tone from the beginning. It was critical, both to the club and the fans, that the feelings of the Juventus club, their supporters and the bereaved families were understood and respected. Among Reds supporters there was generally a heartfelt desire for reconciliation, and there was also the recognition that this required some form of atonement, a willingness from Liverpool, the club and its fans, to clearly, publicly and unambiguously shoulder its share of the responsibility for the tragedy.

But, inevitably, there were very complicated responses at work here, for different individuals had different ideas concerning the exact extent and nature of this responsibility, though no one doubted that it *was* a heavy responsibility. Steve Kelly, in a sensitive piece in *Through the Wind and Rain*, pointed to some of these complex factors. He prefaced his piece by saying that, as he had not been at Heysel, 'I've always felt a bit of a fraud talking about it', but went on:

> Part of the beauty of football is the togetherness you feel, being part of something bigger than ourselves . . . We feel proud of our fellow Reds when they out-sing the opposition or turn up in vast numbers at out of the way places at awkward times, so we inevitably feel shame and revulsion when others "kick off" and drag our name through the mud.

Yet, for Kelly, there were undoubtedly factors other than the totally unacceptable behaviour of some of the Liverpool fans in Brussels that should also be considered: UEFA's decision to stage the match at a crumbling venue, and the inadequacies of the policing, for example. However, Kelly argued that 'Heysel created a cauldron of blame, and everything that was wrong with English football and English society was immediately dumped into our laps – and that's unfair.'

Still, in the final analysis, the guilt felt by many Liverpool supporters was unavoidable, and must be carried: 'We're all Reds together, the good and the bad, and those people are dead because "we" kicked off.'

This welter of emotions had to be tackled in a short space of time, and under the glare of the media spotlight. It was hugely important that Liverpool – all of us – try to get this right. For some supporters, for once, it was genuinely the case that events *off* the pitch were more significant than those on it. Liverpool, the club and the fans, but also the city authorities, worked very hard to make sure that Juventus were welcomed for the first leg. A 'fans' friendly' match took place on the morning of the match at the Academy in Kirkby, and each Juventus supporter received a special programme in Italian that said, unequivocally, 'We are sorry.' The *Echo* carried this message as a banner headline. Importantly, one of the key events at the match involved the parading of a banner declaring '*Memoria e Amicizia*' ('In memory and friendship'), and listing the first names of those who had died. This banner had been produced by local youth workers ten years earlier for the tenth anniversary and had been warmly applauded by fans at that occasion. Before the game kicked off, the Kop also unveiled a mosaic with the 'friendship' motif, and Phil Neal, Michel Platini and Ian Rush (a player for both clubs) carried together the banner and plaque symbolically from the centre circle towards the Juve fans in the Anfield Road end. This last gesture was met with applause from Juve supporters, but some *ultras* turned their backs and made plain their rejection of the move. By and large, though, the efforts were well received by the Italian and British press, as well as UEFA, and the process of reconciliation, though by no means complete, was aided by these pre-match events.

However, Otello Lorentini, the father of Roberto, one of the victims at Heysel, who had set up an Association for the Families of Heysel Victims, was critical of both clubs: 'For 20 years Liverpool and Juventus have maintained an incomprehensible silence,' he said. 'After 20 years this comes out now. It is not sufficient.' He called for a friendly match between the teams as a tribute, 'played in an atmosphere outside competition and the pursuit of money'.

In this emotional atmosphere there was uncertainty about whether the match might prove a secondary distraction, and for some that might have been justified. However, Benítez and his players, along with Fabio Capello and the Juve team, made it clear that they wanted 'an outstanding match in which two famous clubs give everything to progress to the last four . . .'. Benítez had spent some time with Capello during his sabbatical in 1999, visiting the then Milan boss at his training ground and 'learning a lot of things'. Capello also knew Anfield well, having brought his Roma side here on two occasions, first for a 1–0 win in the UEFA Cup in 2001 (but a 2–1 defeat on aggregate), and then, on an emotional night when Gérard Houllier returned from his heart problems in 2002.

Once again the current Liverpool manager was confronted by serious injury problems. Didi Hamann, who many thought would be crucial to our chances of success, was out of both legs after picking up a strain in the derby match; the midfield weight would now rest on Steven Gerrard and Igor Biscan. Of even more concern was the goalkeeping situation: Dudek was out with a strained hamstring (although he did recover to play in the second leg). Kirkland remained on the injury sidelines, so rookie 19-year-old Scott Carson was thrown into the fray for an unlikely debut. We feared he might be busy and hoped he could rise to the occasion. The other improbable selection involved the young French tyro, Anthony Le Tallec, who came in to play just off Milan Baros; it was his first start in 2004–05 for the Reds in any competition. At least it allowed Gerrard to remain squarely behind the ball and in the engine room. Juventus were without their own midfield anchor, Tacchinardi, so their central midfield had an unfamiliar look. But up-front, with the ageing (but still mesmeric) Del Piero and the impressive Ibrahimovic, the threat was obvious. Pavel Nedved and Camoranesi would be raiding down the flanks, so Juve certainly appeared strong going forward. Juve's vastly experienced defence, including Thuram, Cannavaro and keeper Buffon, had conceded only twice in eight previous matches in the competition.

Liverpool started at a tremendous pace, with Emerson caught on the ball by Gerrard straight from kick-off. But just as this early storm threatened to blow itself out, the Reds received some tangible reward for their pressure: a Gerrard corner from the right was flicked on at the near post – possibly by García or Zambrotta – and big Sami, just as he had done in the home leg of the quarter-final in 2002 against Leverkusen, despatched the ball from inside the box. This was a controlled, technically superb volley from a central defender. The Reds supporters really began to believe this team could beat the mighty Juventus after all. With heart and no little skill, Liverpool maintained the high tempo and continued to create chances. The second goal, however, could not be accurately described as a 'chance'. Le Tallec, who was winning plenty of possession in the air, found himself wide on the right flank and played a volley inside: slightly over-hit and probably not intended for García at all. Intuitively, as it dropped beyond Cannavaro, the little Spaniard struck a sumptuous volley from between 25–30 yards which simply flew over Buffon and high into the net.

Juve now showed some much-needed moments of real class. Ibrahimovic struck the post from 18 yards with a lightning left-foot shot, and Carson made a good stop from Del Piero, after the Reds had been carved open by a slick one–two with Nedved. Still, the safety of half-time was reached and the stadium rang to the tune of incredulous excitement. If we could avoid conceding an away goal, this result would give the Reds a real opportunity to progress to the semi-final, where either Bayern Munich or Chelsea awaited. But don't look too far ahead, we told ourselves, not with this team!

Capello made a significant half-time change, with the ineffective Blasi replaced by the more experienced Pessotto. Juve began to exert a grip in midfield, and perhaps Liverpool tired; certainly, Baros seemed less than fully fit, and it was only to be expected that Le Tallec would find the pace difficult. Both would be subbed later. With almost 20 minutes gone in the second half, and just as we were beginning to think Juve could be held at bay, a half-cleared corner was returned by Zambrotta to the far post, where Cannavaro managed a weak header down towards the near post. Carson, who had done excellently up to that point, misread the bounce, and the ball squirmed in. Liverpool were rocked back by this soft concession, but thankfully the Italian mentality now played a part. Whether consciously or not, Juve visibly relaxed. Their thinking was that a 1–2 deficit could definitely be overcome at the Stadio delle Alpi, and they were more concerned with ensuring that Liverpool didn't score again than with pushing on for an equaliser. This caution may have saved a tiring Liverpool.

We savoured a famous European victory under Benítez, and felt we had now given ourselves an outside chance in Turin – not that very many of us would be going. Given the hostile reception to the pre-match memorials from some *bianconeri,* many 'away' regulars among the Reds faithful thought discretion would be the better part of valour for this trip. In the end perhaps 2,500 made the journey, and while there were only sporadic problems of missile-throwing from Juve fans within the ground, it is fair to say that the atmosphere of reconciliation was, at best, muted. Instead there was hostility, which perhaps should not be a surprise, but was nonetheless depressing.

Liverpool welcomed back Xabi Alonso, who had not had a game for four months. He proceeded to have a heroic night, alongside the tremendous (!) Biscan, included only because of Gerrard's suspension. Cissé also made a heroic return to action as a substitute, occasionally hurdling Juve tackles. The Reds were also fortunate that there was a strong referee, the Russian Ivanov, who allowed Liverpool's defensive players to put tackles in and refused to blow every time a Juventus man went down. On the pitch the match was tense – but not intense – with Juve still constrained by fear of being caught on the counter. They seemed to assume that, with patience – that Italian mentality again – a home goal would inevitably come, but Liverpool's back four and defensive midfielders allowed them only the briefest sights of goal. In the end Juve simply couldn't raise the tempo of their game, and the match fizzled out, to the delight of the besieged Reds fans and those many millions who were watching at home. Chelsea now awaited Liverpool in the semi-finals – which is, after all, what you'd wished for, Steven Gerrard.

# Chapter Seven

# THE PEOPLE'S CLUB, A THAI TAKEAWAY AND CHELSKI

## NEW MONEY, NEW GAME

The sport that Rafa Benítez joined in England in the summer of 2004 as Liverpool's new manager was a very different one even to that which had faced Gérard Houllier when he had arrived in England in 1998 to share management duties with Roy Evans. It was remarked upon a little at the time, but when Russian billionaire and Sibneft energy-company owner Roman Abramovich bought our Champions League semi-final opponents Chelsea FC in July 2003 for £150 million, before destabilising the entire international football transfer market with his apparently limitless funding for new players for the club in 2003 – and then under new manager José Mourhino in 2004 – it actually also changed English football radically. It set a new benchmark for competitive advantage at the elite levels of the English game. It broke the new duopoly of Manchester United and Arsenal at the top of the Premiership and made even finishing in the top four a challenging proposition for Liverpool FC and for all the clubs with ambitions to elevate themselves into this exclusive European league. If you wanted a warning sign of the costs of stretching just too hard for this goal, you only needed to look at recent European Cup semi-finalists Leeds United, now down in the Championship with huge debts, a creaky stadium – and no team.

This Chelsea story also set off, or confirmed, a number of connected new developments in the game that put the finances of the very top English clubs into an entirely new orbit. 'This was by no means the first sizeable personal investment in a football club,' said Dan Jones, partner in the sports business group at Deloitte, 'but the scale and speed of it dwarfed anything previously witnessed. Other clubs are not trying to compete in an unwinnable financial contest. That makes sense.' But some clubs *were* trying to stay in touch somehow. In 2003–04 Chelsea spent an extraordinary £115 million on salaries – £38 million more even than Manchester United – even though Premiership salaries in total had increased by only 7 per cent that year, the lowest figure in the history of the League. The fall in transfer payments during 2002–03, as the crazy economics of Premiership football had at last begun to level out, was also reversed in the Year of Abramovich, with one third of the total £250 million spent by Premiership clubs on foreign players and their agents in 2003–04 spent by Chelsea.

Abramovich is one of 23 Russian entrepreneurs, of course, who 'took advantage' of the privatisation of Russia's state assets in the mid-1990s and who now owned around 60 per cent of the Russian economy. Look at that figure again: 60 per cent of a country's economy. Abramovich, a man who enjoyed his sport and needed somewhere to invest his cash before someone – the Russian people, perhaps – tried to claw it back, had also invested in the CSKA Moscow club, and was soon reported to be looking to expand his sporting franchises by planning to import a fully Russian ice-hockey team into the North American National Hockey League, and maybe even buy a Formula One racing team. Not a bad day's shopping. Abramovich was soon being pursued by the Russian authorities for alleged 'irregularities' in his business dealings, though this fact, and the sources of his vast wealth, seemed to disturb Chelsea fans hardly at all, especially as the club's first League title for 50 years began, inexorably, to slide into view in 2005 – a case of never mind the quality, feel the width, if ever there was one.

By 2005 any Premiership football manager pursuing a transfer deal dreaded hearing the footsteps or heavy breathing of Mourhino and his Russian bankers: if 'Chelski' became involved in an auction, either the fee doubled or else you simply lost your quarry to west London in a blur of pound signs. Arsenal were already laying down a response to the emerging new global economics of football by borrowing hundreds of millions of pounds and building a new 60,000-capacity £460-million stadium in north London named, for sponsorship reasons and to their fans' disgust, after the Emirates airline (recently discarded as a sponsor by Chelsea in favour of a better offer). The Highbury club had made a record £33 million from domestic TV income in 2003–04, the highest in the Premiership, but their non-TV revenue was only half that of Manchester United, with a stadium capacity to match. Of course, as Arsenal set off to expand – perhaps to double – their match-day revenues, so United ratcheted up the contest by proposing to grow Old Trafford to a monster 75,000 seats. Hosting the 2004 European Cup final also signalled Manchester as a major player among the European football elite, a market leader with facilities to match.

But things began to spiral out of financial control at United from the moment in 2003 when an American sports and property tycoon, Malcolm Glazer, took a stakeholding in the publicly listed United business. He then set about taking total control of the club by the middle of 2005, mainly by folding into it an alleged half a billion pounds' worth of debt in order to buy out existing major shareholders and de-list the business for a whopping £790 million purchase price. Glazer was no mug. He had successfully turned the NFL's Tampa Bay Buccaneers into a profitable business and a winning sports franchise between 1995 and its Superbowl success in 2003. But in recent years the Buccs had pumped up ticket prices and reverted to type: they were, once again, in a slump. Glazer happily professed to know nothing about 'soccer', but pointed out that his sons would run the United business in his place. He looked like a guy who wanted to make a fast dollar, and now that he had huge debts to service at United, he would certainly need to milk the club for profit. Cue much wailing and burning of effigies from the vast tribes of Old Trafford. It was OK, apparently, to squeeze cash, from Singapore to Salford, out of any possible United 'branding' opportunity, or for a couple of Irish horse-racing grifters to own 29 per cent of your football club, but a geeky, profit-seeking American tycoon in charge? Well, that was just beyond the pale.

Actually, this was no laughing matter for football clubs or their fans – and even for Liverpool supporters. After all, even the awful Abramovich was actually putting money *into* the sports economy, though, admittedly, you had to gag when reflecting on where it had all come from. Chelski fans might also have given a stray thought to where their club might end up if anything were suddenly to happen to their generous Russian benefactor. Malcolm Glazer seemed, by contrast, to be importing huge debt into United purely as a business opportunity, though it was also clear that, unless this was a simple asset-stripping exercise, United would have to continue to win football matches in order for 'the business' to keep on making decent returns for its new owners. He could try to insist, of course, that United now negotiate all their own future domestic TV deals, but who in the Premiership would agree to that? Any United profits would now, definitely, end up in the Glazers' account at the local Co-op, unless they decided to give Sir Alex a few bob to squander on new signings. It was a rum deal, indeed.

There was also the other matter, of course: that of a man who lived thousands of miles away and had no interest in the sport or in the club and its fans now owning the whole United enterprise for his own devices. We believe this sort of thing is known as the unacceptable face of global capitalism. So now we had, unsurprisingly, the United IMUSA (Independent Manchester United Supporters Association) faithful – hard core and true, all United authentics – tearing up their season tickets and arguing that this was no less than the McDonaldisation of the club, that the very soul of United as an institution that was 'owned' by the fan community was now entirely lost (no sniggering at the back, there). United, of course, had taken the football–business couplet to an early extreme in Britain, which is one of the reasons why public support for these protesters now seemed so harshly qualified, to say the least. There were relatively few signs, either, that a call for a boycott on 2005 season-ticket purchase at Old Trafford had taken any real hold on the club's huge fan base. Supply and demand, my friends. Not that any of this deterred the Glazer objectors. They were in it for the long haul. They had even reinvented their club as FC United in the local North West Counties League. But the United protest was likely to run and run and make owning an English football club not an entirely pleasant experience for its American investors. We wished them luck – and we meant it.

Not that anything remotely like this could ever happen at the family business that was Liverpool Football Club. Oh, no. In fact, this very point was one of the issues regularly covered in interviews by Rick Parry and the chairman, with more than a nod and a wink to the doings of the cash-rich football corporation operating at the other end of the East Lancs. Road. As Parry himself had observed: 'There is a paradox for Manchester United that they are simultaneously the most loved and the most hated brand of all, which is quite tough from a commercial perspective.'

Liverpool would never prostitute its identity, nor lose its own local and community sensibilities, Parry promised, certainly not by over-exploiting its brand or by seeking out investments from dubious sources overseas. We would always be a football club first and a business later, and the latter *only* in relation to the central concern, the *raison d'être* of Liverpool Football Club: the production of a team to satisfy the demands of Liverpool's fans. Fair enough, nothing to worry about there.

The problem, though, was that the new economics of the sport – the Arsenal stadium development, Abramovich's millions, Glazer's adventure capitalism, even Newcastle United's expanded St James's Park – made it more and more difficult to rely for funding, as Liverpool had recently done, on TV income, the residue of a family fortune (through the long-standing Moores connection), gate money from a 'mere' 44,000-capacity stadium and a few million quid a year contributed by willing sponsors. Recent Liverpool uncertainty about winning trophies and annual Champions League returns – with Chelsea's arrival, only the fourth qualifying spot had seemed realistically available to Liverpool in recent years – was adding to difficulties in financial planning and, more importantly, the year-on-year supporting of squad development at Anfield. For people like Rick Parry the question was whether the Liverpool club stood still commercially – and therefore fell behind its domestic competitors – or else pursued entirely new sources of funding. In January 2004 *The Guardian* ran a Dominic Fifield story about the leadership and funding of the club headlined: 'Liverpool stuck in a time warp'. The club accountants argued that this was now a no-contest: their view was that Liverpool FC needed a new injection of serious funds.

## STADIUM BLUES

Some of this required new income had already come from a new partnership with Granada TV and had been invested on players – some of it wasted, in fact – by Gérard Houllier. But now some of the projected income streams from the club's tie-in with television and new technology had started to slow and Granada's ardour had also seemed to wane. So, where next for cash? As early as 2002 Liverpool had announced plans to build a new stadium on nearby Stanley Park, initially marked out for 70,000 fans, at a cost of £85 million. The club was losing an estimated £1 million per match on income compared with Manchester United, was behind Newcastle United in this area, and the new Arsenal Stadium – scheduled to open in 2006 – would mean more falling revenues for Anfield compared to the new 'Highbury'. Chelsea was already out of the equation, off the scale, in terms of available funds provided out of Abramovich's deep pockets. The new ground seemed a viable way out.

The new Liverpool stadium plans were eventually revised to a 60,000 capacity, more in keeping with real demand for League matches at the club, where maybe half the games in a season might expect to get close to selling out. We might even get back to a welcome, regular walk-up trade for some League fixtures and European matches, and some sensible ticket prices. Redevelopment of the old Anfield was out of the question, at least according to the club, because the Main Stand would have to be rebuilt, possibly even to a smaller capacity than now, and 250 nearby houses would have to be demolished, for which there was unlikely to be local-authority approval. Although some fans, unsurprisingly, vehemently disagreed with this assessment, it seemed that staying at Anfield in the long term was a non-option, at least in terms of trying to keep in financial touch with the clubs Liverpool was currently competing against at League Championship and European Cup levels.

A report on the effects of the proposed redevelopment for the Anfield and Breckfield community, prepared by GVA Grimley

Development Consultants in 2004, predictably linked the regeneration of the entire area positively with the provision of a new, possibly 60,000-capacity, football stadium, and a new Anfield Plaza at the site of the old ground. The implication was clear: without a new football stadium for Liverpool FC on their doorsteps – slicing into Stanley Park – there were, simply, no regeneration possibilities in the offing at all for any local residents, something of a short straw. But at least some of the club's maths seemed straightforward here: it was estimated that Liverpool could make between £10 and £12 million more per season from income from the new stadium at a cost of around £7 million per annum interest on a suitable loan to help build the ground. This seemed like good business – but suddenly nothing was quite straightforward here any more.

The deputy prime minister, John Prescott, announced in September 2004 that there would be no public inquiry into Liverpool's stadium plans and Rick Parry confirmed that, after local consultations, the club would now look to move into the new ground in 2007. But, by January 2005, after more than 18 months of talks with the city council and the Northwest Development Agency, the costs of the new stadium had now risen to close to £120 million, and Liverpool FC seemed no nearer to raising the necessary investment or really moving the project on. What is more, local and national politicians had warmed to the idea that the near-neighbouring football clubs that had grown from the same shoots – Liverpool and Everton – should look towards *sharing* a single stadium. From outside the city, and from outside football, this might have seemed like the ideal solution, halving costs at a stroke and offering real prospects for a more impressive joint-stadium project. Inside Liverpool, however, it was another agenda entirely. Apart from the small matter of the massive cultural objections from both sets of fans and some club officials – a return, perhaps, to some old-style 1890s falling out – the main obstacle seemed to be the resources available to each club. As Walton MP Peter Kilfoyle put it: 'Realistically, in my view, it comes down to money. It appears that one club [Liverpool] has the money and the other [Everton] does not.' But Kilfoyle went on, in puzzlement: 'What is the point of duplicating facilities 400 yards away when the extra money released could be spent on players? But when talking about football, this seems to go out the window.' Kilfoyle was right in one sense: Everton – mischievously dubbed the 'People's Club' by their cunning manager David Moyes – were definitely struggling for cash, but even in this department, and definitely on the field, things were suddenly beginning to change for the Blues.

The Everton dressing-room that the young Moyes had inherited included the corpulent David Ginola, an ageing Paul Gascoigne and an injury-prone Duncan Ferguson. His was a major managerial challenge, and he was just 38 years of age. Having earlier threatened a European spot, in 2003–04 Everton had struggled all season near the relegation mire. Searching out new ways of bolstering local Blue pride by utilising the new Moyes brand, the club had cleverly tried to set themselves against Liverpool FC's larger national and international fan base and the penchant of Houllier, and later Benítez, for recruiting foreign players. Everton stressed, instead, their British – and especially their supposedly stronger *local* – ties and values on show at Goodison Park. This was smart PR work, but much of it was tosh, of course: Everton recruited their own foreign players, patently did not monopolise football support in the city, and they also drew on fans from outside Liverpool. But the 'People's Club' banners that were now draped around the crumbling blue edifice that resided across Stanley Park had admirably succeeded in annoying every Red Scouser and plenty who lived outside the city boundaries. This, of course, was a central part of the plan.

Moyes, himself, was a figure very well suited to this new ideological campaign waged in Merseyside football; his managerial hero was the flinty Alex Ferguson, and he had many of the steely leadership and stoic qualities associated with that earlier famous generation of Scottish football bosses, which included, of course, Bill Shankly and Matt Busby. He was no Continental technocrat. A plaque in Moyes's Bellefield office read: 'Team spirit cannot be purchased, yet once fostered is prized above all monetary value'. He looked and sounded, in fact, like a crude Anfield boot-room product out of his time and in the wrong club. He was, by any measure, a formidable local rival for Rafa Benítez.

By the start of 2004–05 Everton were, once again, deeply in debt with no rescuer in sight, in a failing ground and were most people's clear relegation favourites. In this emergency, and to much Blue, Walton wailing, Moyes accepted the sale of Croxteth's urchin Wayne Rooney to Manchester United for £27 million and then invested his slice of the fee wisely. With other local products to the fore in the Everton first team, the Blues now dug in and began challenging Liverpool for a Champions League spot, rather than nervously eyeing the relegation places. This was quite a turnaround, but would it last? With Moyes at the helm it looked as if Everton might not be quite the economic basket-case, compared to their Red neighbours, they had appeared even 12 months earlier. After all, Liverpool had also announced record losses of £21.9 million in 2004 and had been scouring the globe, unsuccessfully, for new investors. Where, exactly, was *their* stadium money coming from? Things had not, exactly, gone smoothly in this area: in fact, there had been some embarrassment already.

## MONEY FOR NOTHING?

Back in May 2004 the billionaire prime minister of Thailand, Thaksin Shinawatra, had popped up with an offer of a reported 'no strings attached' £65 million investment in the Liverpool club, equivalent to a 30 per cent stake. How could one football club be so lucky? Not that Liverpool was the *only* club that Thaksin seemed to have in mind. Sure, he was a Reds fan, but if he couldn't make it work at Anfield, then wasn't there another club – a *Blue* one – on Merseyside, perhaps, that also needed some cash? Actually almost any Premiership club would seem to do for this character. Moreover, he had a credible local rival at Liverpool. Multimillionaire builder Steve Morgan, a 'real' Liverpool fan, a man who was there at every old Reds European triumph, came up, very publicly, with another offer. This was a reported £73 million on the table, including £12 million as part of an underwritten rights issue aimed at fans. Anfield democracy, it seemed, awaited just around the corner. The club argued that this 'hostile' offer undervalued Liverpool FC. With a man such as Morgan potentially on board, it was made clear that the future at L4 looked bleak for both Rick Parry and David Moores.

Most Reds fans, naturally, focus on what is happening on the field rather than on the financial malarkey behind, but this proposed Thai deal made more than a few Liverpool heads turn. Even when the offer was clearly in the public domain, neither Parry nor anyone else at the club bothered to try to explain to fans how or why this partnership might work for Liverpool or, indeed, the Thai people. The Liverpool board seemed to think that Thaksin's own money would be simply pumped into the club from 6,000 miles' distance with no other calls on the club apart from, perhaps, Steven Gerrard and others doing a couple of helpful speeches at the forthcoming Thai elections and the setting up of a Bangkok LFC academy. Instead, the Thais proposed agreement on the rights to sell LFC merchandise in Thailand, claimed two seats on the LFC board and declared their capacity to veto 'any large spending by the club'. This sounded like a pretty hands-on deal – and why not, with a proposed 30 per cent club stake? The general trend in global development in football is for European clubs to scope new markets in South-East Asia and elsewhere. But in this case, a developing country and its people were effectively on the brink of buying into control of a major Premiership club – into Liverpool FC. What was going on?

Reds critics of the proposed deal, quite rightly, pointed to human-rights abuses in Thailand and the immoral use of public funds by Thaksin in what looked like a crass piece of electioneering. It was also a major overseas investment of public capital with no guarantee of a financial return. Premiership clubs, let's face it, are usually black holes for investors: and Liverpool's annual profits had just fallen by some 61 per cent. Tragically, in the age of the global sound bite, Third World politicians can make more of their links with Steve Gerrard and his Liverpool mates than they can, say, with local anti-poverty programmes.

This whole deal looked like a desperate measure: a gross mistake for the Thais and a very ill-judged departure for a football club with very different traditions. As Paul Hayward put it, unkindly, in the *Daily Telegraph*: 'Liverpool will take any sort of radical action so long as it lifts the odour of decay.' Politicians and football are poor bedfellows at the best of times, and this deal had the stench of grand larceny. Maybe there were, potentially, real benefits even to

Liverpool's new prospective partners. If so, someone at the club should have urgently spelt them out, otherwise fans were justified in suspecting that this was another case of: 'These are my principles and if you don't like them I have others.' Eventually the Thai money evaporated – including a new offer from a new Thai group headed by GMM Grammy entertainment – much to the relief of most progressive Liverpool supporters. But we still needed investment, it seemed.

By December 2004, with new manager Rafa Benítez now securely in place, Steve Morgan had officially 'lost his patience' with the Liverpool board and he withdrew his offer of new funds. A relieved Rick Parry claimed that Liverpool had now to consider a 'new and exciting' offer from the United States, one 'that could transform the club'. He might have meant interest from the Kraft family, owner of NFL's New England Patriots and supposed wealthy backers of the 'L4' group, a consortium involving two Hollywood-based entertainment executives, Stuart Ford and Mike Davies. Hang on: was this a wolf in wolf's clothing – another potential Glazer fiasco from across the Atlantic? Negotiations between this group and Liverpool's own investment consultants, Hawkpoint Partners, were supposed to be 'ongoing', but as the new season wore on there was no further public news about new money being emptied into Liverpool's coffers. The club confirmed, nevertheless, that things remained somehow 'on track' for the new stadium – but without Everton. Meanwhile, the global search for new cash for Liverpool Football Club apparently goes on.

## BENÍTEZ GOES SHOPPING

This lack of success in tracking down investors failed to deter Rafa Benítez from returning to Spain in the transfer window in 2005 and finally signing the experienced forward Fernando Morientes from Real Madrid for £6 million. He also picked up, on a free, the 33-year-old Argentinian central defender Mauricio Pellegrino from his old club Valencia and the young English goalkeeper Scott Carson from Leeds United for a cut-down £250,000: more worrying news for the flapping Jerzy Dudek. But before these arrivals could check in at Anfield, unstoppable Chelsea had already stolen the New Year's Day points from Anfield, with Xabi Alonso picking up an ankle break in the process, following an innocuous-looking tackle from Frank Lampard. Mourinho argued after this match that 'to play in the north is more difficult. Teams here are brave, have a lot of character. Also the public are different: they can push a home team.' The new man was learning. Arguably, Liverpool were one of the few teams in the season, north or south, to comprehensively outplay Chelsea, as they did here. But referee Mike Riley's woeful miss of a glaring Tiago penalty-area handling offence in the first half, plus Alonso's substitution and missed home chances, rescued the visitors, who scored with a late Joe Cole goal deflected in by Carragher.

'Everybody knows it was a certain penalty,' said JC later.

It was difficult to argue.

At Norwich City three days later a Liverpool side containing Diao, Núñez, García and Mellor – a definite risk – hung on to beat a strangely subdued home team 2–1, but really more by good fortune than judgement.

Manchester United at home is always a big fans' test for a new Liverpool manager: a reliable barometer for how well – or how badly – things are progressing. Reds supporters were lifted by the news that Morientes would start his first match for the club, though this seemed hugely ambitious given the new arrival had hardly played for Real Madrid thus far this season. The striker struggled to make an impact in a strong Liverpool line-up and was eventually substituted. The only goal of the match came from a further Jerzy Dudek howler: this time the Pole allowed newly transferred Wayne Rooney, of all people, to slide a gentle shot under the goalkeeper in front of a stupefied Kop. Young Wayne goaded the Kop and got some brief missile treatment from the Walton Breck Road rotary club in return, in a hugely disappointing contest. Manager Benítez was now in something of a dark tunnel, and rapidly approaching his lowest first-season juncture at the club.

Perhaps an abject FA Cup defeat at Burnley for Anfield's 'reserves' had suddenly depressed Liverpool's first-team players? And who wouldn't be utterly dejected inside the club after that sort of easy dereliction of managerial duty? Whatever the reason, when Liverpool travelled to Southampton for League business on 22 January it was to offer what Alan Hansen described as the worst

Liverpool performance since he had retired as a player. Benítez's team could neither attack nor defend. Pellegrino started, with Hyypiä and Carragher, in what could have been a back three, with Stephen Warnock pushed forward on the left. What it definitely was was a mess. The Liverpool players looked listless and unhappy, with Morientes starved of any service at all from midfield and failing to link up with the perpetually self-obsessed Milan Baros. When Southampton scored two early goals, the new non-English speaking Argentinian defender made the easy-going, loping Sami Hyypiä look positively electric by comparison. Were these the slowest centre-back partners *ever* to play in this League? Benítez looked in a real mini-crisis here: angry Reds fans were calling for blood, his new signings looked questionable at best and his senior players seemed to be registering their protest (a major shock this) by *not trying*. Liverpool had now fallen seven points behind local rivals Everton in the League, were out (apparently by preference) of the FA Cup and were being completely left behind by the top three clubs that Benítez had been hired by Liverpool to pursue. Apart from that, things were hunky-dory.

There was clearly some serious talk now inside Anfield, after the club booked its League Cup final place by edging past Watford. The senior players and the manager began to rally the troops, and not a moment too soon. So it was a very different Liverpool that turned up for the evening League fixture at Charlton Athletic, and then at home to struggling Fulham. Pellegrino was absent once more and Igor Biscan even got his first League start of the season, at Charlton, for Hamann. Although behind at the half, Liverpool looked transformed and they poured all over a disconsolate Charlton in the second period, Morientes scoring his first goal for the club with a stunning solo run and left-foot finish before Riise drove home the winner after good work by García. Morientes scored an even better goal: a header from a García cross in the 3–1 Anfield win over Fulham. The scorer had now begun to look at least something like the penetrating and classy striker we all thought – and hoped – we had bought from Spain. 'We want to play like we play today – it is our idea,' said Benítez brightly at The Valley. A good idea: so why mess about with the shape of the team?

## THE WORST OF TIMES, THE BEST OF TIMES

Birmingham City is a horrible place to have to play your football. It promises a raging, ugly crowd, a physical battle, the wind in your face – and Steve Bruce on the opposing bench. It feels like the 1970s all over again – including the pubs. Above all, you need resolve and solidity here; you must earn the right to play. It is *not* a place – repeat, *not* a place – to start experimenting, to try out fancy new ideas. It took Gérard Houllier *seasons* to learn this hard lesson. You need to keep your best shape and your nerve and just tough it out here until you can dominate. But no one at Anfield, no one who should know better, bothered to convey this vital message to Rafael Benítez. This allowed the Liverpool manager, playing his 'advanced coaching class' card once more, to field a quite ridiculous Liverpool formation today, one which has 'Come and beat us, Blues' stamped all the way through it. Steve Bruce laughs all the way to the bar.

Steven Gerrard started in front of the ball and just behind Morientes, a joke decision here, leaving Hamann and a timid Biscan to 'guard' midfield, while Milan Baros was asked to play – wait for it – on the left of midfield! Predictably, Liverpool looked hopelessly unbalanced. An energised Emile Heskey stole a daft first-half penalty, from Sami Hyypiä, and the on-parole Jermaine Pennant made a complete mess out of Djimi Traoré at left-back to lay on a simple second. At 0–2 down Benítez actually brought on both Pellegrino and Josemi, as if graciously accepting the defeat. We raged in the away end. 'Don't fucking clap that,' we told the gratuitous Liverpool applauders as we left. At Newcastle things were little better: Scott Carson started and let in a wide free-kick over his head, this time from the barely conscious Laurent Robert. Christ, our guy, our young keeper, must be 6 ft 4 in.! Could he not get off the ground? Chalk up: L 0–1. Chalk up: must try harder.

Blackburn Rovers, under Mark Hughes, are willing to battle and scrap down at the bottom, so it was no real surprise when they successfully shut up shop at Anfield for a slumberland 0–0 scoreline. Benítez played Pellegrino, with Hyypiä on the bench. Why? So we had finally reached Everton at home: 20 March – pretty much Liverpool's last chance to stay in the race for fourth place. Did we say 'race'? Because it felt more like a case of whenever the Bluenoses slipped up we supinely followed suit. We still trailed by seven points. Liverpool never seemed to get within striking distance, while *they* seemed to churn out results whenever they really needed them. Moyes had done a brilliant job at Goodison, making the Rooney transfer work well for him and even shoring things up when Thomas Gravesen left for Real in January. And this was a typically bruising battle, but Liverpool went two first-half goals ahead: a free-kick passed through the Everton wall by Steven Gerrard, and then a fantastic Morientes lob volley which deceived Martyn, who palmed it onto the bar for Luis García to head in the rebound. García had been showing us a little more recently, both at home and abroad, enjoying the presence of his new Spanish mate up-front.

As Everton tried, crudely, to up the ante, Liverpool lost three players to injury – Hamann, Morientes and Warnock – and a hobbling García had to struggle on himself for an hour, while clearly suffering. Further forward, Milan Baros was proving frustrating: bags of energy and vim, but little real control and precision. He missed two one-on-ones with Martyn before getting himself sent off, for kicking Stubbs. No court in the land would convict him. Nine-man Liverpool hung on, with Pellegrino actually looking much more secure for once: a battler. We conceded only one, to the horrible – and talented – Tim Cahill. Mission accomplished, local pride assuaged: but don't count on Liverpool catching up on this gap, not even after a totally undeserved next score of Liverpool 1, Bolton 0 (Biscan, 85').

With key Champions League fixtures looming large now, Liverpool seemed to lose even more heart and direction in the League. A 0–1 late defeat at Manchester City, now under an enthused Stuart Pearce, was followed by an entertaining 2–2 draw at home to Spurs and a fighting 1–1 v. Middlesbrough. Pellegrino was mysteriously played on the left against Tottenham – and floundered. Gerrard missed a penalty. García scored another terrific goal and Alonso was back in League action at last. And Cissé also returned, as a substitute: a brave man for all his worrying flaws, including his vivid red hair in this one. A decent 2–1 win in unfamiliar white socks, at Portsmouth on 20 April – a horrible place for Liverpool recently – (Morientes scoring whilst on his arse, and a García header) was a bright surprise, but only because our expectations had been so lowered by recent performances away from home. This was Liverpool's first away win since Charlton on 1 February, and only our fifth all season. It proved hardly cause for celebration, however, because we could make no useful headway at all at lowly Crystal Palace (they won 1–0); and although an Alonso-inspired Liverpool gave Arsenal a scare at Highbury in May, it still ended up 3–1 to the home team, with Benítez, typically, as one newspaper put it, 'communicating his touch-line messages through the medium of interpretive dance'.

It may not be at all conclusive, but Anthony Le Tallec's only seasonal League starts were at Manchester City and Palace: both horrible losses. Harry Kewell was now back from long-term injury and Djibril Cissé even bagged a couple of goals in the final 2–1 home League win v. Aston Villa. He looked justifiably ecstatic. But all these final League matches, worthlessly spent trying to catch Everton, now played a weak second fiddle to Liverpool's raucous meetings with Chelsea in the Champions League semi-final. For some sections of the British press this match was less England v. England than it was Portugal v. Spain and also Big Money v. Proper Football Club.

## CHAMPIONS LEAGUE? WE'RE HAVING KEBABS

Judged by his team's performances in domestic competitions, Rafa Benítez's first season at Liverpool had been a failure: not a cataclysmic one, but a failure nevertheless. Finishing behind Everton was bad enough – the first time in 18 years – but we could get over that. Seeing the Blues in the Champions League while we were languishing in the UEFA Cup, well, that was a different matter entirely. In theory Liverpool could sneak into the big competition next year by actually winning the European Cup in 2005, though UEFA seemed unsure whether the holders qualified by right to defend the trophy. It was hard for Liverpool to argue for this 'principle' now: we knew the rules, so the time for all that, surely, was before the competition started.

The Liverpool League season under Benítez, hampered by serious injuries, had started brightly but had petered out badly.

Since Christmas, Liverpool had won only four home games out of nine: a poor return. Away from home it was much worse: three wins, but six losses and *no* draws. Where was the old Liverpool credo of coming away with something, even if you were not on your game? We have what we hold? In the six away defeats Liverpool could manage only one goal, at Arsenal. Benítez pointed out that his team had failed to win in 12 out of 14 matches in the season following European fixtures: 'Maybe the players think it is more special in the Champions League?' He drew attention to his reduced forward options. 'The statistics are there for analysing,' he said, coyly. His players were also better suited to the less physical 'cat and mouse' of European contests. But, unlike Houllier, the Spaniard didn't look readily for excuses at home. There was also too much dangerous player rotation from the manager, too many experiments not thought through and no reliable Liverpool striker – an Owen or a Fowler – to rescue something from unpromising afternoons away from Anfield. From his Valencia days it seemed that Benítez just didn't believe in conventional strikers. Liverpool ended up fifth, three points behind Everton and a stratospheric thirty-seven behind champions Chelski. Things would have to improve.

Much of this would be forgotten, of course, if Liverpool could only topple the west Londoners in the European Cup semi-final. Liverpool would have many friends here, even among traditional foes. Unlike the polite Benítez, the Machiavellian José Mourhino, the 'master of provocation' according to Paul Hayward in the *Telegraph*, had been stirring up Europe, been accused of 'lying' about alleged meetings between referee Anders Frisk and the Barcelona manager Rijkaard, and described by Bayern Munich officials and the German press as 'arrogant'. Really? Mourhino was also accused of illegally contacting Arsenal's Ashley Cole, so his gloss was dimming in the general public's eyes and people were getting just a bit fed up at Chelsea's perceived bullying and the impression they gave that their wealth meant they could simply make up the rules as they went along. The 'nation' was behind Liverpool, it seemed, for the first all-English European Cup clash since Nottingham Forest beat the holders, Liverpool, way back in 1978. 'Cheering for the Red corner,' argued *The Independent*'s James

Lawton, 'is only natural in the face of Mourhino's mighty empire.'

At Stamford Bridge in the first leg, the sheer ferocity and belief of travelling Liverpool supporters, at a venue hardly known for its productivity for the Anfield club, suggested that these visiting fans believed we now had Chelsea on our own historical terms: in the European Cup, a two-legged competition where we knew the ropes and where *we* were the experienced gaffers. A strong Reds line-up – no Pellegrino, Biscan, Josemi, Le Tallec, etc. – and a tight defensive plan from Benítez proved successful in a surprisingly stress-free goalless draw. Both Duff and Robben were helpfully absent for Chelsea, and Liverpool's only dark cloud here – albeit a big, stormy one – was that the French referee Sars decided to book Alonso late on following a debatable foul on Gudjohnsen. Xabi would now miss the crucial second leg – yet another new Champions League midfield would now be required. We could also expect much more from Chelsea at Anfield. An epic night lay up ahead, with Chelsea probably still slight favourites.

You could feel the buzz around Anfield on the night of the return. In the Flat Iron pub beforehand it was that old European Cup feel, one magical night from glory. Just getting to the final again would be an extraordinary statement of intent from this club and a fantastic trip for these fans, who were now 20 long years out of the European Cup final loop. Benítez had been smart all week, buoying up the fans, calling for a performance in the stands to drive his team home. We were not about to disappoint. Anfield, and the stadium apron, positively shook with emotion and desire, the players reporting that they could hear singing in the ground fully half an hour before kick-off and an utter contrast to the mildness of the home sections in west London just a week earlier. There was no Duff or Robben again for Chelsea and the European warhorse Biscan filled in for Alonso for Liverpool. Baros started alone up-front, instead of the straining Cissé.

Liverpool had to score first to have a chance of victory and, attacking a bristling, frenzied Kop, it took just three and a half electrifying and lung-bursting minutes for the Reds to nose in front. Gerrard forced the ball forward to Baros, who bravely took on goalkeeper Cech. As Liverpool fans cried 'penalty' as the two players collided, Luis García, following up, edged the ball towards the Chelsea goal-line before the retreating Gallas cleared desperately into the Kemlyn Road. But was it already over the line? We were in the Main Stand tonight. We couldn't tell: not really, not conclusively. (Over the next few days entire university departments would have a go with their computer graphic reconstructions: none of them completely convincing.) Tonight we just needed to convince the Slovak officials. They looked now at the Liverpool fans gathered menacingly around them: at the baying, pleading red mobs of Anfield; at the people who could no longer think straight, who could barely communicate in this madhouse any more, at least not beyond a guttural grunt – people, frankly, who looked like they may well pursue you (and your family and all *their* relatives), if you don't get this right. Slovaks are sensible people. Referee Michel gently nodded and loped towards the halfway line, pursued by blue shirts. And this 113-year-old ground, once owned by Everton, went absolutely mental.

What would happen next? None of us were sure. We just shouted and sang and looked at our watches and howled and looked at our watches – and waited. It is exhausting, thrilling, tortured work, watching football like this. And waiting. And at that very moment when we were allowing ourselves to remember all those great Anfield nights, those wonderful European victories, as the marvellous Mr Michel, our friend – who had added *six* minutes of injury-time – was looking at his watch for about the fifteenth fucking time, Jerzy Dudek spilled a cross in front of Gudjohnsen to the right of the Kop goal. We were right behind this incident – saw it unfold perfectly. The Icelander took careful aim and drove the ball towards the Liverpool goal – and *wide*. Gloriously wide. So, after 20 years of penury, and after too many false dawns, we were actually going to Istanbul to bring back what was rightfully ours.

In the Flat Iron, later, joy was unconfined, grown men tearful and beaming older ladyfolk weirdly dancing: until the ale ran out, that was. Call up the websites; get out the maps; tell bosses we all need time off; tell the whole world that Liverpool Football Club is back where it belongs, back in the European Cup final – a proper football club, with proper fans and back in the *real* final once more. And maybe Rafa was right, all along, to say that competing on all fronts was simply unrealistic for this Liverpool: that our current squad was just too thin, and that we had to prioritise. Maybe this had been his plan right from the start: a concerted assault on the European Cup – a trophy he hadn't been able to deliver for Valencia and one that he knew meant so much to us. He would need time to sort out his League problems and to realise the FA Cup was also important to all Reds fans. But for now, gratefully, we tipped our hats to him: Señor, you have already joined the Liverpool managerial elite.

Later that night, author Steve and partner Cath would go home flushed with victory and the worse for drink, naturally. In their house in the middle of Liverpool they drunkenly went to bed leaving their front door wide open. Nobody ventured in. It was that sort of night: it's a wonderful life.

# Chapter Eight

# HEART AS BIG AS LIVERPOOL: THE SOUNDS OF THE LIVERPOOL CROWD
## (with Cathy Long)

Ian McCulloch's a massive Liverpool fan – but how can you be as cool as he is, and look as cool as he does, and be a fan of Liverpool? Imagine a whole crowd like him at the match!

Pete Wylie

## GONE – BUT NEVER FORGOTTEN

The sudden death in 2004 of the much venerated BBC Radio veteran DJ, broadcaster and Liverpool FC long-distance devotee, John Robert Parker Ravenscroft – better known, of course, as John Peel – was a very public reminder that football and music had been synonymous with the city of Liverpool for quite some time. John Peel's death was a cause for national mourning and provoked articles on music in *Through the Wind and Rain*, and even a back-page memorial. 'I can take or leave celeb supporters,' wrote fanzine editor Steve Kelly, movingly (ahem, we think that means 'leave', Steve), 'and while I'm glad men like [Ian] McCulloch and [Pete] Wylie follow the one true religion, there are only three people that I'd praise God because they are Liverpool fans: my dad, myself (which are one and the same thing, I suppose) – and John Peel.'

Amen. The Liverpool match programme also carried a tribute to Peel, and the songs played at the Birmingham City home match were all Peel favourites, including his favourite single, 'Teenage Kicks' by The Undertones. John Peel, perhaps more than any other Liverpool football fan, would have enjoyed the club's return to the pinnacle of European football in the spring of 2005 in Istanbul.

Peel was much loved in BBC broadcasting and in the independent music industry, and in Liverpool his studied devotion to some of the great names of Liverpool FC's past – especially, perhaps, Bill Shankly, Billy Liddell and Kenny Dalglish – was well known and authentic. Peel was no man to pull strings in order to mix with 'other' celebrities, drawn from sport: though he famously carried Bill Shankly's bag at the 1981 European Cup final – a treasured memory, and one he talked often and humbly about. But, more typically, he once avoided seeing Dalglish during a Radio One visit by the Scot, for fear that he might burst into tears on meeting his football hero. On another famous occasion he did burst into uncontrollable tears whilst broadcasting live: as the Liverpool death toll mounted after Hillsborough.

Peel, a middle-class boy from Cheshire and a Shrewsbury public schoolboy, once revealed that he favoured football in part as a statement of class solidarity and rebellion, saying the more that people told him 'only proletarian folk supported a professional football team . . . the more interested I became'. He hated the public-school ethos and elitism – and the many beatings it brought him. His love of Liverpool FC from the early 1950s was cemented by the fact that, as a seven year old, he found himself in a boarding school full of Manchester United fans. Not much changes, after all. Later, Peel gave his son William and daughter Alex a novel and honoured middle name – Anfield – while son Tom rejoiced in the moniker 'Dalglish' and daughter Florence 'Shankly'. As the subject for the BBC Radio Four show *Desert Island Discs* in 1989, Peel asked for a football as his luxury item on the island. He explained this choice by saying – like many men of his generation from Liverpool might – that he was a graceless, inhibited dancer, but 'When I was playing football, I always felt graceful. I feel as other people would feel when they were dancing, so a football would be essential.' At Peel's funeral at Bury St Edmunds Cathedral in November 2004 the men of his family wore Liverpool-red ties. Respect.

John Peel alluded, obliquely, to the links between Liverpool fan culture and music when he accepted his Sony Award in 1993 and tearfully told his audience that music radio was, 'a wonderful medium for short, fat Liverpool supporters'. Twelve years on and Elvis Costello – who was present at the Liverpool UEFA Cup final victory in Dortmund in 2001 – had little planned for Liverpool making it all the way to the European Cup final in Istanbul in 2005. This meant that on the night of the final he was reduced to pacing his dressing-room before a gig in Norwich, watching the first-half torture on TV. As his band The Imposters were about to take the stage, and still thinking his beloved Reds were down 3–0, out of the corner of his eye Costello saw that Gerrard and Smicer had pulled back two goals. 'Hold on,' he told the band. The gig was massively delayed, 16 people asked for their money back and East Anglian music lovers almost rioted as Elvis and the band simply carried on watching. Costello commented later: 'Despite the greed, vanity and vile bigotry that lurks within and sometimes overwhelms the game today, it can still be magical. For those two hours it was certainly more important than rock and roll.' And who, for a moment, could doubt that?

As Liverpool fans gathered outside the cathedral in the desert that was to host the 2005 European Cup final, the familiar strains of some legendary Liverpool music could be heard. In a wonderfully chaotic Liverpool *music* night, Pete Wylie, Amsterdam and DJ Danny Hunt from Ladytron were all onstage entertaining the mass gathering. Set in a car park, with no food or drink in sight, this was a strange gig indeed. Danny put together a John Peel tribute, and first up was the Liverpool fans' song of the season, Johnny Cash's 'Ring of Fire'. 'Teenage Kicks', 'Roadrunner' and a version of 'The Fields of Anfield Road' all made it into the set. An avid Red, Danny had thought he wouldn't make it to the match, never mind be playing to thousands of fellow fans outside the stadium. With a tour starting the day after the final, his only route would be to get himself on an official party flying back that night. Some chance. But these days, if you're a musical Red and your team's in *this* sort of final, there's always the chance that the club might give you a call and ask you to come along.

At Dortmund in 2001 Liverpool organised a gig in the main square before the UEFA Cup final. John Power of Cast, Pete Wylie and assorted others played in the rain in front of a delighted crowd. In 2005 Wylie was invited along again, following on Danny's lead with some neat adaptations of his own songs. 'Blitzkreig Bop' became 'Anfield Kop' and the opportunity to sing 'The Story of Emlyn Hughes (Blues)' and 'Heart as Big as Liverpool' gave Wylie 'the best two nights of my life in one night – playing in front of that many fans and the response, and then the comeback in the match. We weren't there to entertain the troops: we were there to lift them, and I like to think we played our part.' A rousing rendition of 'You'll Never Walk Alone' led to a crowd invasion of the stage, and the panicked Turks declared the gig over.

The music may have stopped here to give way to the match, but how have the music and football traditions of the city of Liverpool become so uniquely intertwined?

## YEAH, YEAH, YEAH

Emlyn Hughes was still growing up strong in the north-west of England, and John Ravenscroft was but an office boy over in Dallas, Texas, when The Beatles signed their first record deal in the early 1960s and Everton, and then Liverpool FC, began periods of domination of the English and – more briefly – the European game up until the five-year Heysel ban in 1985. Liverpudlians travelling abroad – and it was small numbers of adventurers then, rather than the tens of thousands we had out in Turkey in 2005 – had, typically, ploughed cross-cultural common ground with fellow Europeans, from whom they were otherwise divided by language and by culture. Their basic communication tool: references and allusions to *both* the football and the musical traditions that define the city from which they come.

And in many ways, both then and today, 'Liverpool-ness' is

popularly described through the pleasures and meanings attached to both music and football in the city, and such central cultural activities are used to define localities and to tell stories in the city – and outside it – about Liverpool people's strong attachment to place. So, for all the talk in the red-top press about poverty and drink, crime and drugs and the decline of work, and even of the alleged loss of dignity in Liverpool, around Europe and beyond, the city of Liverpool is probably still best known for something else: for its cultural *creativity*, in both its football and its music cultures.

This all goes back, of course, at least to the early 1960s, when Liverpool had established something of a popular cultural primacy in Britain; the city was already internationally known for its music, but it was also thriving in sport, especially football. The black, American-infused cosmopolitanism of the city of Liverpool, its immigrant peoples and shifting community cultures, helps account for the emergence of the distinctive R&B-influenced pop: the 'Mersey sound'. The Beatles, as the leaders of the movement, were probably the first big 'pop' product in Britain to be quite so closely and exclusively associated with a particular place outside London, and with a specific provincial cultural milieu. The proliferation of other bands from the city – the Searchers, the Merseybeats, Billy J. Kramer and Gerry and the Pacemakers, to name but a few from the time – meant that Liverpool soon became celebrated, albeit briefly, as the early British 'home' of pop music. In a similar way to Tony Blair's more avowedly political 'Britpop' project of the 1990s, under Labour's 'modernising' Harold Wilson government the pop music the city produced became, for a while, the central symbol of fashionable, metropolitan British culture.

It was during this period of intense working-class cultural creativity that the Liverpool football Kop developed much of its extraordinary reputation for terrace songs, humour and, marshalled by its arch-showman and leader, Bill Shankly, a thrilling capacity to intimidate and subjugate the footballing opposition. In 1964 the BBC current affairs flagship *Panorama* programme even visited Anfield, and an astonished reporter, speaking in the familiar tongue of received Home Counties BBC-speech, described the strong links between the new Merseybeat and the songs of the terraces. He also evoked the cultural richness and tropes of northern English football-terrace life as if they were the sorts of mysteries that might be found elsewhere only by anthropologists, perhaps on distant South Sea Islands.

It was easy, then, to assert that the two cultures of football and music in Liverpool were intrinsically and inextricably linked, and not just with the city but with each other. After all, the younger members of Shankly's Liverpool Kop 'naturally' sang Beatles-influenced songs as a means of asserting an identity distinctive from bland, post-war English football-supporter traditions. 'She Loves You' and 'We all live in a red and white Kop' (to the tune of 'Yellow Submarine') were soon staple features of the new singing terrace cultures. They were still being sung in 2005 – though 'submarine' had now become the updated and raucous salute to a new local hero: 'We all dream of a team of Carraghers'. In 1965, while Liverpool FC won the FA Cup for the first time, beating Leeds United in the final, the *Liverpool Echo* proclaimed the final victory as a sign that it was: 'Liverpool's year, yeah, yeah'. The *Echo* later produced a special Cup-final supplement for the city, rather painfully entitled: 'Hail the Beatleeds'. In 2005 the Spanish press called Liverpool FC the 'Benitles'.

The reality, however, was rather different, at least as far as local musicians themselves were concerned. Paul McCartney's family supported Everton, but despite occasional rumours since that he, himself, might invest in the Blues (wishful thinking, perhaps, on the part of some Evertonians), Macca has shown little obvious interest in the club his father favoured: he is certainly not what most supporters would call 'a fan'. Whilst none of the original Beatles had especially privileged backgrounds, by local standards they lived in more affluent areas – in the south end of the city – and in relative, semi-detached comfort. The band's key creative figure, John Lennon, and also Paul McCartney himself were actually part of the exclusive Liverpool art-school crowd of the period, and 'proletarian' football was simply defined as 'off limits' in these bohemian Liverpool circles in the 1960s, where art and music, rather than sport, ruled.

## LET'S ALL GO TO ERIC'S

During the mid-1970s, when Liverpool FC began to win trophies at home and abroad and firmly laid down its intention of establishing routine footballing dominance across the Continent, Liverpool music also began to recover from its inevitable post-Beatles trough. In 1976 things began to change with the opening of Eric's: a small, dingy nightclub in the city centre. Situated in Mathew Street, directly opposite the original site of The Cavern club, Eric's became home for music lovers, art students and just about anybody with an eclectic taste and a liking for the sort of nightclub where your feet stick to the carpet. The club was owned and run by Peter Fulwell and Roger Eagle, two adopted Liverpudlians with an entrepreneurial spirit and a love of music.

The Clash, The Jam, Elvis Costello and many more of the post-punk bands of that era played at Eric's, and they inspired a new generation of young Liverpool-based pretenders to take to the stage. Pete Wylie's Wah! Heat, The Teardrop Explodes, Echo and the Bunnymen and Orchestral Manoeuvres in the Dark all played their first professional gigs at Eric's, and by the turn of the decade these bands started to enjoy some national chart success. In fact, by the early 1980s Liverpool bands threatened to dominate the pop airwaves once again. It was during this time, of course, that Liverpool FC began to tower over European football, winning four European Cups. So, was this new cohort of Liverpool musicians also made up of football fans? Or did they immerse themselves solely in their art and music, as had The Beatles and the Liverpool music insiders before them? Many of the local boys (and they were almost always boys) *were* interested in football, but, early on, at least, and in an arena where music was definitely king, football talk just wasn't appropriate.

Pete Wylie, legendary Liverpool figurehead and blagger, Istanbul 2005 star and now a fixture at Reds music shows abroad for all major football finals, shows well how football played poorly against the aesthetics and 'politics' of musical subcultures at the time in Liverpool. He recalls: 'No one at Eric's talked about football – you were either a swot or a jock and you couldn't be both. I was into music completely and at the time that was an important thing. You would have been seen as a part-timer if you could also like football. The idea of being able to like two things at once was bizarre! Football was working class, and although we were working class we also had this thing of being "class-less" and we weren't going to be categorised and we were beyond all those definitions.'

In these sorts of circles, at this time, owning up to being a footy fan was not a smart move. Wylie again: 'To some extent we rebelled against that football culture – but then we rebelled against everything. I rebelled against being from Norris Green, from being from that kind of background. At Eric's and in that whole scene I had mates like Paul [Rutherford], Holly [Johnson], Pete Burns, who were openly, outrageously gay. They could be totally out of the gay closet, yet you hid in the shadows as a football fan. I lived in the football closet! It was like, you can be gay, you can be anything you want, but you can't be into footy. It's bizarre! I'm sure if the subject of football had come up there would have been snobbery about it.'

Music journalist and football fan Kev McManus remembers attending the Saturday-afternoon matinée shows at Eric's: 'It would have been impossible for me to have gone to the match as well, and I clearly chose music over football at the time.' So, it was clear that many of the 'young and trendy' set who spent their days and nights in and around the Mathew Street area, in cafés, nightclubs and record shops, simply didn't talk much about football, in an era when Liverpool and Everton were both extraordinarily successful. The two cultures simply didn't mix, at least not for these fellas. This was clearly no simple matter of being 'cool' and ignoring the hysteria drifting from the football grounds across Stanley Park.

Michael Head of the Pale Fountains, a popular 'underground' Liverpool band producing soft, pretty, melodic songs, and now the critically acclaimed band Shack, agrees with Wylie: 'No one ever talked about football then, when we were in the Pale Fountains. I was from Kenny [Kensington, an area in south Liverpool], so being brought up on the streets of Kenny, for me to get into music – it just wasn't what people there did. I felt like I was leaving things behind, which was, like, bus rides with my mates, playing footy, going to the match. To get into music, start going to places like the Everyman [Theatre], I was leaving something behind, going into a totally different territory. I *wanted* something different and I felt excited by the music. So I left all the people I'd been hanging around with. So forming the band, doing what we did, was all part of leaving that culture in Kenny behind, and football had been a part of that. We weren't betraying it, or letting it down, we'd just had enough of all that went with it.'

'All that went with it', of course, included the bravado and violence that often went hand-in-hand for many 'smart' young urban scals following football in the early 1980s. Many Liverpool fans who had seen the fighting en route to matches felt they either had to opt in or out. You could 'stand and fight' or you could 'pick up a guitar' was one trusted (and clichéd) line of thinking. A few did both.

The violence, or threat of it, which ran through much of the late 1970s and '80s football-terrace culture did occasionally spill over into club culture, however. Despite the fact that football didn't matter much to most of the Eric's crowd, owners Roger Eagle and Pete Fulwell were astute enough to realise that many of their male punters *did* actually attend matches. The author Kev Sampson, who also manages The Farm, recalled that 'Eric's were so on the ball at predicting movements, and getting in first. They put Secret Affair on when everyone was just getting into the mod thing, on the night of Liverpool's first home game of the season against West Ham.' It was a great idea but, sadly, not wonderfully organised. 'Unfortunately,' said Kev, 'they didn't open until late, so there was a big brawl outside as the Reds fans came out of the Why Not? pub and met the West Ham fans waiting for Eric's to open.'

On those occasions when, eventually, Liverpool music artists began, themselves, to bring up the subject of football in press interviews, it was often to deal with questions in the city and elsewhere about acceptable forms of masculinity. Ian McCulloch was an art-house Irish-Liverpudlian sporting a wild cockatoo hairstyle who explored, in his music, mythical and romantic allusions for Echo and the Bunnymen. This might have been 'troublesome' material for some Kopites and local terrace hard-cases. Mac confessed to using his local football affiliations – he is a staunch Liverpool fan – to reinforce his heterosexual identity: 'I don't remember anyone bringing up the subject of footy – apart from Rod Stewart,' recalls McCulloch. 'But I was the first bastard to say I like music and I go to the match. No one would ask me about it in interviews, but I'd bring it up. I'd say, "I'm a sodding Liverpool fan" because I didn't want to come across like some fop.' Immediately after the 2005 Liverpool FC Istanbul triumph, the Bunnymen took the stage for their next gig in front of an enormous red Liverpool FC flag.

Later, in a music-hall-style pastiche of 'All You Need Is Love', the Bunnymen would, unusually, bring together the great musical and football inspirations in the city by tagging on a lengthy musical *homage* at the end of the Beatles song to Bill Shankly, 'Bobbie' Paisley and the coaching staff of Liverpool FC.

Like the Bunnymen, members of the Pale Fountains, didn't want to be seen as lacking in the masculine 'right stuff' because of their musical preoccupations. And if the 'Paleys' weren't playing football in Liverpool in the 1980s then they were certainly *talking* about playing football, as Mick Head remembers: 'At the time, the Paleys were, like, soft guitars and this image and all that, but we had a shit-hot little team going. And Test Department had this German, industrial sort of sound, and we thrashed the shit out of them. They probably didn't expect us to be such a good team. Our music was acoustic and folky, and we probably surprised people, 'cos we are actually very good footballers!'

Johnny Mellor, a local musician who played with the Bunnymen and the Pale Fountains, notes the usefulness, for football-mad musicians, of the Liverpool connection. It somehow added legitimacy to their claims that they were also 'serious' about their football. It could open doors. 'Mick Head is a great footballer. The Paleys were the thoroughbreds of Liverpool football. There used to be a load of people who would play football at Sefton Park on Sunday afternoons – McCulloch, the Pale Fountains, the Christians, Colin from Black, and Ian Broudie [Lightning Seeds]. One time, Broudie threw a tantrum and walked off because Mac mistimed a tackle.' This was not a great outcome: Broudie was the only one with a car so he had to be coaxed back to play the following week. Mellor travelled around Europe with various bands and made a point of cycling to local football clubs: 'We'd try and get a game with the apprentices. The Liverpool thing definitely helped. I'd just say, "We're from Liverpool" and they'd let us look around the ground because everyone associates Liverpool with football.'

## ALL TOGETHER NOW?

The Farm, perhaps the Liverpool band most closely associated with football, and in particular with the 'scally culture' that went with it in the late-1980s, found themselves in a rather different situation than most. Keith Mullin, guitarist in The Farm, was asked in 1990 about the band being labelled the 'original scallies'. He pointed to the deep roots of the concept of 'scallying' in the city: 'It was over five years ago . . . it was just a word that was bandied about . . . someone who went to football matches, robbers and that . . . me grandma used to call me old fella a scally.' The Farm quickly became known in music circles as football fans, largely due to the fact that their lead singer, Pete Hooton, had also edited the Liverpool fanzine *The End* from the late-1970s, a forerunner of the shoal of local football fanzines which followed.

Music fanzines had grown up as part of the 'do-it-yourself' ideology of the punk era, and there were a number of music fanzines in Liverpool in the early 1980s, but none covered football. Later, of course, dedicated *football* fanzines would emerge as part of an irreverent, populist – and sometimes polemical – opposition to mainstream football journalism and to the game's administrators. *The End* was something very different: it pioneered the 'musicalisation' of football. In Liverpool, and drawing, uniquely and evenly, on *both* of the main popular cultural traditions in the city, *The End* was a completely new form of fanzine that actually bridged the two cultures, and included features on both music *and* football. Perhaps most importantly it also relentlessly covered forms of male street fashion which linked for the first time the local (football) clubs to other (night) clubs in the city. As Pete Hooton puts it: 'People used to say that we would never get football supporters to buy a fanzine, particularly one that included music, and trying to sell the first few issues was almost impossible. But soon people realised what it was all about.'

So, did any of this overt football enthusiasm and self-conscious northern 'laddism' really contribute in a big way to The Farm's national success? In the early days the band certainly struggled to get any sort of attention from the major record labels. Dressed in jeans, trainers or even plastic sandals, they embraced the working-class 'boy [read scally] next door' look. In Liverpool 'lads in the know' who went to the match adopted, from the late 1970s, what they considered be an 'anti-football' casual look, and The Farm and their readers and supporters inevitably became leaders and arbiters in these obsessive and increasingly narcissistic fashion stakes. The Farm claim to be the first band actually to wear football trainers onstage, and they tracked the new developments in Liverpool back as early as 1978. Kev Sampson recalls the way in which, in the early days, the band were some way ahead of what record executives *thought* they were looking for: 'The Farm "look" was so alien to the people at the record companies, they shook their heads in dumb confusion and said, "It looks like an identity parade: a load of convicts on a day out."' These same record-company executives now have their own private boxes at Arsenal, Spurs and Chelsea, of course, as football later became the cultural and commercial currency of the age.

One man who certainly *did* understand terrace culture and saw the real commercial potential of the booming football/street-style phenomenon on Merseyside was Robert Wade-Smith. In the early 1980s he worked in an Adidas concession in Top Shop in Church Street, the main shopping street in Liverpool city centre. The concession sold an incredible number of training shoes; only the much larger Adidas concession in London's Oxford Circus sold more. Wade-Smith realised that the new competition in football aesthetics meant that the young football fans from Liverpool wanted more, and different, sporting styles, and in 1982 he opened his own shop selling rare imported trainers from Europe and the US. He never looked back. These new sporting styles were popular in Liverpool in part because trainers and tracksuits were flexible, all-purpose wear, if 'reassuringly' expensive. They also helped to emphasise, albeit indirectly, the consistent *footballing* power of the city, when much else in the region seemed to be failing.

Smart 'trackies' were also one important way of dealing, symbolically at least, with the economic exclusion which had hit Liverpool hard in the 1980s; the price tag of the 'right' sportswear revealed a determination of young scals not to be excluded from the 'good life' at all. Finally the trainer fashions and the liking in the city, especially, for more exclusive foreign football tops stemmed from the fact that Liverpool FC had been so remarkably successful in Europe in the 1970s and 1980s. Fans from the city could travel abroad for the games, on a regular basis, bringing back 'clothes gear' from beyond the usual local sources. Jegsy Dodd, local poet and Liverpool football fan, recalled shopping abroad for 'ski-jackets, Lacoste jackets, Fila, stuff you couldn't buy in England. Some fans made legitimate purchases, but many stole – they'd swarm into a shop like locusts and take the lot. The whole fashion of the time was influenced by the nature of the football trips – by the fact that many of the fans would be "on the rob".' How did they get away with it? 'They'd have less chance of being suspected in a shop with the tweed jacket and the wedge haircut, etc., than looking like the rest. A nice sensible side-parting could cover up a multitude of sins!'

The Farm and Liverpool football fans now began exploring the symbolic combinations of streetwear, combining Continental sportswear with 'country fashion' by dressing mysteriously in 'gentlemen's' Harris tweed jackets and Adidas Samba trainers. A small number of those at Eric's might dare to sport 'football' wedge haircuts and Lois jeans, but Kevin Sampson remembers well the fashion 'apartheid' established between music and football in Liverpool at the time: 'All the musical movements throughout the '70s and the '80s, from a stylistic point of view, were quite bohemian – there was the goth thing, new romantic, wearing black. It was only in the 1990s that you see anyone at a match wearing black. You would have been seen as a "weirdo" by the football fans.'

## TV, 'E' CULTURE AND COMMERCE
Bands who dared to *sing* about football were still generally seen as more than a little quirky, a bit of an English oddity. Some, clearly, enjoyed and played up to this image. The John Peel-championed and Birkenhead's own Half Man, Half Biscuit's wilfully obscure, brilliant football classics such as 'All I Want for Christmas is a Dukla Prague Away Kit', 'I was a Teenage Armchair Honved Fan'

and the marvellous 'Friday Nights and the Gates are Low' (an Abba 'Dancing Queen' spoof, of course, and a critique of the commercialisation of football) passed by critically acclaimed but commercially largely unnoticed. The Biscuits were sometimes match sponsors at lowly Tranmere Rovers, and the band famously failed to turn up for a live appearance on Channel 4's *The Tube* in the 1980s because it clashed with a Rovers match. Football and music was still, largely, in a state of 'them' and 'us'. As Pete Hooton, again, points out: 'Football was unfashionable in London media circles during the 1980s. It was looked down on as a horrific game. But it was never unfashionable in the circles I mixed in.'

Some local musicians in Liverpool had other reasons for rejecting football, including the crippling 1980s economic depression that had hit Merseyside especially hard. Between 1979 and 1984 alone almost half of all manufacturing jobs in Liverpool were lost, as the city became known as the 'Bermuda Triangle' of British capitalism. With no significant white-collar sector in the local economy and with only one of the twenty largest manufacturing companies in the city actually locally owned, Liverpool had effectively lost control of its own economic destiny. Unlike neighbouring Manchester the city also lacked a grounded professional media base and the sort of mixed night-time economy which might be built around such a core. Severe economic decline had, however, brought artistic and cultural responses from the city, including Alan Bleasdale's politically challenging and darkly comic Liverpool-based TV series *Boys from the Blackstuff*, and also his football-based comedy series *Scully*.

Football is not usually featured, of course, even in working-class British TV drama. Today, implausibly, discussion of football is still almost entirely absent from the two national soap operas: the north's *Coronation Street* and the south's *EastEnders*. The *Blackstuff*, an elegiac account of the adventures of a Liverpool tarmac gang and also of how unemployment in the city could push people right over the edge, unusually contained TV drama scenes involving *real* footballers. These included contemporaneous Liverpool FC players, ironically including the club's 'Thatcherite' midfield architect and enforcer, Graeme Souness. The club's general association with a 'political' TV programme, one that was clearly sympathetic to the plight of the city's unemployed, was no bad thing, both from a marketing and a public image point of view.

*Scully* was a rather different TV piece from *Blackstuff*. It was a popular comedy drama series based around a young man's fantasy of playing for Liverpool FC. Implicit here, however, was the strong notion that in post-industrial Liverpool this football fantasy was possibly the *only* available means of escape from enforced drudgery for many working-class lads in the city. *Scully* included scenes shot at Liverpool FC, and Elvis Costello appeared in the series (with Kenny Dalglish). Costello, naturally, also wrote the music and the theme tune for this hard-edged, 'heart of gold' comedy, the catchy and pointed 'Painting the Town Red'.

The stark contrast, which was not always consciously highlighted in these programmes, between the all-conquering fortunes of Liverpool FC and the dire state of the economics of the city, proved too much for some locals to bear. Kop season-ticket holder Philip Hayes, of the High Five band, and later manager of the Liverpool Picket music venue, was not the only cultural worker or political activist in the city to become disillusioned with the game, especially in the wake of Thatcherite political and social attacks on the city and its people: 'To go to a match on a Saturday and to follow your team religiously and obsessively was a distraction from what people should really be doing, which was campaigning against the conditions they're brought up in, or government cuts in education, and attempting to destroy capitalism.' 'Destroying capitalism' may not have been a realistic option – or even one which could have solved Liverpool's many problems – but the feeling in parts of the city in the depressed 1980s was that doing so could barely make them much worse.

Arguably the single biggest influence on the blending of musical and football cultures in the late-1980s in Liverpool and elsewhere was the arrival of the 'designer drug' Ecstasy, and its strong association with techno and dance cultures. Although their influence on terrace culture has probably been exaggerated, the arrival of Ecstasy and dance *together* as part of the 'new mainstream' in the late 1980s almost certainly did play an important part in changing the lifestyles of at least some of those who had previously followed football, as well as changing the musical landscape of the country. It was also probably the beginning of the end of the national music success for popular Liverpool 'good time' bands such as The Farm, who now looked a little off the pace of the new music and increasingly youthful club scenes.

Dave Pichilingi of the Liverpool band 35 Summers recalls: 'Ecstasy played a big part in changing the way people acted. Lads that were in 1987 slashing each other – within 12 months those same people were hugging each other. Liverpool, Man U., Chelsea, West Ham all fought each other and had away crowds. And then Ecstasy broke down that barrier. It didn't last long, maybe three or four years. After that the tablets weren't as good, and people started taking other drugs – Charlie [cocaine], for example, which had a completely different effect. Football fans went to nightclubs, so they were part of that big scene.'

Inevitably there is more than a little nostalgia and some distortion here. Not all 'lads' downed their football fighting tools in the 'summer of love' from 1988, far from it. But, substituting Ecstasy for beer and dance cultures for lads' gangs did help to 'chill out' some previously fierce football rivalries. Soon after, in 1990, 35 Summers seized the moment and produced a promotional T-shirt carrying a picture of Bill Shankly. The band had brought out their first single, a cover version of The Beatles song 'Come Together', which now included a spoken football excerpt sampled from the *Shankly Speaks* LP owned by one of the band members, Dave Pichilingi. But the John Peel favourite Bim Sherman's 'Sharp as a Needle' sampling of football commentary on the Liverpool strikers Dalglish and Rush remains the top music–football reference in this area.

In 1990, for the first time, an official England World Cup song was no novelty shocker sung by the England squad. Instead, 'World in Motion' was put together and performed by New Order, a 'cool' rock band, accompanied by Liverpool's John Barnes. Indeed, English football itself was now officially cool. Originally called, transparently and provocatively, 'E for England', the Italia '90 song's lyrics and emphasis was changed considerably before its final recording. New Order singer Bernard Sumner told the *NME* that the FA had made it clear that the song had to distance itself from hooliganism, but he also claimed that there was a 'deliberate ambiguity' about the words in that they could be read to refer to both music and football. 'Pop and football,' he concluded, 'are nearer than they have been for a long time.'

As national support for Merseyside's The Farm waned further under the assault from dance culture, new football–pop connections were beginning to emerge openly around the new dance genres. Cultural critic Paul Morley commented, for example, on how the dance music of Manchester's 808 State connected to the way fans felt on the terrace: 'The mood and the rhythm, and the motion and the excitement, and the boredom and the intermission, and the before the match and the after the match. So, for me, if I was going to do a soundtrack to a football match musically, I would always use 808 State.'

Few Liverpool bands were now able to make any real impact on the national music charts. The Las, The Real People and Rain were all bands that were lauded, locally. The Las' heavily Beatles-influenced 'There She Goes' was an obvious and acknowledged influence on the music produced later by the madcap, Manchester City-supporting Gallagher brothers of Oasis.

Like other parts of the Merseyside economy, however, the music industry in Liverpool was fragile and lacked even one small, but strong, local record label on which these new artists might successfully establish themselves. Later signed up by major London labels, these late-Liverpool bands, nevertheless, have failed to fulfil their early potential. Whilst 'baggy' bands from Manchester began to dominate the national music scene from the late-1980s, it was not until 1995, when The Las' guitarist, John Power, formed his own new band, Cast, that Liverpool began to make another impact on the mainstream charts. A slightly quirky and unpredictable new Liverpool band, Space, then took many by surprise in 1996, with their single 'Female of the Species' launching the band into a period of some critical and popular success. A 'new' Liverpool sound had begun to emerge.

These new Liverpool bands were managed by local companies that were able to combine the necessary business acumen for negotiating in the murky world of pop with an understanding of the cultural and musical roots of the bands. John Power is an avid Liverpool football fan and, like many pop stars in the late 1990s, he was astute enough to state publicly his football-club allegiance. When asked by music industry magazine *Music Week* who had been the most important person in the Merseyside *music* industry, his reply was both perverse and unerring – he said it was Liverpool FC's iconic ex-manager Bill Shankly. Space's lead singer, Tommy Scott, spoke in a similar vein: 'Shankly and Paisley have been major influences on me in my music career. I love their dedication – anyone who has that sort of dedication to their cause has to be an inspiration. Football is so important to us. We've called our new album *Love You More Than Football*. You know, all of us in the band wish we were footballers.'

Dedicated? What, pop stars? The old Liverpool trainer, the fearsome Reuben Bennett, would have asked some harsh questions – and no doubt wondered how the Liverpool 'boot room' of the 1960s and '70s was still inspiring even young *musicians* in the city some 25 years later.

Liverpool pop–football 'veterans', Echo and the Bunnymen, made an 'England' comeback in 1998. The band had reformed in 1997, ten years after an acrimonious split. Ian McCulloch, still keen on making any possible allusion to his beloved Reds, told *The Guardian*, mysteriously, 'We're like Ian Rush: he went to Juventus for a year; felt like a fish out of water because he couldn't speak the language, then came back and was brilliant. Sometimes you have to go elsewhere.' McCulloch had been seduced by the FA dollar to produce '(How Does it Feel to Be) On Top of the World' for World Cup 1998. In fact the verses of an original Bunnymen song were altered to fit the FA's own concept of a terrace chant, and none other than the Spice Girls were recruited to sing on the record. McCulloch seemed less than pleased with the outcome; it lacked real fizz and credibility and, worse, the football and music public were still wedded to their favourite 'Three Lions' anthem at matches. McCulloch claimed to be really more concerned about the football, telling *Melody Maker*: 'To be honest, I'm more worried about the England team than the song. I don't know what the sod's going on with Hoddle at the moment.' Mercifully, Mac's rather strange venture into England football–music territory was soon forgotten in favour of the Bunnymen's sublime back catalogue.

## CREATIVITY AND THE CITY OF LIVERPOOL

So is there anything about the city of Liverpool itself which stimulates this sort of musical and poetic creativity, both at the match and in the clubs, bars and various venues of the city? Born out of transcultural exchanges and immigrant performance cultures imported from both Ireland and the USA, combined with hard times, Liverpool does seem to produce footballers, musicians, comedians, poets, writers and actors by the plenty. Cliché? Coincidence? Not for Space's precocious young Tommy Scott: 'It's no coincidence that Liverpool has had both footballing and musical success,' he argues. 'Liverpool people are hungry. When people are poor, they're brought up to strive for something different, and Liverpool people seem to have this more than most. We probably wouldn't be doing what we do if we'd lived anywhere else. I don't know why, but it does seem to be a particularly Liverpudlian thing.'

'Hardship produces innovation' might be an overly simplistic slogan made for the cultural politics of Britain in the 1980s and early '90s. Liverpool had had plenty of recent hardship, certainly. Ian Broudie may well have been thinking of the creative charge he got from the chaotic struggles and the sheer pace of life in the city when he told *The Times,* enigmatically, in 1997 that he used to be afraid that if he left Liverpool, 'something would leave me musically'. Indeed, a common theme running through much of the city's music has been the special sense of place in Liverpool, and especially the work of the river. Even without the obvious reference to Gerry Marsden's 'Ferry Across the Mersey' 1960s anthem occasionally taken up today by the Liverpool Kop, references to the river and the sea appear many times as a theme in songs written by Echo and the Bunnymen, the Pale Fountains and others, and is a subject band members frequently like to return to in interviews.

The sea as an influence on local music is long established in the city, of course, especially in the Beatles' early debt to American black rhythm and blues artists. For Ian Broudie, the sea represents the freedom and romantic allure of the 'other': 'I even used to love the docks before they were regenerated – I would go cycling there when they were deserted and there was this great romantic atmosphere.' Pete Wylie, too, refers to the sea and the river as having a 'profound effect' on his writing; he even called his daughter Mersey.

Perhaps echoing again the historical influences on music and popular culture in what was essentially a northern decaying seaport, Ian McCulloch is also in no doubt about the 'soothing' importance of the River Mersey for stimulating the creative musical juices. But in the pre-2008 City of Culture era for the city he also recognises the importance of the unique and intoxicatingly 'dangerous' character of Liverpool and its people, as well as the decaying architectural legacy and its many shambolic, but iconic, public spaces: 'The Pier Head, it's wide open. It's peaceful and soothing being down there. Other places do up their waterfronts and spoil them but Liverpool hasn't. It retains that feel of days gone by and I think that's one of the strengths of Liverpool. I mean they are doing it up, but to do it up completely would make it just like other cities.' He goes on: 'Some of the buildings in town that are derelict, it's the only major city in Britain that has this now. It's real and it's part of the city . . . A lot of it's kind of self-inflicted. You go down Park Road and they burn buildings in their own street – generally the Tory club! It's that self-destruction that's part of our character. Most Scousers I know have that self-destructive thing. It's better than graffiti, isn't it, to kind of just blow the gaff up? The "edge" is what's good about the city. The Bunnymen tend to be liked in "proper" places, where there's a spirit to the city.'

## ENDPIECE: LIVING *WITH* THE PAST, AND SELLING THE FUTURE?

In May 2005 Rafa Benítez's Liverpool FC won the European Cup for the first time in 21 years. Pete Wylie and many other Liverpool musicians were in Istanbul to see that great night – sadly John Peel could not be. Whilst some Liverpool bands can claim some measure of commercial success in the past 30 years, none, of course, have come close to that of the 1960s musical pioneers of Merseyside. By the same token could the new Benítez football era at Anfield ever hope to challenge those of Shankly and Paisley? The legacy of the extraordinary dominance, in sport and music, of these men and of The Beatles over the past three decades has, at times, hung heavily over today's Liverpool like a dark and forbidding cloud.

Rafa Benítez now promises to lift that veil in the football arena. But no matter how much football is promoted and celebrated as a new success story for the city, the use of it by the authorities, along with other sports, music and the arts, to sell a 'new' Liverpool to tourists or to visiting fans from outside the city will not solve some of the area's wider problems. There are real dangers in institutionalising pop music and football consumption in Liverpool, and thus sanitising or diluting its local appeal. In an era of multinational corporations and global flows, it is almost certainly *cities*, rather than nations, that are likely to be the key economic units and actors of the future. This is why Liverpool FC's place in the Champions League football elite is so crucial to the future of both football at Anfield and to the city itself.

The power of cities – and of football clubs – in this regard may be exaggerated, but the eventual 'recovery' of both Liverpool FC and, indeed, Everton under David Moyes, may yet play an important part in revitalising, in a wider sense, the city of Liverpool. Of course, thoughts of the past will always trouble those who have to follow in the wake of great success. Manchester United have only recently exorcised their own football 'ghosts' from the 1960s. But, mostly, this now historic success, in both football and music, is not regarded as a burden in Liverpool; it is still celebrated and enjoyed by its people, who have slowly begun to learn how to live in these incredibly long shadows. Moreover, with Liverpool bands such as The Coral and The Zutons now riding high again, and with key local boys – Carragher and Gerrard – playing for the European Champions in 2005, the future is looking brighter, both for Liverpool's footballers and for its many musicians, many of whom are also, of course, committed Reds football fans.

All original interviews for this chapter were conducted by Cathy Long.

# Chapter Nine

# THE MIRACLE OF ISTANBUL

My brother rang me and described the save from
Shevchenko as the Hand of God.

Jerzy Dudek

## COME FLY WITH ME

How many ways to get to Istanbul in May 2005? How many do you
need? Immediately after Chelsea, even as we are gleefully driving
home, the Liverpool Flat Iron internet-travel elves, working deep
into the night, are doing their wondrous stuff. By the next morning
we have our answer. Fly from Lennon to Amsterdam at 6 a.m.
Monday, 23 May. Catch a train from Amsterdam to Brussels, then
fly on to Istanbul on some weird Dutch airline, if it stays afloat
until then. Fly back on Thursday morning, May 26 – no sleeping
that night – via Eindhoven and then Amsterdam. Simple.
Accommodation? A little homely number not far from the Blue
Mosque: three nights sharing for €35 each, in total. Which means
3,400 miles travelled, three nights in one of the most exotic cities
of the world and a ticket for the European Cup final, all for around
£420. It costs you almost as much to go to Chelsea away. How on
earth did we manage in Rome in 1977, by coach, cars and
charters? Back then 25,000 did it, and most of us even got home.

Chris, Paul, Barnesy, Ross, Mandy, Steve K., 'Moany' Simon, Cathy, Kelly, Sheila, John and Alan join with us for this excursion. We follow Alan's giant red flag, our mantra: 'Liverpool: My Passion, My Love, My Life'. His (heavily) pregnant missus is very impressed by it, apparently.

We would like to tell you that we saw plenty of the local sights during our stay in Istanbul and, to be fair, we did trawl the city streets, visit a local mosque and do some gentle bargaining in the extraordinary Grand Bazaar. The people of Istanbul are actually very like those from Liverpool: friendly and charming, street traders and grifters. Deal-makers. But today we are football fans, charged with representing our great club and our city as fans for a *football* match. Reaching this final is our greatest achievement in almost 20 years of painful trying. We want now to show the locals exactly how we support and how deeply we care. And to impress on them that what they might have read about our supposed brutal behaviour from 20 years ago is not who we are at all. We also want a drink and to see who is in the advance Liverpool party. We set off for the supporter gathering-spots.

Liverpool fans have been told to congregate in Tacsim Square, which is a short (and alarming) taxi ride across the Bosporus from where we are staying. We soon learn that one reason for UEFA choosing Istanbul to host this final is that the city allows a sterile and near perfect segregation of rival supporters at almost all times during their stay: separate airports; separate parts of the city; separate transport; separate and impenetrable stadium access and segregation. In fact, most Liverpool fans are allowed no sight or contact with any Milan fans – a huge disappointment. Whatever happened to great international football matches being staged as wonderful opportunities for fellow Europeans to meet together in friendly rivalry and healthy competition – as Liverpool fans had been doing for decades, and all this season in Europe, despite the inevitable tensions in Turin? Actually, this is UEFA's rather terrible, small-minded vision of the future: rival football fans in hermetically sealed parts of the city, who only get to stare at each other as complete strangers from across the stadium divides. And they think they are doing a good job, these guys! Do they understand anything at all about us?

Tacsim will be our base from now on. We take root in a small-fronted bar at its corner, which is soon draped in Liverpool flags, Alan's 'Passion' effort chief among them. The owner, a gold-star grifter, gets the picture right away: he is soon wearing a Liverpool shirt, hiring more staff and sending out urgently for more ale. All his birthdays have come at once, as the local cash registers sing. And now the Liverpool singing really begins. For lots of fans of English football clubs the prospects of trying to fill, say, a gentle four- or five-hour stint some 1,700 miles from home with their football songs for the entertainment of locals and themselves might prove just a little daunting – or boring. After ten minutes you start again. Not here. Not for this club. All right, 'You'll Never Walk Alone' and 'The Fields of Anfield Road' get a right pasting now, but there are dozens of other songs also in play here; more are probably being written yards from where we speak and thirstily empty our glasses.

This kind of thing is vitally important production-line work for the keepers of the club's heritage and its crucial oral traditions. Just look around you now. Look at the sheer invention and the many extraordinary examples of urban cultural expression revealed in the carefully crafted messages and quotations on the literally *hundreds* of Liverpool flags and banners that have been lovingly and *individually* made for this contest, and are now gathering here. It was suggested recently on a fans website – only half-jokingly – that new Liverpool supporters should be required to compose a 60-verse song about the club as an initiation rite: a reasonable test, we would say. Is there any football club – Celtic, perhaps – quite like this one? Are there, really, any other supporters with quite such a sense of their own aesthetic and their almost poetic role in shaping the historical and cultural identity of their club and of the game? Are there any other English fans who show quite such a knowledge and such respect for the traditions of their club and for its great players and managers? We honestly doubt it, we really do.

The locals have now started to gather round, wide-eyed, to watch us perform, the bar owner keeping them at a decent distance to ensure that he misses no passing Liverpool trade. These people, our audience, need to be entertained. So a scrawny Scouser decides to climb a nearby tree, beer mug in hand, and to lead the singing from here. He has his 15 minutes of fame as 'Tree Boy' and appears in all the Istanbul papers the next day, nursing his ale like some emaciated Walton King Kong. He almost falls asleep – and out of his tree. Our own man, Steve, will later reveal his treasured copy of a Bill Shankly autobiography which he produces for public 'readings' and scripture study of the sayings of the great man, our spiritual leader. Meanwhile the roof platform above the bars has begun to attract thousands of new arrivals, their flags and banners at hand. On and on they go, a veritable red-and-white Scrabble board of intentions, scriptures, messages and in-jokes.

Over the next couple of hours, in the Istanbul sunshine, the Liverpool-supporting 'celebrities' will also, slowly, start to show: the boxer Amir Khan, a pocket powerhouse with arms like steel rods; Alan Kennedy, two European Cups won and spending hours now, uncomplainingly, signing autographs and being endlessly photographed by Scousers who are much too young to remember him play; and the young Liverpool bands who will play in the concert before the match itself.

Tacsim Square is now joyfully filling with Scandies and Indians (the Punjabi Reds have their own Reds flag) and Australians and Americans and Dutch and Israelis and Japanese Reds, a wonderful international gathering of the far-flung Liverpool FC clans. Gangs of glossy Liverpool women commandeer some of the best bar tables. This is a very different event from that very first time in 1977, when pretty much only pasty Scouse men travelled to Rome: we are now a global football club, and we should be very proud to take on that mantle – while respecting always, of course, our authentic, our utterly indispensable, Scouse roots.

## THE GREAT JOURNEY

Buses, we are told, will take us to our destination, to the Atatürk Olympic Stadium. A cab would be a crazy option: it would take us fully two hours for 40 km on a single road from here (two hours!). We leave at 5 p.m. for a 9.45 p.m. kick-off. We want to try to catch Pete Wylie and some of the Liverpool concert stage show outside the ground. This amazing, twisting bus journey takes us through industrial sites and picturesque hill towns and pastures; through desolate wastelands and through rural villages; through high streets and near mountain routes. We wave to the clergy and to milkmaids, to farmhands and factory workers, to grandmothers and to schoolchildren. All Turkish life is here – including ale-selling urchins – and we have suddenly invaded their horizons, the strange urban football tribes of northern Italy and England. They all return our greetings, smiling, wondering at our ridiculous hats and banners and at exactly how we have ended up here, in the middle of their lost worlds.

Where *is* this stadium? We know something about its brief history. Designed by French architects and built to support Turkish bids to host the Olympic Games, the Atatürk cost $126 million (£67 million) to build. It is a failing stadium: it failed to attract the Olympic Games for Turkey in 2000, 2004 and for 2008. Its main, crescent-shaped roof weighs 3,420 tonnes. Proper roads to the stadium were only completed last month, and it was only on 11 May 2005 that it hosted the Turkish Cup final between Fenerbahce (Asia) and Galatasaray (Europe) as a rehearsal for tonight's match, which should play host to around 70,000 fans. This all sounds bad. We hear that it was built at such distance from the centre of Istanbul in order, partly, to keep warring local football factions safely outside the city – which also sounds like a desperate route to despair. And we are *miles* from anywhere now – in 584 hectares of open land, actually – surrounded only by cattle and goats and what look like abandoned cottage shells. We have already lost some idiot scally out of the back window of our bus, a man surely cut loose forever in the barren reaches of outer-outer Istanbul. Eventually, after what seems like hours of nothingness, we can begin to see the shape of the stadium in the far distance. With vehicles backed up bumper to bumper on the only road to the ground, we get off the bus – everyone is doing it now – and set off across open fields to the Holy Grail, the stadium. It feels positively Biblical – or else a scene from an Iranian art-house movie.

Look at us closely, now, for we are the much-cherished UEFA customers, the prized consumers of the European game for whom no expense has been spared in organising this blue-chip event. We are the Chosen Ones. And we are now, in the twenty-first century and having spent, in some cases, thousands of pounds just to get here, walking miles across muddied open fields just to reach this ludicrous venue for Europe's – the world's – premier club-football match. Did the corporates have to do just the same thing? Did they – and their media mates – get here by helicopter? It is ironic, don't you think, that the football authorities are constantly trying to make football stadia more plush, sterile and bland, often against the wishes of supporters. And now we have miles of this rutted assault course for men, women and their kids to overcome! It is a show of utter contempt for fans by the organising officials. As we look back now from the stadium apron, watching thousands of Liverpool fans still streaming towards their goal, a florid red wave across the landscape, it looks nothing like a northern European sports crowd excitedly approaching a state-of the-art venue for the football experience of a lifetime. It actually looks more like a despondent refugee trail: a scene, perhaps, from a Balkan siege. 'It is the management's boast' (we are told about the Atatürk Stadium) 'that no spectator needs to walk more than 60 metres from his or her seat to find a toilet or a buffet.' How about not having to walk three or four miles on hostile terrain to reach the fucking place?

Pete Wylie and the bands are gamely playing on a stage on what looks like a vast open car park outside the Liverpool end of the ground. We are totally sealed off from the Milan supporters. Later, as hundreds of Liverpool fans invade the stage for a wild dance, we get plaintive loudspeaker appeals for them to vacate it – in case it collapses. Thousands of fans are standing listening and dreaming as a cold wind begins to whip across the site. Apart from match programmes – soon gone – and crisps, nuts and water, there is nothing to buy here, no hot food or facilities of any sort. It is miles just to get here, so there are no willing street vendors, no local food providers or merchandisers to benefit from this night and offer us their much needed services. We are in a wasteland. Some Liverpool fans have brought pallets of ale with them and the area is soon awash with empties. Inside the ground, later, the tiny hot-food areas will be utterly besieged by angry Liverpool fans, many of whom – and their kids – have not eaten for hours. The prices at these official outlets soon begin to double and even treble. Many of them, too, are quickly sold out and are closed early. Maybe someone should have warned the organisers that a European Cup final was being played here tonight – and that they should expect some football supporters to attend.

As we try to get into the ground the bar-code ticket-reader system breaks down, so, after a long and largely patient wait, tickets are checked manually – though the signage outside is so appalling that some people are forced to join two or three different queues before finally making it inside. On the East Tribune we are engulfed in a sea of red, as is about three-quarters of the stadium. On the pitch some impenetrable opening ceremony is going on involving half the population of a small town and, no doubt, costing more than anything laid on tonight for the fans of these two famous football clubs. The Milan supporters to our left are passionate and organised, their collective expressions of support including massed coloured flags, coordinated plastic coloured tunics, a massive 'devil' banner and a joint message with IMUSA against 'the commercialisation of football': just in time, then. The Liverpool support, by contrast, sprawls incoherently around the stadium in an anarchic red splash, red flags and banners offering insistent but silent stadium chatter. But all this stuff is so much talk and event-dressing now. We await impatiently the kick-off to the 2005 European Cup final: our Liverpool hearts are now pounding. After all this waiting – 20 long years – we have a first-minute surprise.

## THE FIRST MINUTE: THERE OUGHT TO BE A LAW AGAINST IT

We think there should be a new football law: we would vote for it tomorrow. We don't exactly have the right wording yet, but it goes something like this: nothing of any significance should be allowed to happen in any major football match, in any big final abroad, during the first minute of play. Not while the fans are still busy scraping the country mud off their heels, or settling in to watching the game, getting their flags and these weird stadium sight-lines sorted out. And not while they are still practising their best European Cup songs, perhaps only halfway through a first, serious chorus. Or still looking for close mates among 40,000 others, or else trying to get a decent handle on the opposition line-up: 'Who's the no. 21 for them?' Or, 'Is that Rui Costa fella playing tonight?' Not while you're still trying to work out who is on the Liverpool bench who could possibly affect the outcome later. Or trying to assess the price of the stadium coffee: 'What, 300 million Turkish lira for *that* shite?' And definitely not while you are still examining exactly what is going on down the left-hand side of Liverpool FC's defence. Get in touch now to lend your weight to this campaign: we really need your support.

Why are we so keen for this change? Because it took precisely six seconds of the 2005 European Cup final in the Atatürk Olympic Stadium for Liverpool's left-back Djimi Traoré to give the ball away for the first time. He slowed down from here, because it took him fully another 15 seconds to commit his first foul in a dangerous position, on the rapid, boy-band Brazilian kid Kaka. This was not a promising start, not what we had hoped for at all. But shit happens: especially, it seems, down this vulnerable Liverpool flank. As a very young man in 2002 Djimi had been virtually destroyed in defence by FC Valencia – by Rufete and Pablo Aimar, if you must know – in the Champions League, playing under Houllier for Liverpool against Benítez's formidable side. Lesser men might have crumbled, but the determined Djimi got more experienced and he fought on.

The Spaniard clearly paid that little episode no mind, either, because earlier this year, with Benítez now at the Liverpool helm, Djimi was still firmly Liverpool's left-back. But he now bagged a truly dreadful own goal at Burnley – a piece of football grotesque – to help knock his own club out of the FA Cup. Rafa said, 'Don't worry, he will learn from it.' Traoré soon regained his place. In between times Djimi had suffered numerous, smaller catastrophes whilst trying gamely, but usually inadequately, to seal up Liverpool's left side. But Benítez had stuck with him – while we, the mere concerned onlookers, still had our serious doubts. Was this *really* a potential European Cup-winning left-back? Even Joey Jones and Alan Kennedy have him by miles – and, unlike AK, he scores no crucial goals. And now here we are, in the very first minute of the final we have waited 20 years to see, already forced to defend one of Djimi's familiar early failings. The Italian midfielder Pirlo (*he* is the Milan no. 21) is standing on the ball, wide on Liverpool's left, near the edge of the penalty area. Forty-five seconds have already flown by in the 2005 European Cup final. Our proposed new football law would stop, right here, what is about to happen happening. That is its simple (and only) beauty.

This Milan free-kick, awarded too early in the game for any real precision, is certainly no work of science or art. Pirlo is probably aiming for that 'ugly man' Jaap Stam at the back post, but he actually under-hits the cross and it arrives shallower and behind the Dutchman, and also behind his captain, Paolo Maldini, who has withdrawn slightly outside the penalty area scrum and so has not been picked up by anybody in red at all. Instinctively Maldini now swings his right foot back and through the ball at waist height – old Paolo actually began his career as a *right*-back and was predominantly right-footed into his late teens, so this is no chore – and as the nearby Alonso grimaces and recoils, this shot arrows downwards through the bodies piled in front of Dudek. It then pings off the turf before bouncing high into the Liverpool net, which offers a soft and large black hole of welcome. To our left, where all this horror has just occurred, the Milan fans erupt, their carefully choreographed stadium tableau now shivering and dislocating with early, unplanned glee.

At the match you don't always 'see' all of this stuff happen on the pitch: not right away. Unless, of course, you are in the boss seats, and people are actually *sitting* down on them. From our modest €100 vantage point, low down and near the other end of the ground, this is mainly a chilling mystery, involving someone else's unfamiliar players. No, a lot of this is guesswork and sheer speculation, hewn from a land far beyond rational thought and informed analysis. 'Should Dudek have saved that?' 'Was it deflected?' And here, among the dreamers and the exhausted Liverpool foot-soldiers, you don't have Andy Gray and his mates instantly plying you with helpful TV camera angles and bundles of statistics, whilst telling you exactly who should have been marking whom. And that in 1959 someone else scored a first-minute goal in the European Cup final and the team which scores first almost always wins these matches. Not that these guys know much. And not that you really want to hear this kind of thing at this stage – not right now.

We don't even have big-screen replays of the offending event here. Instead, we have to piece it all together – as our fathers did, and theirs before them – from all the other available, similarly half-arsed perspectives and commentaries around you, and wait until the celebratory Milan player-pyramid unpeels from the far corner to see that they have, indeed, been congratulating the gorgeous Maldini – only his third goal in a record 148 UEFA club matches. His name now goes up proudly under Milan's badge on the red screen to our right: 'Maldini, 1'. It is official: officially bad, that is. The defender lopes back towards us now, feigning modesty and preparing to do his serious work tonight, of defending Milan's left side. Traoré could do with a crash course in the Italian's masterclass. But it is all too little, too late for poor Djimi – and for Liverpool.

One-nil down in less than a minute: a harsh lesson. In the cheap(er) seats we are deflated, but not discouraged, and songs of Liverpool defiance immediately fill the Turkish skies. This is exactly why we are needed here tonight, and we will rise to the occasion, don't worry about that. A calm and rational Rafa Benítez – the only man in the ground, probably – almost certainly thinks now, his 'Mr Positive' hat jauntily on, 'It is very good that I have selected my attacking Liverpool team tonight. We will need Harry Kewell to respond to this setback.' The Liverpool manager is soon out on the touch-line, dispassionately pointing and cajoling. And for the next five minutes his hopes seem entirely justified, because Liverpool storm back at Milan, a vicious (goal-bound?) Riise volley being blocked by Stam. Then a powerful Hyypiä header, from Gerrard's cross, finds Dida's midriff when it could easily have found the Milan net. We feel good again: we will score in a minute and start dismantling this ageing Milan defence. It is only a matter of time before Liverpool will be level. Our no. 10 needs to help the cause.

Little Luis García had played under Rafa Benítez at Tenerife, back in the Spanish second-division promotion year of 2000–01, and had scored 16 goals for his manager from a favoured position just behind the forwards. This was no bad return, even in the soft underbelly of Spanish football. With Vladdy Smicer in injury trouble again in Liverpool's pre-season training in 2004, and with the Czech hardly likely, in any case, to produce goals in this sort of quantity from this area of the field, Rafa went back to García, gambling that the man from Spain could adapt quickly to the English game.

Thus far the manager has been proved half-right: at Anfield García has frequently thrilled, setting up colleagues and rifling in goals. He has scored out of nothing, and spectacular goals at that. He has seemingly taken a special liking to attacking the Anfield Road end, but the Kop understands his preference. He now even had his own jaunty fans' song, especially coined for this trip, about him being 'five foot seven' and 'football heaven', and he 'came from Barca, to bring us joy'. After the plodding pragmatism of the later Houllier years the romance of the prancing García and his little headband was seductive. He made some of us dream again. But all this, remember, was at *home*.

Away from home, freed from the warm, protective bosom of the Liverpool faithful and with the need to commit completely to defence as well as to attack, García has often looked lightweight and a dangerous luxury. He has attracted scowls and reprimands from the travelling Liverpool crowd, not the love he so craves. Here his flicks look like indulgences: weightless, light snacks when what we need are more solid, meaty interventions. He has given the ball away, casually and alarmingly so, thus inviting more pressure on Liverpool's creaking defence. He has been a liability, a man who hides from Jamie Carragher's high-pitched public admonishments from the rearguard. And here, in Turkey, even in front of tens of thousands of his supplicants, Luis is defiantly in away-match mode. In fact he is slowly helping Milan establish control of this first half.

On the quarter-hour mark Dudek throws an early ball to Luis on the halfway line – which is fine: as long as you don't lose the ball, don't turn over possession here (we know a bit about this and shout as much now: 'Don't fucking lose it there!'). Because if you *do* lose it here, your defence is misshapen and off-guard: it is trying to move out together as the ball comes back in. Imagine Bob Paisley's withering response to this sort of absolute failure of duty. Inevitably, Luis loses out. He simply *gives* the ball away, and from the resultant Milan corner he has to rescue the situation himself, forcing Crespo's header off the Liverpool goal-line with his chest, or even his shoulder.

Milan are visibly lifted by this moment and probably by Harry Kewell's departure, which seems to take an age and convinces some supporters near us that the Liverpool man is *asking* to come off when Benítez thinks he is OK. In fact, Harry knows, right away, that his groin is gone, after a hefty, but hardly brutal, halfway-line challenge from Nesta. The delay is that Smicer is simply not ready to replace him. As he leaves, Kewell applauds the boos that spill, uncharitably, out of the Liverpool sections of the Atatürk.

Vladdy finally joins up, just in time to watch Shevchenko threaten, once more, to undo Traoré on Liverpool's left. The silky Andriy Shevchenko, a product of the great Valeriy Lobanovsky's production line at Dynamo Kiev, looks like a brown-eyed, post-Soviet film star. But his unlined face masks serious dental work following a penalty-area kick to the mouth in 2003 and the insertion of five titanium plates around his eye socket, which was recently smashed in two places by a Serie A defender's carefully planted elbow. He also once watched a heart transplant in Italy in order to get a measure of perspective on the game and on life. This guy is tough as well as intelligent. Twenty-four goals in just thirty-two brutal Serie A matches in 2003–04 tells you all you need to know – or 144 goals in a total of 253 Milan appearances. He is called '*un animale da goal*' by the Italian press: a goal animal. It fits him well, but he is much more than a simple goal-poacher. What you really notice here is how he glides around the field and how, as honest tryers like Baros and Cissé fight the ball, the Ukrainian brings it instantly to attention before moving on, unthinkingly, to his next fatal manoeuvre. This boy has real class.

As is often the way in this sport, Liverpool had had an indirect role to play in lining up Shevchenko against them now. The great Liverpool North-Walian Ian Rush had once presented the 14-year-old Ukrainian with a pair of undersized boots at a European youth tournament and the young striker had worn them out, patched up and tattered, even as his toes began to poke through the leather seams. 'I couldn't get nicer ones,' he said. He claimed later that it was this early experience, with Rushie's too-small boots, that had helped him develop his incredible feel for the ball and his exemplary close control. Today's Liverpool might even have moved in to sign a young prospect like this one. But what we also see here, tonight, is the way in which, like a true assassin, Shevchenko sniffs out uncertainty and weakness anywhere in the Liverpool back line, appearing one minute beyond and outside the eye line of the floundering Traoré, the next in the soft hole between Carragher and Finnan on the right side of Liverpool's defence. Shevchenko's is a forensic study of defensive pliability and corrosion, but we have not had anyone with a native striker's instincts since a still-young Robbie Fowler.

AC Milan are now coming on strong in this match. Liverpool are losing control of key midfield areas, with Pirlo, from deep, regularly picking out Kaka, who is getting between the Liverpool midfield and their deep-lying back four. Near the half-hour mark, García loses the ball cheaply again, this time trying an extravagant flick past Seedorf near the Milan box, which leads to Kaka breaking for fully 30 yards at the retreating Liverpool defence, pursued all the way by Steven Gerrard. The Liverpool man catches him at the critical point, but now succeeds only in tackling the Brazilian and inadvertently offering a perfect 'pass' between Liverpool's right-side defenders and through to the deadly and clear Shevchenko. The Ukrainian looks up, misses a beat – and then unerringly *passes* the ball past Dudek and low into the Liverpool net. The reaction around us is one of deep gloom, a momentary crisis – and then elation. Offside! 'But didn't Stevie get there?' Who cares?

Luis García needs to sort himself out, and we badly need to push up now from the back, close up that space that Kaka is living in – killing us from. Benítez himself waves the Liverpool defence forward from his technical area. He has to, because the sheer pace at which Milan are moving the ball from back to front means that the game is beginning to bypass our own prospective match controller, Xabi Alonso. He is anonymous. We are starting to hang on now, maybe even hoping we can get to half-time to sort some of this out. For the first time we can hear the Milan supporters really singing. But 0–1 down to the mighty AC Milan at this stage is no tragedy, no insurmountable barrier. Rafa can make the necessary adjustments – and we will be stronger in the second half. This match is ours still to win. This is what we tell ourselves. And then it happens.

## THREE STRIKES – AND YOU'RE (SURELY) OUT

Vladdy Smicer has done OK since he replaced Kewell: he has kept the ball and has worked hard without ever threatening once to really damage Milan. But now, with Maldini drawn forward, he picks up a poor Stam clearance and instantly finds Luis García with an incisive little pass down the Milan left: 37 minutes show on the digital stadium clock. Luis, buoyant once more – he is never discouraged – targets and threatens to expose Nesta and, for once, even gets him out of his slick comfort zone. We are all on tiptoes now, trying to track this Liverpool attack – our best moment for some time. As García drives inside and into the Milan penalty area, Nesta, shuffling across and caught on the turn moving backwards, loses his balance and falls, arms flailing. This is absolutely crucial, what happens next. Critical. Because in what circumstances, exactly, does a football accidentally strike an arm? Or when does an arm control the ball, offering some real advantage to a defender? Let us know your answer on a postcard. Some idiot referees will give penalties for anything that hits a hand or an arm in the box: what are defenders supposed to do, cut off the offending limbs? Others will see no offence at all in almost any defender's arm actions. You decide.

OK: referees are faced every season with hundreds of impossible decisions, potential match-turners – we all know that. But they are not *all* impossible. Remember Tiago's similarly obvious, but neglected, handiwork at Anfield, when Liverpool actually had Chelsea on the rack? This is payback time. It looks to us – all right, we see what we want to see, and this all happens in a split-second, but we do have a decent view of it – as if Nesta has moved his arm (or cleverly left it) on the ground in order to play the ball away or obstruct it from Luis. Otherwise, García is definitely around him and in on goal. Nesta is lying helpless. So this could be – should be – a Liverpool penalty *and* possibly a sending off. But let's just talk about the penalty now: a sure Liverpool equaliser just before half-time. Let's just think, for a minute, exactly where that would leave us under this cooling Turkish night sky. We see a García or maybe Vladdy sticking it to the Italians from the penalty spot. We then sniff victory.

'Handball! He's fucking handled that!' Ten thousand voices, at least, offer useful, uncomplicated advice. It should not be needed. All the attacking Liverpool players appeal immediately. But the Spanish officials shake their heads – they can't see it; it's ball to hand. It's so obvious to them. And then inarticulate Liverpool anger follows, all around us – García is still furiously pointing to his own arm – which, in an instant, turns to despair.

Even as we remonstrate with ourselves and our near neighbours, curse our misfortune and these Spanish officials, four Liverpool players are now sucked towards where this incident has so enraged us, and where the ball has ended up. Alonso, Smicer, Gerrard and, crucially, Finnan – they are all directly in front of us, right now, a hopeless, stranded little red cabal. Hopeless, because the ball is quickly and cleverly squeezed out of the Milan defence by Seedorf and Pirlo (who else?) and beyond all of those in this red posse. It reaches the fleet-footed Brazilian Kaka, near the centre circle. And this is now a booming, deafening signal, just like in those B horror movies, when the music gets louder and darker immediately before somebody has their head bitten off or is attacked with a kitchen knife or a machete – a danger signal that Liverpool Football Club is about to suffer a terrible, possibly a fatal, wound in this final. But it is a wound inflicted with a stiletto, not an axe.

Liverpool are stretched and at risk here, precisely because it is now Kaka, Shevchenko and Crespo, together and at pace, against Carragher, Hyypiä and Traoré. Finnan is really struggling, simply cannot get back. This looks horribly uneven, a completely unbalanced three against three. It is. Shevchenko and Crespo now make clever little crossing diagonal runs (no Liverpool strikers ever work together quite like this), and Traoré, trying to follow his man Crespo, going right, almost collides with the distraught Hyypiä. This little comedy moment – not for us a comic interlude, we are horror-struck – allows Shevchenko a free run down the Liverpool left, with Traoré trailing and flummoxed. Kaka sees all of this instantly and feeds the Ukrainian, who is now in open water. The Argentinian Crespo – still actually a Chelsea player – has drifted to the far post, hoping (expecting) his striker mate can pick him out. In fact Shevchenko, for once, scuffs his low cross, so it is behind the Argentinian and has no real pace. But for truly great strikers, even mistakes can work out OK, because the retreating Jamie Carragher is now off-balance and is flailing and twisting in blind panic, like a monkey falling out of a tree, in the Liverpool six-yard box. This confusion allows Crespo, calmly, to pull a yard off the far post, pick up the cross from Shevchenko and score easily, right-footed. Jerzy Dudek is nowhere.

And this goal really sucks our lives away: it is a dagger to the Liverpool heart. Just 18 seconds before this we had had a clear penalty and a route back into this match. Since their early Maldini 'fluke', Milan have made a few chances, sure, but we have also had our moments. Now we look lost. The Liverpool protests continue, Baros and García leading the pointless campaign. The ugly seminars also continue in the stands. It is all *so* obvious to us now, that we have been robbed, cheated. It is just like the Inter Milan European Cup match in 1965, when even the late, great Bill Shankly was reduced – by incompetent (or worse) refereeing – to a silent rage. Blow up now for half-time, for God's sake, while we can still speak, and while we still have even an outside chance to repair this dishonest, this undeserved, damage.

But still it goes on and Milan are now strutting, their fans positively alive with joy. They sense a kill. As Liverpool press forward, Gerrard gives the ball away, carelessly, to Pirlo and then, limply, gets the wrong side of Kaka, who speeds up-field in possession once more. Didi Hamann – who should be Kaka's keeper – watches it all, helpless, on the Liverpool bench. Before he has even reached the Liverpool half of the field, the imperious Kaka has already seen Crespo powering forward between Finnan and Carragher. He bends a raking low pass around JC, who stretches to try to intercept on his right side but, agonisingly, just can't make it. Crespo is clear: this pass is calibrated over a 40-yard distance right into his stride. Jerzy has decided to come off his line, but is really nowhere useful at all, because Crespo is able to act instantly, his mind made up by the goalkeeper's positioning, and he dinks a gentle little shot, with his leading right boot, up and over Dudek's left arm and into the unguarded Liverpool net. Three hundred and four seconds have now passed since Alessandro Nesta handled, without conceding a penalty, in the Milan box: enough time – plenty of time – for AC Milan to win, irrefutably, the 2005

European Cup. In the stands we slump, absolutely devastated, crushed beyond hope.

\* \* \*

## THE IMPOSSIBLE DREAM

How do you explain it: a second-half recovery in a match of this magnitude, a revival such as this one, from certain defeat? AC Milan have nine European finals to their name and six victories, a team full of battle-hardened internationals: Serie A, Champions League and World Cup veterans among them. It is Liverpool that have no recent record of play at this exalted level. Looking back, though, one thing was probably more important here than we realised: Milan, almost certainly, expected Liverpool to accede to the inevitable in the second half, to bow to defeat as any Italian club might have done. In Italy there can still be honour in a defeat gracefully accepted. Take your beating and move on. The Dutchman Seedorf had warned his colleagues about Liverpool's grit: 'They have a European tradition, they have tremendous fans [us again] and the beating heart of the team is still English. They get really fired up. That is the British spirit.' Maybe Liverpool's heart and sheer unwillingness to give up, even from this seemingly impossible deficit, simply shocked Milan, and fed on the Italians' own lurking uncertainties? They had definitely been there, on show, in the Italian championship and also in Eindhoven in the weeks before the final. Maybe this was a Milan team that was mentally soft, just a little too long in the tooth, especially in defence, and unaccountably uncertain in goal.

The tactical changes for Liverpool made by Rafael Benítez at half-time were obviously also crucial here: but are we to praise the Liverpool manager or execrate him? Were these changes a manager's last desperate throws to salvage a self-inflicted crisis? His chosen Liverpool line-up – and variants on it – had been shattered by Milan in the first half and especially by the unfettered Kaka. Moderate coaches – and most knowledgeable fans – might have predicted the same. Rafa's management at this stage was a little like watching the act of a farmer viewing hungry foxes as they wreak havoc through his favourite flock of sheep: at what exact moment shall I release my own dog? In the end he took action when it was all but too late. Didi Hamann eventually offered the sort of dedicated midfield policing so sorely missed by Liverpool in the first half. It was a simple option, badly misjudged. In the end it was, unavoidably, Benítez's players that saved Liverpool this night, not the manager's inexplicably belated actions to put things right.

More generally, today's sports coaches are probably guilty – like the rest of us sometimes are – of complicating the game and, possibly, of over-emphasising their own importance. They have a crucial role to play in sport, of course. But their technocratic stress – a professional's occasional conceit – on the tiny bits of technical advice and on the back-room know-how and impression-management that, they maintain, can make a real difference in team sports at this level, actually becomes worthless and self-defeating if the basics are missed as a consequence: if, for example, the wrong players are chosen for the wrong contests, or if the wrong strategies are adopted. Or, indeed, if top players are simply unable to show their true skills because of the application of a coaching straitjacket. In the end it is always players who win sporting contests, not the back-room staff. Bob Paisley, of course, had it right in the 1980s when he was asked about the 'secret' of Liverpool's success. It was not rocket science for Bob: 'It's simple: good players.' If you think otherwise, then you need to step back and look at the situation again. If you ever think that the coach is the main story in the camp, rather than the players, then you are in deep, deep trouble. Witness, if you will, the recent Sir Clive Woodward 'I know best' coaching debacle with rugby's touring British Lions in 2005. There are important lessons here for all sport, as there were in the Atatürk Stadium on 25 May 2005. Hubris, in the end, makes fools of us all.

Two other things got Liverpool into extra-time in this match: the performances of the contrary club captain Steven Gerrard and his committed Scouse mate Jamie Carragher; and the extraordinary contribution of the Liverpool crowd.

As we know, Gerrard was a troubled and controversial figure for Liverpool pretty much throughout this season, starting with his summer 2004 prevarications about joining Chelsea. Too often, for many fans, his loyalty to the Liverpool club seemed stretched – beyond breaking point, it seemed later in 2005. Although his form had been patchy through the season, he could deliver in the major contests. Here in Turkey Gerrard produced 20 incredible, possibly match-turning, second-half minutes when his team needed them most, and also another dedicated and inspirational half an hour in extra-time to snuff out Milan's newest threat, Serginho. He played in three different positions in the final for Liverpool and excelled in two of them. Despite his self-obsessed problems, without him Liverpool would not – could not – have won the 2005 European Cup. What was his reward for this stunning contribution? His manager now asks if he will take a penalty in the shoot-out (he has missed one recently). What is he to say? He is the Scouse captain, a man who feels he owes the fans for all the heartaches of this season. 'Sure, boss,' he mutters. 'Good,' replies Benítez, walking away. 'You are taking the fifth one.'

Jamie Carragher has also been a seminal figure for Liverpool tonight and through the season, though he has had absolutely none of Gerrard's own personal conflicts to resolve in 2005. Carra's heroic last line of defence tonight, and above all his courage and resolve when Liverpool were simply exhausted in extra-time, was beyond measure and value. As he has done all season, he fed off the Liverpool fans who, in turn, recharged the players on the field. This symbiosis has dragged the team and its manager through much of the 2004–05 European competition, from Graz to Olympiakos, to Turin and against Chelsea, and it was still working strongly here in Turkey. Who could ever doubt the importance of the presence of we, the Liverpool fans tonight – in our tens of thousands – to that astonishing Liverpool comeback? Who else was there to play *for* out in the Turkish wilderness?

* * *

## NO TIME FOR LOSERS

After *that* second-half six minutes, if the truth be told, Liverpool are hanging on for dear life in this concrete pod outside Istanbul for much of what follows. We, the fans, are hanging on too: thrilled, astounded, exhausted, astonished, *proud*. Virtually the whole of the second half contains – is shaped by – Liverpool songs; or Liverpool noise; or Liverpool complaints; or Liverpool flares; or Scouse jeers; or all of these things mixed up at the same time. It seems as if the Milan fans in the South Tribune have been replaced by a painted mural. Except this area isn't loud enough any more even to be a mural. Off the field, in fact, it is pretty much all Liverpool. We are drained, but glad to be alive and in Istanbul, and to be wearing red.

On the footballing side the sheer physical and mental effort of the players in equalising from such a hopeless position can mean that trying to push on beyond your opponents seems like a step too far, an unnecessary risk on a night such as this one. Milan look shell-shocked too – who could blame them? Shevchenko and Crespo had virtually disappeared as influences in the second half, as their supply line, from Pirlo, was cut out by a much more advanced Steven Gerrard, and as the restored Hamann took care of Kaka, thus offering Alonso much more time and space to play. There are still the heart-stopping Liverpool escapes, of course: Dudek shovelling a Kaka cross into Shevchenko's path only for the Ukrainian's shot to be cleared off the line by Traoré; Jamie Carragher's incredible last-ditch tackles, on Kaka, and, later, on Shevchenko; Stam's late header wide. And with extra-time drawing nearer, the Liverpool fans around us – the big teases – even start chanting, cheekily: 'Attack, attack, attack.' *We* aren't joining in. How much can you ask of these guys in red? And how much stress can you take? Instead, to keep ourselves entertained, we start to cheer Liverpool possession now and whistle and boo Milan's. There was more booing than cheering. Much more. The minutes tick on.

Late on, Cissé replaces a brave Baros, the Frenchman sporting what seems to be a couple of black spiders on his head – a new gobshite hairstyle. As far as we, the authors, are concerned, he also plays pretty much like the fool he now looks, a largely wasteful presence. By this stage, too, Riise is really struggling with obvious injury, no longer getting forward at all on the left. What a season he has had under Benítez. Smicer is starting to cramp up, his last heroic minutes in a Liverpool jersey, and this after so much stick. We are out on our feet. Which means that the Liverpool team-talk at full-time is pretty much all about surviving, about simply staying in the game. Stevie Gerrard is, sensibly, moved by Benítez to right-back to cope with the Milan substitute Serginho. This tells you all you need to know about our intentions now. Pedants might argue that it could have occurred earlier to Milan coach Ancelotti to bring on a really dangerous left-winger when Liverpool had gone three at the back and Carragher was bombing dangerously forward on the Liverpool right. But, by then, Milan were leading 3–0 – why did he need to change anything at all? That 3–0 thing seems like an age ago now, by the way: another contest all together.

At full-time we, the fans, the crucial extras for this drama, produce the seventh – or is it the eighth – complete version of 'You'll Never Walk Alone' of the night. There are more still to come. These versions had all been carefully toned and presented for every available occasion tonight. Each version symbolised a different message about us, about our football club and about the fragile state of the contest. They have covered: expectation; hope; inspiration; mourning; defiance; joy; and now, pride. Think about it: how many evenings in your life do you go through *all* these emotions – or even a few of them – in a couple of hours? Here is a life's emotional work, completed in one spring evening. In a contest like this one you are on the brink of cheering or crying, screaming or withdrawing, hoping or despairing, most of the time. Try not to look too hard at the shattered people around you now: you look like all of them – hollowed out, mangled.

Extra-time, from the Liverpool perspective, is basically made up of three or four basic components only: Steven Gerrard routinely tackling and dispossessing the lively Serginho, to louder and louder Liverpool roars; Cissé wasting the little decent Liverpool possession that is generated high up the field; Hyypiä and Carragher with a series of brave, muscle-clenching, clearing headers and tackles to defy Milan to the last; and finally, right at the death, Jerzy Dudek's geometry-defying double save from the deadly Shevchenko. Ah, Jerzy: what a Polish enigma. Rafa Benítez is already committed to bringing in another keeper for next season, Reina from Villarreal, so this could also be Jerzy's last match for Liverpool. Tonight he has missed crosses, shovelled balls out, made great saves, watched low drives bounce off his knees – pretty much the usual crazy Jerzy journey. And now we have this amazing last Dudek moment to suffer and to marvel at. None of us can work out what has happened and exactly why the Liverpool net does not bulge with a football full of UEFA's little stars and the tears of 40,000 Reds supporters.

This is, in fact, one of the very few occasions that Gerrard has allowed Serginho to cross high into the Liverpool box. It is also the only header missed by Sami Hyypiä all night – it is approaching midnight by now. And there is no sensible explanation as to why the vulture Shevchenko doesn't score. He has a clear header from six yards out that Dudek somehow claws out. Maybe the Ukrainian is tired and just too casual with the rebound, from four yards, because he flicks at it with his right foot when his left would be better, more assured. The rising, half-kneeling Dudek just raises his arm, as if in self-defence, and the ball somehow cannons off him and over the bar. Why not into the net? Actually it is probably the sheer *pace* of the rebound shot that helps take it over the bar. For a split-second all the players simply look at each other, bemused, astonished; the Milan forwards do this with hands clasped on their heads. They fear the worst.

Jerzy simply looks sheepish. Goalkeepers who make really great saves instantly start to chivvy up their colleagues with backslaps and clapping as if to say: 'Look at how great I'm playing: you can do this, too.' We get none of that here, and no false modesty. Jerzy knows he's been lucky. Didi Hamann says later that when he saw this certain goal disappear instead into the night sky he knew Liverpool would win the European Cup. Didi even has time for one last run at the Milan defence and a role in an abortive free-kick for the injured Riise. As if this makes any sense at all. The referee blows up as we all gulp for one last breath. Thank God we have made it here. Penalties.

## THE MIRACLE OF ISTANBUL

Patrick Barclay, a serious football journalist, a civilised and educated man, an intelligent member of a rather dubious profession and a Liverpool FC sympathiser, said immediately after the final whistle that he had realised while at the match in Turkey that penalty kicks were no sane way to decide a contest of this kind.

A much better way, he argued, was to decide the winners on the basis of how few fouls they had committed in the match. This would encourage and reward fair play, he suggested. This sort of tells you that, like it or not, penalties *are* the only way to deal with these deadlocks. Imagine the extra-time diving and the complete faking we would get with dear Paddy's proposed solution. We doubt we would even reach the final whistle. No other ideas make any better sense – play fifteen minutes of nine-a-side here, with players collapsing from exhaustion? We don't think so. In any case, unsatisfactory as they are, penalties are no simple lottery: they are a test of technique, nerve and accuracy, key components of the game itself. We have to live with them – if not exactly learn to love them.

Frankly there is little point trying to convey here, in these pages of a mere book, exactly how nerve-wracking, how gut-churningly stressful it is watching all this. And we are only the put-upon Liverpool fans, the seen-it-all-before European football commandos: we can sit, and cry, and cheer, and hide, and even refuse to watch if we really want to. Many people do that now. We could even leave right here, step out into the Istanbul rural wilderness. John Peel used to go for a drive when Liverpool were playing live on TV. It was too stressful for him to watch: he recorded it and watched the game later, but only if we had won. We could do with the 'winding on' video function now, seeing the outcome in advance. And even if the Liverpool manager himself strolls over to ask one of us, right now, to take a kick, to help out this team we *profess* to love, then a simple, polite refusal will usually suffice. But not for the Liverpool players: not for our heroes tonight. They must shake the tiredness out of their legs and their minds and step up again now. Alone.

All we can say is that the psychology of where we are right at this moment is both simple and complicated. The AC Milan players (and fans) must be thinking: 'Why, exactly, are we still here? Why are *we* having to take these kicks at all? Almost an hour ago we were 3–0 up, coasting. We have messed this up badly. Even if we win with these penalties, what sort of sullied glory is that?' They will take the victory, of course, sullied or not. They would rather take home the European Cup than not. But it must be a negative mindset on the Milan side, surely. Having been so close to victory, they must now expect to lose. Psychologically, they are already losers.

The Liverpool players must be thinking: 'We are already heroes tonight.' (This is dangerous territory, negative thinking.) 'We have come back from the dead and now we have a better than even chance to win this European Cup, because our name must be on this trophy.' (More danger.) 'The gods are with us. We can't lose this from here.' The key, of course, is for the Liverpool players to continue to act positively, not to settle for the glory of this fantastic comeback: to act out the 'winning mentality' that Benítez is always stressing so strongly and which is also so central to the Liverpool Way. If Liverpool can just get ahead in the count, they will win: it will be impossible for this damaged Milan to recover. *If.*

And here is where Liverpool's great European heritage now plays its real part. And why you need deep students of the game in your ranks, players who really understand the club they play for, its fans and its importance to the people of the city, players who really do care about the past and about what it means. Because amidst all the good-luck backslapping and the general chivvying up of Jerzy Dudek by the Liverpool staff – and who wouldn't be a goalkeeper now: a real chance for glory and no blame for failure – Jamie Carragher, with his Ph.D. (with distinction) in the History of Liverpool FC, pulls Jerzy aside. And he brooks no arguments here, the Bootle chronicler. He doesn't just 'suggest' to Jerzy that he might try calling upon the wobbly-legged ghost of Brucie G. in Rome in 1984. He doesn't raise it as perhaps an option to consider. He doesn't ask Dudek if he might have seen the tapes, possibly. He absolutely *insists* on it, pulling the keeper back to him as Jerzy tries to slip away to gather his own fragile thoughts. Even from where we are in the ground wondering, distractedly, exactly who will step up to the spot for Liverpool, we can see Carra in a hugely animated talk with Jerzy, throwing his arms and legs around like a madman. *We* know.

So, actually, we are not *that* surprised when Jerzy does his crazy little star jumps as Serginho approaches to take the first penalty for Milan. And skies it way, way into Turkish orbit. Nor are we *that* bemused when the Pole does the same to Andrea Pirlo, adding an illegal two-yard step off his line, for good measure, to make the save. (Alan Kennedy is in the ground tonight with his son Michael: he will be reliving all of this, thinking back to Brucie's antics and to *that* kick in 1984 and his own little celebratory leap.) And even John Arne Riise's miss for Liverpool seems somehow bearable now. Because, like in some corny Frank Capra movie, a shimmering, golden glow is beginning, slowly, to rise in front of us over the West Tribune at the pretty darn fantastic Atatürk Olympic Stadium, which is so many, many millions of miles outside Istanbul.

Because with Didi Hamann, Cissé and the God-like Vladdy Smicer all scoring easily from the spot – embarrassingly easily – for Liverpool, when faced with a statuesque Dida, it suddenly all seems to make sense to us: exactly why we have been brought together, with 40,000 other worshippers, at this very moment approaching 1 a.m. on Thursday, 26 May 2005, in the heart of the Turkish countryside and near the exact point where Asia and Europe meet. We suddenly all know that this is already scripted. We know with an absolutely crystal clarity, just as surely as we know that Shankly, Fagan and Paisley – and John Peel and Emlyn – are all watching overhead, that the man who is currently Europe's best footballer, the staggeringly talented Andriy Shevchenko will not – cannot – now score past our fumbling, error prone, wonderful Polish goalkeeper. Which means that Steven Gerrard, who is ashen-faced and dumb with fear at the halfway line, can safely forget the fifth penalty he has promised to his manager, and to the Liverpool supporters who now grip each other in rapt anticipation. It will not be needed.

How else do you explain it? Do you have a rational account? What else is it, exactly, if not this greater Liverpool presence, that snags right now at the Ukrainian Sheva's deadly right leg, that clips his follow-through at the very moment he addresses the ball on the penalty spot? And which means that he barely chips the very gentlest of kicks – a back-pass really – to Dudek's skywards left hand? One final save to win the 2005 European Cup for Liverpool. Call it karma, call it psychic energy, call it history repeating itself, call it whatever you want. Looking at the Asian night skies, we call it – because we want to – The Miracle of Istanbul. It was, somehow, meant to be. And right now, even as a catatonic Jamie Carragher is running wide-eyed towards us, socks rolled down to his ankles, red heart beating loudly, tears of sheer relief and joy are starting to cloud our vision of him. We *are* the people.

## EPILOGUE: THE (NON) LEAVING OF STEVEN GERRARD

Almost six weeks on and the memories of Istanbul are still strong. We were not in Liverpool, of course, to see the European Cup paraded before an estimated 500,000 people, but we could imagine the scenes. We had our own little parties in Istanbul at 4 a.m. that Thursday morning, before trying to negotiate the chaos of the Istanbul airports to find our bleary way home. Let us mention one crucial matter now, 20 years after the horrors of Heysel: 40,000 Liverpool fans were in Istanbul, warmly welcomed by local people, but tested to the very limits of endurance by the appalling arrangements made for them at this game. There was not a single Red arrest during this trip. Incredibly, the Turkish authorities crowed about this later as if it was their doing, rather than ours. We are decent, proud people, true football devotees. We have this stain against us, not wholly of our making. Unlike others, we will accept our responsibilities and what happened 20 years ago is now part of our history. Fair enough. But it should not be seen – and it is not seen by Liverpool fans – as the defining part of our identity. On TV later we saw our often reluctant captain this past season, Steven Gerrard, ask, rhetorically, how could he possibly leave Liverpool Football Club now, after all that had happened? He was a Liverpool lad, raising a trophy that was in the very DNA of this club, the pinnacle of any footballer's club career. He had dreamt of this moment. Steven was now looking forward to signing a new contract at Anfield and was anticipating winning new trophies at the football club he truly loved. Or so we thought.

Today (5 July 2005), exactly 41 days after the final, Gerrard, 282 appearances for a club he joined at 8 years of age, has announced that he is leaving Liverpool Football Club after all. The manager Benítez, and Rick Parry, insist that they want Gerrard to stay. The player and his agent imply that the club has somehow 'disrespected' him, as if this is some sort of macho street stand-off between peers. Liverpool have offered Gerrard a reported £100,000 per week for five years. Some disrespect. 'Think of Istanbul, think of the fans,' implored Rick Parry. His message seemed to fall on deaf ears. Liverpool fans were interviewed on TV and most have been hostile to Gerrard: the word 'betrayal' has been used a few times, and someone has, kindly, burned a Gerrard no. 17 shirt outside Anfield for the benefit of the TV cameras. He is rumoured to be moving to Chelsea or to Real Madrid, and Gerrard says that the ambitions of Liverpool Football Club, the 2005 European Champions, still do not match his own. Frankly, we are bored with this stuff now. David Fairclough is interviewed, and he offers a calm and accurate Liverpool perspective: Gerrard must be allowed to leave if he wants to. At least this is all finally out in the open and over. Liverpool FC will continue its special work, and he will be replaced. No player is bigger than the club. Onwards and upwards: but it is still a bitter taste.

It is now 42 days after the final. A day is a long time in football. Steven Gerrard has changed his mind. He is staying (for the next 24 hours at least)! Walk on.